CIVIC ENGAGEMENT IN HIGHER EDUCATION

Concepts and Practices

Barbara Jacoby and Associates

Foreword by Thomas Ehrlich

JOSSEY-BASS
A Wiley Imprint
www.josseybass.com

Published by Jossey-Bass
A Wiley Imprint
989 Market Street, San Francisco, CA 94103-1741—www.josseybass.com

Jossey-Bass books and products are available through most bookstores. To contact Jossey-Bass directly call our Customer Care Department within the U.S. at 800-956-7739, outside the U.S. at 317-572-3986, or fax 317-572-4002.

Jossey-Bass also publishes its books in a variety of electronic formats. Some content that appears in print may not be available in electronic books.

Library of Congress Cataloging-in-Publication Data
Jacoby, Barbara.
    Civic engagement in higher education : concepts and practices / Barbara Jacoby and Associates ; foreword by Thomas Ehrlich.
      p. cm.—(The Jossey-Bass higher and adult education series)
  Includes bibliographical references and index.
    ISBN 978-0-470-38846-4 (cloth)
      1. Service learning—United States. 2. Civics—Study and teaching (Higher—United States. 3 Education, Higher–Social aspects—United States. I. Title. II. Series.
  LC220.5.J33 2009
  378'.015—dc22
                                                2008036103

FIRST EDITION
HB Printing 10 9 8 7 6 5 4 3 2

CONTENTS

FOREWORD

Thirty-five years ago, the Carnegie Foundation for the Advancement of Teaching published the first Carnegie Classification of colleges and universities. The classification quickly became the gold standard for those seeking to differentiate among and between institutions of higher education. Complaints were often made that the classification was misused for unintended purposes, such as the ranking of campuses. But no one seriously argued that institutional groupings could be made without some consideration of the Carnegie Classification. So when the Carnegie Foundation announced that—starting with its 2005 classification—it would undertake multiple classifications rather than a single approach based on terminal degrees, interest was particularly high. This was especially true because the announcement stated that one of the new classifications would be a voluntary one focused on community engagement. Colleges and universities could apply for this designation and would be accepted if they showed that they met a defined set of criteria, including just the kinds of teaching and learning that Barbara Jacoby and Associates examine in this splendid volume. As much as any marker that one could imagine, this new classification means that civic engagement has come of age for American higher education. Appropriately enough, its birth as a movement was a little more than twenty-one years ago.

Campus Compact, the organization that led the movement, was created in the mid-1980s because a small group of leaders in higher education thought that the "me generation" was a bum rap for their students. They believed that students should have a wide range of opportunities for community service, and these leaders committed themselves to providing those opportunities for students on their campuses. There was certainly civic engagement work by faculty and students before this time, but I count this as the founding of the civic engagement movement because it was the first time that a national organization of campus presidents agreed that the issues involved in promoting civic engagement ought to be high on the institutional agendas of their campuses. Preparing civic leaders had certainly long been part of the mission statement of campuses across the country. But in the main the rhetoric of civic engagement was unmatched by reality.

The movement got off to a somewhat slow start, in part because many of us involved did not realize that it would not be enough simply to provide opportunities for students to engage in community service. Those opportunities were too often perceived by students and faculty as one more set of optional after-school activities. By the 1990s, it was clear that civic engagement by students would never be viewed as central to the educational mission of their institutions unless it was linked to the curriculum through community service-learning.

In the years that followed, community service-learning has become a major force in American higher education. An impressive array of scholarly works has been published on this mode of teaching and learning, and new studies in the field are appearing regularly. For a time, however, it was not clear that to achieve learning outcomes that extend beyond academic learning to civic learning, care is needed in shaping the structured opportunities for reflection that link the academic and community experiences. Civic learning means coming to understand how a community functions, what problems it faces, the richness of its diversity, the need for individual commitments of time and energy to enhance community life, and most of all, the importance of working as a community to resolve community concerns.

This remarkable volume of essays offers superb insights on every aspect of civic engagement. Faculty members, campus administrators, and others seriously interested in the field should start with this volume as an essential text. Barbara Jacoby has been a national leader in promoting civic engagement, and she has assembled an extraordinary group of authors as her collaborators.

As this book makes clear, civic engagement has come a long way in recent years. Those gains are in no small measure because of the tireless effort of Barbara and her associates. But these essays also provide abundant evidence that much work remains to be done. My colleagues at the Carnegie Foundation and I think this is particularly true in terms of that subset of civic engagement that involves politics and public policymaking. Even though the proportion of the U.S. population attending college has increased dramatically in the past fifty years, political knowledge and engagement have not increased. According to some indicators, they have actually decreased. Our own book, *Educating for Democracy: Preparing Undergraduates for Responsible Political Engagement* (Jossey-Bass, 2007), examines the ways that students can gain the knowledge, skills, and dispositions to be politically engaged. We build on thoughtful analysis done by Barbara and other scholars represented in these pages. Civic learning is pedagogy in progress, and they have made major contributions to every aspect.

It has become a cliché that democracy is not a spectator sport. It demands the active participation of its citizenry. Yet the evidence is overwhelming that Americans are not learning what they need to know to be civically engaged. This volume should become an indispensable tool in guiding faculty and administrators who want to be sure that students are well prepared to become responsible civic leaders in their communities.

Thomas Ehrlich
Senior Scholar
The Carnegie Foundation for the Advancement of Teaching

For my beloved parents,
Pearl and Herb Gendler

PREFACE

There is much work to be done. Local, national, and global social problems are growing on many fronts, including poverty, education, health, the environment, and the escalation of violent conflicts. Virtually every local problem has a global dimension, and the reverse is equally true. The vitality of our democracy is in question, even as it was at the time of the Constitutional Convention in 1787, when, after three and a half months of deliberation, a woman asked Benjamin Franklin, "'Well, Doctor, what have we got, a republic or a monarchy?' 'A republic,' replied the Doctor, 'if you can keep it'" (Ferrand, 1911). More recently, the popular film character President Andrew Shepherd, in *The American President,* put it this way: "America isn't easy. America is advanced citizenship. You've got to want it bad."

To further complicate matters, more and more people shun politics as corrupt and ineffectual. Unfortunately, many studies have shown that Americans' involvement in volunteering has increased in recent years but that their interest in and knowledge about civic and political issues and processes have significantly declined (Colby, Ehrlich, Beaumont, and Stephens, 2003; Ehrlich, 2000; Gibson, 2006). This is particularly true of youth, who, in addition, tend to "view politics as a way for the powerful to keep power to themselves" (Kiesa et al., 2007). The public is also repeatedly disgusted by the altogether too many examples of corporate corruption that have deeply harmed many innocent people. The horrific events of September 11, 2001 have left us trying to understand why they occurred and how such acts can be prevented in the future. And more of us are "bowling alone," as Robert Putnam's memorable title (2000) characterizes the decline in civic participation and engagement in community life.

As a result, higher education experts and critics, government and business leaders, civil society, and the public are more loudly and more frequently calling on colleges and universities to focus sharply on educating students for democratic empowerment and global citizenship. Employers in all sectors are clamoring for higher education to teach students such important civic skills as active listening, deliberation, engaging diverse perspectives, collaboration, creative problem solving, civility, ethical decision making, and information literacy. A crisis in the nation's ability to fill public service positions in the federal government and to recruit qualified teachers is rapidly approaching, if not already upon us. Simultaneously, the demands for compassionate, skilled, and committed individuals to roll up their sleeves and go to work in our local communities and in our interconnected global society are huge. Furthermore, it is critical for citizens to reclaim politics as an essential means by which they can—and believe that they can—engage with their democracy.

So there is indeed much work to be done, and higher education must prepare and motivate the next generations to do it. Colleges and universities must educate students to understand how democracy and governments function and to appreciate freedom, self-determination, and the responsibility of citizens to actively engage in the welfare of their own and other countries. As Carmen Sirianni and Lewis A. Friedland (2005) explain, "Democracy is, in some fundamental sense, the shared work of citizens acting pragmatically to solve public problems and to build a commonwealth" (p. 135). It is higher education's historical and altogether fitting contemporary role to encourage students to view themselves as problem solvers and to invest in developing the civic knowledge and skills needed to work with others to make a difference. We must provide opportunities for students to learn about and practice civic engagement so they can create their own civic identities—as neighbors, family and community members, volunteers, organization participants and leaders, advocates and activists, professionals, politicians and elected officials, public servants, and leaders in business and civil society. Henry Giroux (2002) reminds us that higher education is "one of the few public spaces left where students can learn the power of questioning authority, recover the ideals of engaged citizenship, reaffirm the importance of the public good, and expand their capacities to make a difference" (p. 450).

It is for these reasons that this book is crucial and timely. It is in this spirit that I and my fellow contributors invite our colleagues to join us in educating the next generations of civically engaged citizens, scholars, and leaders.

References

Colby, A., Ehrlich, T., Beaumont, E., and Stephens, J. *Educating Citizens: Preparing Undergraduates for Lives of Moral and Civic Responsibility.* San Francisco: Jossey-Bass, 2003.

Ehrlich, T. *Civic Responsibility and Higher Education.* Phoenix, AZ: Oryx Press, 2000.

Ferrand, M. *The Records of the Federal Convention of 1787.* Vol. 3, Appendix A, 1911.

Gibson, C. M. *New Times Demand New Scholarship.* Medford, MA: Tufts University, 2006.

Giroux, H. A. "Neoliberalism, Corporate Culture, and the Promise of Higher Education: The University as a Democratic Public Sphere," *Harvard Educational Review,* 2002, 72(4), 425–462.

Kiesa, A., Orlowski, A. P., Levine, P. L., Both, D., Kirby, E. H., Lopez, M. H., et al. *Millennials Talk Politics: A Study of College Student Political Engagement.* College Park, MD: Center for Information & Research on Civic Learning & Engagement, 2007.

Putnam, R. D. *Bowling Alone: The Collapse and Revival of American Community.* New York: Simon & Schuster, 2000.

Sirianni, C., and Friedland, L. A. *The Civic Renewal Movement: Community Building and Democracy in the U.S.* Dayton, OH: Charles F. Kettering Foundation, 2005.

The Jossey-Bass

Higher and Adult Education Series

ACKNOWLEDGMENTS

Many people have contributed to and enriched this book. I am indebted to all of them.

I appreciate the chapter authors for so generously and so articulately sharing their knowledge and experience with us. It has been an honor to work with such an incredible group of educators and writers. I thank the many colleagues across the country whose examples of good practice are featured in this book and also those whose examples could not be included.

As always, I am grateful for the wisdom and dedication of my colleagues in Campus Compact and The Research University Civic Engagement Network, as well as the members of the Coalition for Civic Engagement and Leadership on my campus. The book is considerably stronger as a result of the invaluable guidance of Elizabeth Hollander. I thank David Brightman, Aneesa Davenport, and Cathy Mallon of Jossey-Bass for their assistance and support. Michelle Cain is an awesome copyeditor, and I am happy to acknowledge her outstanding work.

Most of all, I am continually inspired by the many talented and committed University of Maryland students with whom I have been privileged to work. You never cease to amaze me. There is no doubt that you are the civically engaged leaders we have been waiting for.

Last but surely not least, I thank my adored husband of thirty-seven years, Steve Jacoby. He is always my most loyal and supportive fan.

THE AUTHORS

Barbara Jacoby is senior scholar for the Adele H. Stamp Student Union–Center for Campus Life at the University of Maryland, College Park. In this role, she facilitates initiatives involving academic partnerships, assessment, scholarship, and student learning. Jacoby is also chair of the university's Coalition for Civic Engagement and Leadership. She is a fellow of the Academy for Excellence in Teaching and Learning and was a Center for Teaching Excellence–Lilly Fellow during the 2007–2008 academic year. She served as director of the Office of Community Service-Learning from 2003 to 2005, director of Commuter Affairs and Community Service from 1992 to 2003, and director of the Office of Commuter Affairs from 1983 to 2003—all at the University of Maryland. Jacoby has served as Campus Compact's Engaged Scholar for Professional Development. In addition, she is senior scholar for the National Clearinghouse for Commuter Programs. She was director of the National Clearinghouse for Commuter Programs from 1983 to 2003.

Jacoby received her BA (1971), MA (1972), and PhD (1978)—all summa cum laude—in French language and literature from the University of Maryland. She taught French honors courses for ten years and is currently affiliate associate professor of college student personnel.

Jacoby's publications include five books: *The Student as Commuter: Developing a Comprehensive Institutional Response* (ASHE-ERIC Higher Education Reports, 1989), *Service-Learning in Higher Education: Concepts and Practices* (Jossey-Bass, 1996), *Involving Commuter Students in Learning* (Jossey-Bass New Directions for Higher Education, 2000), *Building Partnerships for Service-Learning* (Jossey-Bass, 2003), and *Essential Information and Tools of the Trade for Community Service and Service-Learning Professionals* (working title, with Pamela Mutascio, Campus Compact, in press).

She has served on the board of directors of the Council for the Advancement of Standards in Higher Education since 1980. She has held many leadership positions in NASPA–Student Affairs Administrators in Higher Education and ACPA–College Student Educators International. Jacoby writes and consults extensively and makes numerous speeches and presentations across the country each year. Her institution and professional associations have recognized her outstanding work on behalf of commuter students and service-learning.

Nevin C. Brown is president of the International Partnership for Service-Learning and Leadership (IPSL). He oversees advocacy efforts as well as academic programs for fifteen undergraduate international service-learning programs offered by IPSL in thirteen nations, as well as a graduate program in international service involving IPSL and universities in three nations. Before joining IPSL in 2003, Brown held various positions over a twenty-year period with U.S.-based higher education associations. He also has been active professionally in the field of urban studies both in North America and in Europe. His MA (1973) is in American history from the University of Virginia, and his BA (1972) is in history from the University of California, Santa Barbara.

Michelle R. Dunlap is associate professor and chair of the human development department at Connecticut College. She is also an educational and community consultant. She has published several books and many articles on service-learning, multicultural families, and diversity and feminist issues. Dunlap is coeditor with Stephanie Evans, Colette Taylor, and DeMond Miller of the forthcoming book *African Americans and Community Engagement in Higher Education: Perspectives of Race in Community Service, Service-Learning, and Community-Based Research* (SUNY Press). She received her BS from Wayne State University and her MS and PhD from the University of Florida.

Elizabeth Hollander is a senior fellow at the Jonathan M. Tisch College of Citizenship and Public Service at Tufts University. Before that, she served for ten years as executive director of Campus Compact. She is a fellow of the National Academy of Public Administration. In 2008, she spent a semester as a residential fellow at the Spencer Foundation. Hollander holds honorary doctorate degrees from Millikin University (2001) and DePaul University (2003). She received a BA cum laude in political science from Bryn Mawr College (1961).

Mary Stuart Hunter is assistant vice provost for University 101 programs and the National Resource Center for the First-Year Experience and Students in Transition at the University of South Carolina. Her work centers on providing educators with resources to develop personal and professional skills while creating and refining innovative programs to increase undergraduate student learning and success. In addition to her administrative and teaching responsibilities at the University of South Carolina, she speaks, conducts workshops, and writes about the first-year experience, first-year seminars, the sophomore year, academic advising, faculty development, and teaching on campuses and at national and international conferences. She was recently recognized as outstanding alumna of the year from the higher education and student affairs graduate program at the University of South Carolina. She holds a BA in English from Queens University of Charlotte and an MEd from the University of South Carolina.

Kevin Kecskes is the director for community-university partnerships at Portland State University. Before joining Portland State's Center for Academic Excellence in 2002, he was program director of the Western Region Campus Compact Consortium. Kecskes cofounded the Boston College International Volunteer Program and has spent a dozen years working, serving, and studying in the developing world, primarily in Latin America and Asia. He has run his own small business and has taught in both secondary and higher education. His formal studies include biology, philosophy, education, and public administration and policy at Boston College (BS, 1982), Harvard University (EdM, 1995), and Portland State University (PhD, Mark O. Hatfield School of Government, expected 2008). His recent publications focus on the nexus between cultural theory and community-campus partnerships, faculty and institutional development for civic engagement, and service-learning's impact on community partners. Kecskes edited *Engaging Departments: Moving Faculty Culture from Private to Public, Individual to Collective Focus for the Common Good* (Anker, 2006).

Seanna Kerrigan brings a decade of experience to her current position as the capstone program director at Portland State

University. In this role, she works collaboratively with community-based organizations and faculty to develop over two hundred and twenty service-learning courses that engage more than thirty-three hundred students each academic year. She also assists faculty in the design, implementation, and assessment of these courses; works on an administrative level within the university to ensure the ongoing success of this cutting-edge program; and promotes the concept of service-learning to faculty, students, and staff locally and nationally. Her scholarship focuses on assessing capstone courses with a special interest in expressing the voices of the students and the community members involved. Kerrigan received her BA (1991) summa cum laude in psychology from Ohio University, her MEd (1994) in college student personnel from Ohio University, and her EdD (2004) in postsecondary education from Portland State University.

Abby Kiesa is the youth coordinator at the Center for Information & Research on Civic Learning & Engagement (CIRCLE). She led the research and writing of CIRCLE's national study of college student political engagement, entitled *Millennials Talk Politics: A Study of College Student Political Engagement.* Kiesa came to CIRCLE from the national office of Campus Compact, where she codirected a national campaign to increase college students' involvement in public life. She is currently a cochair of IMPACT: National Student Conference on Service, Advocacy, and Social Action and serves on the board of Break Away. Kiesa's BA (2001) with honors in sociology is from Villanova University. She is a graduate student in American studies at the University of Maryland.

Nicholas V. Longo is the director of the global studies program and assistant professor of public and community service studies at Providence College. From 2006 to 2008, he directed the Harry T. Wilks Leadership Institute at Miami University in Ohio and was an assistant professor in the department of educational leadership. Longo is the author of *Why Community Matters: Connecting Education with Civic Life* (SUNY Press, 2007) and coeditor of *Students as Colleagues: Expanding the Circle of Service-Learning Leadership* (Campus Compact, 2006). He is also an associate at the Kettering Foundation. He received his PhD (2005) in work, community, and family education and his MPA (1999), concentrating on public work, both from the University of Minnesota.

Mark Hugo Lopez served as the research director of the Center for Information & Research on Civic Learning & Engagement (CIRCLE) and as a research assistant professor at the University of Maryland's School of Public Policy during the writing of the chapter for this book. In his work at CIRCLE, he studied young people's electoral participation, the civic engagement of immigrants, young people's views of the First Amendment, and the link between college attendance and civic engagement. He currently serves as the associate director of the Pew Hispanic Center, a project of the Pew Research Center in Washington, DC. He also is second vice president of the American Society of Hispanic Economists and a member of the American Economic Association's Committee on the Status of Minority Groups in the Economics Profession. Lopez holds a PhD (1996) and an MA (1993) in economics from Princeton University. His BA (1989) is in economics from the University of California, Berkeley.

Nance Lucas is the associate dean of New Century College at George Mason University, where she also serves as associate professor. She is an adjunct faculty member with the Gallup Organization and an affiliate faculty member of the Robert H. Smith School of Business at the University of Maryland. Her previous positions include special assistant to the provost, director of the James MacGregor Burns Academy of Leadership, and cofounder and first director of the National Clearinghouse for Leadership Programs—all at the University of Maryland. Her research and scholarship interests focus on ethics and leadership. Among other publications, she is the coauthor of *Exploring Leadership: For College Students Who Want to Make a Difference* (Jossey-Bass, 1998, 2007). Lucas received a PhD in college student personnel with a concentration in leadership studies and ethics at the University of Maryland. Her MA (1984) in college student personnel administration and her BA (1982) in industrial psychology are from the Pennsylvania State University.

Blaire L. Moody is an admissions counselor at the University of Michigan, Ann Arbor. Before that, she was a graduate assistant at the National Resource Center for the First-Year Experience and Students in Transition. She served as a graduate leader and coteacher for first-year and peer leader seminars. Her first professional position was as a residential life coordinator at Ohio

Wesleyan University. Her professional and research interests include social justice initiatives, the experience and influence of peer leadership, and the reflection process associated with community service. Moody obtained her MEd (2007) in higher education and student affairs at the University of South Carolina and her BA (2004) in psychology from Ohio Wesleyan University.

Caryn McTighe Musil is senior vice president at the Association of American Colleges and Universities (AAC&U), where she is also in charge of the Office of Diversity, Equity, and Global Initiatives. She has expertise in curriculum transformation, faculty development, civic engagement, diversity in the United States and globally, and women's issues. Musil directs AAC&U's Center on Liberal Education and Civic Engagement as well as AAC&U's multiproject initiative Core Commitments: Educating Students for Personal and Social Responsibility. She also serves on the steering committees of both the Democracy Imperative and the International Consortium for Higher Education, Civic Responsibility, and Democracy, which involves a partnership with the Council of Europe. Musil's interests focus on mobilizing the three powerful and overlapping educational reform movements—civic, diversity, and global learning—to advance democratic competencies and commitments. Musil received her BA in English from Duke University and her MA and PhD in English from Northwestern University.

Elizabeth L. Paul is vice provost at the College of New Jersey in Ewing, New Jersey, where she holds the rank of professor of psychology and has served as interim provost and vice president for academic affairs, interim vice president for student life, and chair of the department of psychology. She is recognized for her expertise in higher education and community-based assessment, as well as pedagogical innovations in undergraduate research and community-based research. She was the inaugural chair of the social sciences division of the Council on Undergraduate Research (CUR) and has served for years as a facilitator at CUR institutes on growing undergraduate research programs on campuses nationwide. From 2000 to 2006, Paul directed the Trenton Youth Community-Based Research Corps at the College of New Jersey, in which she worked with undergraduate students in partnership with nonprofit community agencies to accomplish research in service of agency needs. In 2006, she was recognized with an honorable mention for the Ernest A. Lynton Faculty Award for the Scholarship of Engagement. Paul also conducts scholarship on relational challenges of late adolescence and young adulthood, particularly youths' risky sexual experiences. Her PhD in personality psychology is from Boston University.

Marguerite S. Shaffer is director of American studies and an associate professor of American studies and history at Miami University in Oxford, Ohio. She is the author of *See America First: Tourism and National Identity, 1880–1940* (Smithsonian Institution Press, 2001). Her essays have appeared in the *Pacific Historical Review* and *Planning Perspectives* and in the collections *Reopening the American West; Being Elsewhere: Tourism, Consumer Culture, and Identity in Modern Europe and North America; Seeing and Being Seen; The Culture of Tourism and the Tourism of Culture;* and *The Blackwell Companion to the American West.* She has received grants and fellowships from the National Endowment for the Humanities, the Smithsonian Institution, the Huntington Library, Dumbarton Oaks, and the James J. Hill Reference Library. Her current work focuses on public culture in the United States. Shaffer received a BA (1985) in history from the University of Pennsylvania and a PhD (1994) in the history of American civilization from Harvard University.

Kim Spiezio is professor of political science and dean of graduate studies at Cedar Crest College. Before that, he was on the faculty at the University of Minnesota and Virginia Polytechnic Institute. His research and teaching interests center on the relationship between law and public policy in the United States, with a particular emphasis on issues relating to education, globalization, and national security. His most recent publications address the role that general education can play in promoting civic engagement and character education among students. Spiezio's PhD (1987) is in political science from the State University of New York at Binghamton.

Nicole Webster is an associate professor in the department of agricultural and extension education and an affiliate for the Center for Human Development and Family Research in Diverse Contexts at the Pennsylvania State University. She specializes in, and has published on, service-learning as it relates to multicultural issues and urban and at-risk youth. In 2001, she was a visiting scholar and instructor at the University of Limpopo in Pietersburg, South Africa. From 1999 to 2001, she served as an extension agent in 4-H youth development at Virginia Cooperative Extension. In 2007, she was recognized by the John Glenn School of Public Affairs at the Ohio State University as one of twenty-five service-learning scholars. Webster received her BS in food and resource economics from the University of Florida. Her MS (1996) and PhD (2002) are from Michigan State University.

Marshall Welch is the director of the Catholic Institute for Lasallian Social Action at St. Mary's College of California. Before coming to St. Mary's College, Welch served as director of the Lowell Bennion Community Service Center at the University of Utah and as a faculty fellow assisting colleagues in establishing service-learning courses. Previously, Welch was a professor in the university's department of special education. He has written articles and made numerous presentations on service-learning and civic engagement nationally and internationally. Welch coedited a book on the research on service-learning and has been recognized as a national leader in the field. His research interests include the social justice and spiritual development of students. Welch earned his PhD (1987) in special education from Southern Illinois University.

Introduction

Higher education is being called on to renew its historical commitment to its public purposes. It is clear that American colleges and universities have always included among their core purposes responding to society's most pressing issues and preparing graduates for responsible citizenship. However, in the past two or three decades, higher education's foremost experts, together with its most outspoken critics, have been urging colleges and universities to take a leadership role in addressing our global society's increasing problems and meeting growing human needs. In 1982, Derek Bok stated, "There is no reason for universities to feel uncomfortable in taking account of society's needs; in fact, they have a clear obligation to do so" (p. 301). Ernest Boyer (1994) directly admonished colleges to "respond to the challenges that confront our children, our schools, and our cities, just as the land-grant colleges responded to the needs of agriculture and industry a century ago" (p. 48). Bok's and Boyer's urgent calls for the civic engagement of higher education were echoed in 1999 by Harry Boyte and Elizabeth Hollander, who lamented, "Whereas universities were once centrally concerned with 'education for democracy' and 'knowledge for society,' today's institutions have often drifted away from their civic mission" (p. 7).

In the context of these broad challenges for higher education to revitalize its civic purpose, the specific focus of this book is on educating students for civic engagement, or preparation for active democratic citizenship. As Richard Morrill (1982) states, "Education for democratic citizenship involves human capacities relating to judgment, to choice, and above all, to action. To be literate as a citizen requires more than knowledge and information; it includes the exercise of personal responsibility, active participation, and personal commitment to a set of values. Democratic

1

literacy is a literacy of doing, not simply of knowing. Knowledge is a necessary, but not sufficient, condition of democratic responsibility" (p. 365).

Civic engagement has become more prominent in undergraduate education in the first decade of the new millennium. Cynthia M. Gibson (2006) notes: "During recent years, increasing numbers of colleges and universities have engaged in innovative efforts to reinvigorate the civic mission of their institutions" (p. 2). *Civic engagement* is a frequent catchphrase in current publications and conversations regarding the public purposes of higher education. A 2006 Ford Foundation report on liberal education and civic engagement emphasizes that "the role of colleges and universities in furthering civic engagement and public participation has come to be seen as a matter of increasingly pressing concern" (Lawry, Laurison, and VanAntwerpen, p. 4). Educators have grown much more conscious that we live in a global society and that we must prepare our students to be active global citizens.

If civic engagement is to gain real traction in today's higher education, it must be clearly defined, and civic learning outcomes must be established. Opportunities to learn about and practice civic engagement must be embedded throughout the curriculum and the cocurriculum. This book shows how all this can be done, and is being done, at higher education institutions around the country.

AUDIENCES

Because nearly all colleges and universities include citizenship education in their mission statements and offer some type of program to achieve this goal, the intended readership for this book is broad. It includes presidents (more than eleven hundred have demonstrated their interest in civic engagement by joining Campus Compact), academic officers, and student affairs professionals. Faculty members across disciplines will find multiple ways to enliven their teaching through civically engaged pedagogy. A primary audience is likely to be the entry- and midlevel professionals and graduate students who generally work in the trenches of service-learning, leadership development, campus activities, and civic engagement. Another is the mid- to senior-level professionals—directors, assistant/associate directors, assistant/

associate deans—who supervise these frontline staff and who oversee civic engagement offices or initiatives. This book also contains
important implications for trustees, public policymakers, foundation leaders, and government officials whose understanding and
support are critical if civic engagement in higher education is to
fulfill its promise and to be sustainable over time.

Overview of the Contents

The first chapter provides the background and fundamentals of
civic engagement in higher education, including its history and
current state of practice. Chapter 2, by Mark Hugo Lopez
and Abby Kiesa, addresses what we know about college students'
civic engagement. In chapter 3, Caryn McTighe Musil presents the
Civic Learning Spiral, which creatively portrays what students
should know and be able to do to be active and engaged citizens
locally, nationally, and globally.

Chapters 4 through 12 describe numerous examples of and
approaches to civic engagement from a wide range of institutions
across the United States. It is important that colleges and universities offer a spectrum of curricular and cocurricular opportunities
to learn about and practice civic engagement that are intentionally designed for students at different points in their education
and at various stages of development. In chapter 4, Mary Stuart
Hunter and Blaire L. Moody profile civic engagement in first-year
experiences. Kim Spiezio, in chapter 5, thoughtfully examines
how democratic practices can be integrated into courses across
disciplines. The focus of chapter 6, by Nance Lucas, is on innovative practices that combine interdisciplinary and integrative learning with civic engagement. Kevin Kecskes and Seanna Kerrigan
describe capstone experiences as the culmination of students' education for engaged citizenship in chapter 7. In chapter 8, Michelle
R. Dunlap and Nicole Webster integrate civic engagement and
education for intercultural competency. Chapter 9, by Nicholas
V. Longo and Marguerite S. Shaffer, focuses on leadership education and its role in the revitalization of public life. Moving from
service to civic engagement is the topic of chapter 10, by Marshall
Welch. Elizabeth L. Paul, in chapter 11, provides examples of good
practice for community-based undergraduate research, together

with practical guidance for initiating and sustaining community research partnerships. Chapter 12, by Barbara Jacoby and Nevin C. Brown, offers principles, options, and institutional models of international civic engagement experiences. In the final chapter, Barbara Jacoby and Elizabeth Hollander examine strategies for securing the future of civic engagement in higher education, on campus and beyond.

The book is organized sequentially so that it will reward readers who read it from cover to cover. Each chapter also stands up well individually to allow readers to pick and choose among the chapters at will.

References

Bok, D. *Beyond the Ivory Tower: Social Responsibilities of the Modern University.* Cambridge, MA: Harvard University Press, 1982.

Boyer, E. L. "Creating the New American College." *Chronicle of Higher Education*, March 9, 1994, p. 48.

Boyte, H., and Hollander, E. *Wingspread Declaration on Renewing the Civic Mission of the American Research University.* Providence, RI: Campus Compact, 1999.

Gibson, C. M. *New Times Demand New Scholarship: Research Universities and Civic Engagement.* Medford, MA: Tufts University and Campus Compact, 2006.

Lawry, S., Laurison, D. L., and VanAntwerpen, J. *Liberal Education and Civic Engagement: A Project of the Ford Foundation's Knowledge, Creativity and Freedom Program.* http://www.fordfound.org/elibrary/documents/5029/toc.cfm, 2006.

Morrill, R. L. "Educating for Democratic Values," *Liberal Education*, 1982, *68*(4), 365–376.

CHAPTER ONE

CIVIC ENGAGEMENT IN TODAY'S HIGHER EDUCATION
An Overview

Barbara Jacoby

This chapter begins by addressing the inherent challenges in defining civic engagement and proposes a working definition. It continues with a brief history of civic engagement in higher education. Finally, it offers an overview of contemporary initiatives. While acknowledging that the term *civic engagement* can be applied to both individuals and institutions, it is important to state up front that this book is about *educating students for civic engagement*. This, therefore, is the focus of the definition of civic engagement, the history and the overview contained in this chapter, and the practices described in the following chapters. Although they are not covered in detail here, institutional civic engagement with communities, both local and global, and recognition of engaged scholarship in the faculty reward system provide an essential context for the purpose of educating students for civic engagement. Chapter 13 highlights the role of these institutional factors.

DEFINING CIVIC ENGAGEMENT

There is widespread recognition that defining civic engagement presents formidable challenges. In fact, there are probably as many definitions of civic engagement as there are scholars and practitioners who are concerned with it. Civic engagement is a

5

complex and polyonymous concept. In addition, scholars and practitioners use a multiplicity of terms to name it, including social capital, citizenship, democratic participation/citizenship/ practice, public work/public problem solving, political engagement, community engagement, social responsibility, social justice, civic professionalism, public agency, community building, civic or public leadership, development of public intellectuals, and preservation and expansion of the commons (Battistoni, 2002; Levine, 2007).

Challenges of Defining Civic Engagement

As John Saltmarsh (2005) notes: "A lack of clarity about what is meant by the term 'civic engagement' is evident when, at almost any gathering convened for the purpose of furthering civic engagement in higher education, questions inevitably arise about what is meant by civic engagement and about how it relates to civic education, service learning, democratic education, political engagement, civics, education for citizenship, or moral education. Moreover, the lack of clarity fuels a latent confusion about how to operationalize a civic engagement agenda on campus" (p. 2). Saltmarsh's dilemma is quite real for me because I am frequently asked by colleague educators, "What *is* civic engagement, anyway?" Another typical comment is "We do not have a definition of civic engagement here at XYZ University, but we are in the process of putting together a center for civic engagement." Others have wondered, is civic engagement a content area, a process for skill development, or a lifestyle? Is it a program, a pedagogy, or a philosophy? Can it be all of these? Peter Levine (2007) muses that civic engagement's lack of definition may to some extent account for its popularity: "It is a Rorschach blot within which anyone can find her own priorities" (p. 1).

Other scholars have suggested further difficulties in defining civic engagement. Among these is the concern of political partisanship. Battistoni (2002) elucidates the nature of the ideological barrier to the language of civic engagement or citizenship education: "Faculty on the left complain that citizenship education tends to convey images of patriotic flag-waving. More conservative faculty see civic engagement as masking a leftist, activist agenda"

(p. 10). These troublesome misconceptions are shared by many others besides faculty, both inside and outside the academy. Levine agrees that the definition of civic engagement is "extremely value laden and controversial" because it is impossible to define civic engagement without a clear understanding of what is a good society and what it would take to make our society better (personal communication, March 6, 2007). The issue of the relationship of civic engagement to social justice is often raised as well. Is the purpose of civic engagement to create a socially just world? Like the concepts of "a good society" and "the common good," the term *social justice* is confounded because what constitutes justice to one person may be dramatically different from what another construes it to be.

Another common issue is that students and educators alike wonder whether community service and civic engagement are the same thing. Several colleges and universities have renamed their community service or service-learning offices "civic engagement" but have not changed the programs or services they offer. This interchangeability of terminology, as well as the avoidance of defining civic engagement, are reinforced by the comprehensive *Review of Service Learning Research* prepared by Jaime Lester and Margaret Salle (2006), under the direction of Adrianna Kezar, at the University of Southern California and in collaboration with that university's Civic Engagement Initiative. Their review lists thirty-three recent studies, only three of which include a definition of civic engagement.

WORKING DEFINITION OF CIVIC ENGAGEMENT

There is widespread agreement that definitions of civic engagement for the purpose of educating students to become civically engaged citizens, scholars, and leaders are broad and multifaceted. Knowledge and skills are acknowledged to be necessary but not sufficient. Values, motivation, and commitment are also required. In *College Learning for the New Global Century,* the Association of American Colleges and Universities states, "In a democracy that is diverse, globally engaged, and dependent on citizen responsibilities, all students need an informed concern for the larger good because nothing less will renew our fractured and diminished commons" (National Leadership Council for Liberal Education and America's Promise, 2007, p. 13). To further complicate matters, Barry Checkoway, in "Renewing the Civic Mission of the American Research University" (2001), elaborates: "Education for citizenship becomes more complex in a diverse democratic society in which communities are not 'monocultural,' consisting of people who share the same social and cultural characteristics, but 'multicultural,' with significant differences among groups. For democracy to function successfully in the future, students must be prepared to understand their own identities, communicate with people who are different from themselves, and build bridges across cultural differences in the transition to a more diverse society" (p. 127).

In a report for the Ford Foundation, Steven Lawry, Daniel L. Laurison, and Jonathan VanAntwerpen (2006) acknowledge that, in recent years, "the concept of civic engagement has been subject to a profusion of sometimes overlapping, sometimes competing attempts at a greater definition" and conclude that "civic engagement has become the rubric under which faculty, administrators and students think about, argue about and attempt to implement a variety of visions of higher education in service to society" (p. 12). The Ford Foundation's report focuses on civic engagement initiatives aimed at students, as does this volume. In it, the authors acknowledge that "there is near consensus that an essential part of civic engagement is feeling responsible to part of something beyond individual interests" (Lawry et al., 2006, p. 13).

Most programs they studied want students to develop a sense of involvement, investment, or responsibility with regard to some group or context. Such civic values are characterized in multiple ways, ranging from generally caring about one's community, to committing to making the world a better place, to believing that voting is an important duty (Lawry et al., 2006). The report also states that knowledge and skills are critical building blocks for civic engagement. Being informed and knowledgeable about local, national, and world affairs is necessary, as is an understanding of the workings of democratic processes (Lawry et al., 2006). Lawry et al. further report that the kinds of actions that constitute civic engagement are construed quite broadly and often cover a wide range of possibilities, with community service the most

often advocated type of civic engagement, with political participation next, and with activism or advocacy promoted the least
frequently. Levine (2007) concurs that civic engagement, while
"rarely defined in a coherent sentence or paragraph . . . is often
operationalized as a list of variables" (p. 1). The work of the Center for Information & Research on Civic Learning & Engagement
has measured civic engagement along nineteen core indicators in
three categories: community participation, political engagement,
and political voice (Levine, 2007).

The working definition of civic engagement for the purposes
of this book is a slight variation of the definition created and
embraced by the Coalition for Civic Engagement and Leadership at the University of Maryland. Civic engagement is defined
as "acting upon a heightened sense of responsibility to one's communities. This includes a wide range of activities, including developing civic sensitivity, participation in building civil society, and
benefiting the common good. Civic engagement encompasses
the notions of global citizenship and interdependence. Through
civic engagement, individuals—as citizens of their communities,
their nations, and the world—are empowered as agents of positive
social change for a more democratic world" (Coalition for Civic
Engagement and Leadership, 2005).

Civic engagement involves one or more of the following:

- Learning from others, self, and environment to develop
  informed perspectives on social issues
- Valuing diversity and building bridges across difference
- Behaving, and working through controversy, with civility
- Taking an active role in the political process
- Participating actively in public life, public problem solving, and
  community service
- Assuming leadership and membership roles in organizations
- Developing empathy, ethics, values, and sense of social
  responsibility
- Promoting social justice locally and globally (Coalition for Civic
  Engagement and Leadership, 2005)

While other terms are used to denote civic engagement, I
have chosen to use *civic engagement* as the most common and most
inclusive term. It does not bear the exclusionary connotation of
citizenship, which also refers to a government-determined legal

status. It offers a "big tent" that allows individuals and initiatives representing a range of perspectives to gather beneath it for the purpose of creating a cohesive whole that advances responsibility for the common good.

However, it is important that each institution choose the term, definition, and approach that best suits its unique mission, culture, and traditions. Faith-based institutions often gravitate to a social justice focus, while historically black institutions, community colleges, and urban universities may prefer a definition grounded in community partnerships or public problem solving. Others, including some Ivy League universities, emphasize citizenship or public service.

A BRIEF HISTORY OF CIVIC ENGAGEMENT IN HIGHER EDUCATION

American higher education has always included among its core mission the preparation of effective citizens: "As long as there have been colleges and universities in this country, there has been a commitment at the heart of the curriculum to preparation for what we might call civic engagement" (Lawry et al., 2006, p. 7). Since the founding of Harvard College in 1636, one of the articulated purposes of higher education in this country has been the preparation of graduates for active involvement in community life (Smith, 1994). Benjamin Franklin and Thomas Jefferson, two of the greatest thinkers of the Revolutionary period, put considerable energy into reforming higher education to be even more responsive to the needs of citizens in the emerging nation: "They considered informed and responsible participation, at least by qualified men, essential to the success of the democratic experiment" (Lawry et al., 2006, p. 7). Colonial colleges taught the classics and emphasized piety until politically sensitive presidents like Yale's Ezra Stiles encouraged students to debate issues related to independence (Kezar, Chambers, and Burkhardt, 2005).

Following the Revolutionary War, the focus of higher education slowly began to shift from the preparation of the individual to the building of a new nation (Boyer, 1994). In Jefferson's time, state legislatures first chartered universities to educate national leaders. In 1862, the passage of the Land-Grant Act created institutions that inextricably linked public higher education and the concept of civic engagement, as it specifically relates to agriculture and industry.

Arguably, John Dewey was the single most influential advocate for the civic role of higher education, particularly in the liberal arts. In *Democracy and Education,* he wrote that the liberal arts experience should consist of "three essential elements: it should engage students in the surrounding community; it should be focused on problems to be solved rather than academic discipline; and it should collaboratively involve students and faculty" (as cited in Lawry et al., 2006, p. 7). Unfortunately, in the first half of the twentieth century, there were few national or institutional initiatives in response to Dewey's call (Stanton and Wagner, 2006).

Even though educating students for responsible citizenship was not a priority for higher education in the early and middle years of the last century, when the economy collapsed and caused the Great Depression, President Franklin D. Roosevelt recruited outstanding scholars to serve as consultants. During World War II, research universities worked closely with the federal government to create solutions to new problems. In the wake of the war, two important partnerships between the federal government and higher education were founded: the GI Bill and the National Science Foundation. Once the Soviet Union launched *Sputnik* in 1957, higher education formed yet another partnership with the federal government to advance national interests by improving education in primary and secondary schools: the National Defense Education Act. Boyer (1994) points out that "the very title of the National Defense Education Act of 1958 clearly linked higher education to the security of our country" (p. 48).

With the launch of the Peace Corps in 1961 and Volunteers in Service to America in 1965, college student involvement in community service came to the fore on the national scene. Despite the lack of broad and concerted national initiatives before the 1960s, there had been a long history of college student community service that includes the YMCA, 4-H, the Scouting movement, fraternities and sororities, and many programs sponsored by campus ministries (Jacoby, 1996). Simultaneously, a small, loosely connected group of pioneers of a pedagogy they called "service-learning" began to combine community service with academic study (Stanton, Giles, and Cruz, 1999). Many campus-based service programs were started in the 1960s and 1970s, along with several regional and consortium programs. In 1978, the National Society for Internships and Experiential Education (as of 1994, the National Society for Experiential Education) was formed by fusing separate groups for field experience education and service internships.

Also, in the 1980s, Americans were alarmed by growing concern over the apathy of citizens in general and of college students in particular. In *Habits of the Heart,* Robert Bellah, Richard M. Madsen, William M. Sullivan, Ann Swidler, and Steven M. Tipton (1985) argued that Americans had become more individualistic and less concerned with the common good. Far-reaching thinkers like Richard Morrill (1982) challenged fellow academicians to focus their energies squarely on education for civic engagement that combines knowledge and action, "the empowerment of persons and the cultivation of minds" (p. 365). Campus Compact was formed in 1985 by college and university presidents who pledged to encourage and support education in service of civic responsibility. Campus Compact presently has more than eleven hundred presidents as members and remains dedicated to both institutional and individual civic engagement in higher education. Through the support of the National Society for Experiential Education, Campus Compact, and the student-driven Campus Outreach Opportunity League, community service and service-learning grew dramatically on college campuses through the 1980s and 1990s.

The passage of the National and Community Service Act in 1990, which was signed into law by President George H. W. Bush, authorized a new independent federal agency, the Commission on National and Community Service. The commission provided support for service and service-learning programs for school-aged youth and college students, along with national service demonstration models. The National and Community Service Trust Act of 1993, under the Bill Clinton administration, created the Corporation for National and Community Service, which administers several programs to mobilize Americans into service. These include Senior Corps, AmeriCorps, USA Freedom Corps, and Learn and Serve America. The latter three programs have since provided substantial technical and financial support to service, service-learning, and civic engagement in higher education (Corporation for National and Community Service, n.d.).

As service-learning soared to prominence on college campuses of all types, it has been integrated into academic courses and majors as well as into initiatives such as living-learning programs, course-based learning communities, new student orientation, leadership development, and multicultural education. We have more research about its effects, more models and principles to guide its practice, and more support from private and public sources. We know from national and institutional research that service-learning done well combines service with academic content and reflection to serve as a powerful introduction to developing an understanding of the root causes of social problems and where to begin to find solutions (Jacoby, 2003). In addition, viewing service-learning in terms of civic engagement enables educators to "make room in [their] practices and in [their] curriculum for conversations where students name for themselves what it is they are doing and its connections to community, citizenship, and democratic politics" (Morton and Battistoni, 1995, p. 18). Chapter 10 further discusses the relationship between service-learning and civic engagement.

The 1990s also saw a dramatic increase in efforts to bring college and university resources to bear on both broad social issues and local problems, giving rise to terms such as "the engaged campus" and "universities as citizens." The concept of college and university outreach is as old as American higher education itself. It took firm root with the creation of the land-grant universities in the nineteenth century and the subsequent launch of the Wisconsin Idea early in the twentieth century. More recently, campus-community engagement has thrived, inspired by the trailblazing work at institutions like the University of Pennsylvania, Portland State University, and Trinity College in Hartford, Connecticut (Butin, 2007; Harkavy, 1992; Harkavy and Puckett, 1994). Numerous campus-community partnerships were initiated through funding from the U.S. Department of Housing and Urban Development's Office of University Partnerships and subsequent Community Outreach Partnership Center (Soska and Johnson Butterfield, 2004). Through service-learning and other engaged pedagogies, campus-community partnerships provide myriad opportunities for student civic engagement.

In 1990, Boyer redefined scholarship, which went a long way to open up the idea of what counts as scholarly work in the academy (Zlotkowski, 2005). He "also provided much of the intellectual scaffolding needed to create new ties between the academy and society in general" (Zlotkowski, 2005, p. 148). According to Boyer (1990), the scholarship of engagement means connecting the rich resources of higher education institutions to our most pressing social, civic, and ethical problems. He urged scholars to ask, "How can knowledge be responsibly applied to consequential problems? How can it be helpful to individuals as well as to institutions? Can social problems themselves define an agenda for scholarly investigation?" (p. 21). Many scholars have echoed and elaborated on Boyer's call for engaged scholarship to be valued and rewarded by the academy to the same extent as "pure," or traditional, research and have noted the challenges of achieving recognition for engaged scholarship in the faculty reward system (Gibson, 2006; O'Meara, 1997; O'Meara and Rice, 2005).

The late 1990s saw a rise in the prominence of the concept of civic engagement, together with "a blossoming of intellectual and institutional concern with the issue" (Lawry et al., 2006, p. 8). It was in 1995 that Robert D. Putnam's article "Bowling Alone: America's Declining Social Capital" won a wide audience by arguing that social capital has eroded in the United States. Putnam (1995) documented the decline of our "longstanding traditions of civic engagement" and lamented, "Whatever happened to civic engagement?" (pp. 65–67). He struck a chord.

The rise of service-learning, engaged scholarship, and campus-community partnerships spurred by Putnam's lament about American society and by clarion calls for higher education to rededicate itself to its public mission (Boyte and Hollander, 1999; Kezar et al., 2005) led to the development of a movement in the past ten or so years to restore preparing students for civic engagement to the forefront of higher education. This movement, as its proponents would call it, is not only national but also international in scope. The following section briefly outlines the contemporary landscape of the movement for civic engagement in higher education.

MAJOR CIVIC ENGAGEMENT INITIATIVES IN HIGHER EDUCATION IN THE TWENTY-FIRST CENTURY

As Scott London (2001) notes: "A new movement is taking shape in American higher education, one aimed at education for democracy, nurturing community, and promoting civic participation. Across the country, colleges, universities, and academic associations are striving to make civic engagement an integral part of the way they do their work" (p. 17). There is no doubt that major civic engagement initiatives are in place and growing across higher education. Higher education associations of all sizes and membership bases have embraced civic engagement and included it in their missions, as have foundations, research organizations, and individual institutions. This section provides an overview of some of these to highlight their breadth and depth.

CAMPUS COMPACT

Campus Compact's mission (n.d.) is to advance the public purpose of colleges and universities "by deepening their ability to improve community life and to educate students for civic and social responsibility." As previously mentioned, the organization's civic engagement work encompasses both institutional engagement with communities and educating students for responsible citizenship. Of particular note in regard to the latter, Campus Compact published in 2006 two volumes that focus on mobilizing students to be effective leaders for change while enhancing their academic and civic learning: *Raise Your Voice: A Student Guide to Positive Social Change* (Cone, Kiesa, and Longo) and *Students as Colleagues: Expanding the Circle of Service-Learning Leadership* (Zlotkowski, Longo, and Williams). Campus Compact's network of state compacts, currently in thirty-four states, provide leadership at the local, state, and regional levels to mobilize resources and provide support for member institutions. The state compacts have been instrumental in leading national efforts on cutting-edge practices. For example, two regional colloquiums, one in the West and one in the upper Midwest, have explored issues related to civic engagement in graduate education (O'Meara, 2007).

ASSOCIATION OF AMERICAN COLLEGES AND UNIVERSITIES

Liberal education, civic engagement, and diversity are at the hub of the extensive work of the Association of American Colleges and Universities (AAC&U), which includes publications, projects, and conferences. The organization advocates "a philosophy of education that empowers individuals, liberates the mind, and cultivates social responsibility" (AAC&U, 2002, p. x). AAC&U (n.d.) views civic engagement as "an essential principle in today's discussions of higher learning." In 2007, AAC&U unveiled its essential learning outcomes in a report entitled *College Learning for the New Global Century:* knowledge of human cultures and the physical and natural world, intellectual and practical skills, personal and social responsibility, and integrative learning. The outcome for personal and social responsibility includes civic knowledge and engagement, both local and global, together with intercultural knowledge and competence, ethical reasoning and action, and foundations and skills for lifelong learning (National Leadership Council for Liberal Education and America's Promise, 2007). Chapter 3 of this volume describes the Civic Learning Spiral developed by AAC&U's Civic Engagement Working Group (Musil et al., in press).

The Bringing Theory to Practice Project (BTtoP) is an independent national effort funded by the Charles Engelhard Foundation that functions in partnership with AAC&U to enable colleges and universities "to build capacity for institutionalizing forms of engaged learning and to understand their relation to outcomes affecting the well-being and civic development of students" (Bringing Theory to Practice, 2007, p. 1). The project originated out of concerns for rising levels of academic disengagement among college students, abuse of alcohol and drugs, and civic disengagement "increasing to levels which are alarming and may jeopardize the scope and quality of a democratic society" (Bringing Theory to Practice, 2007, p. 3). Through grants, national conferences, and publications, BTtoP seeks to encourage the development and practice of innovative, engaged learning strategies to address these concerns.

AMERICAN DEMOCRACY PROJECT, AMERICAN ASSOCIATION OF STATE COLLEGES AND UNIVERSITIES

In 2003, the American Association of State Colleges and Universities and the *New York Times* joined forces to launch the American Democracy Project for the purpose of preparing "the next generation of active, engaged citizens for our democracy" (C. Orphan, personal communication, October 10, 2007). Initially more than 130 university presidents responded to the call for participation. By 2007, there were 228 participating institutions. Initiatives of the American Democracy Project focus on global competencies, stewardship of public lands, political engagement, jury duty as an essential element of democracy, deliberative polling, and measurement of institutional performance in civic engagement (C. Orphan, personal communication, October 10, 2007). Intended for faculty of all disciplines, the American Democracy Project published its *Toolkit for Teaching in a Democratic Academy* to encourage them to transform their courses into democratic classrooms (Meade and Weaver, 2004). The toolkit provides a range of practical techniques for faculty that are designed to enable students to gain civic skills by taking responsibility for their learning and participating actively in the classroom community. The democratic classroom is further discussed in chapter 5.

ASSOCIATIONS SUPPORTING COMMUNITY COLLEGES

From both the pedagogical and community partnership standpoints, community colleges and the associations that support them are deeply involved in civic engagement. According to three national surveys by the American Association of Community Colleges (2006), nearly 60 percent of community colleges offer service-learning in their curricular programs. The association's national project, Community Colleges Broadening Horizons through Service Learning, provides an information clearinghouse, publications, training and technical assistance, and model programs to increase the number, quality, and sustainability of service-learning programs in its member institutions. The project is funded by the Corporation for National and Community Service. The association's publication *A Practical Guide for Integrating Civic*

Responsibility into the Curriculum (2006) is widely used and available online (see http://www.aacc.nche.edu/Content/NavigationMenu/ ResourceCenter/Projects_Partnerships/Current/HorizonsService LearningProject/Publications/CR_guide_2nd.pdf).

The Community College National Center for Community Engagement also offers a wide range of resources and services, such as course syllabi, funding opportunities, conferences, program models, publications, awards, and training and technical assistance. It also publishes the online *Journal for Civic Commitment* (see http://www.mc.maricopa.edu/other/engagement/Journal). In addition, Campus Compact's resources include some developed specifically for community colleges.

DISCIPLINARY ASSOCIATIONS

Disciplinary associations in a variety of fields have been embracing Boyer's concept of the scholarship of engagement and focusing on educating students for civic engagement. Among these are the Association of American Geographers, the American Chemical Society, the American Psychological Association, the American Institute of Biological Sciences, the American Sociological Association, the American Political Science Association, and the National Communication Association (Zlotkowski, 2005). Similarly, sector-based associations provide resources to related groups of disciplines. Community-Campus Partnerships for Health (n.d.) has members from a wide range of health professions and emphasizes the improvement of "health professional education, civic responsibility and the overall health of communities." Imagining America is a national consortium of higher education and cultural institutions dedicated to supporting the civic work of university artists, humanists, and designers. Like Community-Campus Partnerships for Health (CCPH), Imagining America provides resources to facilitate engaged scholarship, teaching, and community-based programs (Zlotkowski, 2005). Science Education for New Civic Engagements and Responsibilities (SENCER) was initiated in 2001 by AAC&U with funding from the National Science Foundation. SENCER supports the improvement of undergraduate science, technology, engineering, and mathematics education by connecting learning to critical civic questions. Unlike CCPH and

Imagining America, SENCER (http://www.sencer.net/About/ projectoverview.cfm) focuses less on community partnerships and more on curriculum and faculty development to make science more real, accessible, and civically important to college students who are not science majors. Resources published by Campus Compact and the now-defunct American Association for Higher Education support discipline-based service-learning and civic engagement as well as the creation of "engaged departments" and can be found at http://www.styluspub.com/Books/ BookDetail.aspx?productID=117889 and http://www.compact. org/publications/detail/engaged_department_toolkit.

OTHER ASSOCIATIONS

Through its nonpartisan National Campus Voter Registration Project, the National Association of Independent Colleges and Universities (see http://www.naicu.edu) helps member institutions conduct both voter education programs and campaigns to register students and employees. The Council of Independent Colleges' Engaging Communities and Campuses program created the Effective Practices Exchange, a rich online source of both conceptual and practical resources (see http://www.cic.edu/projects_services/epe).

The Higher Education Network for Community Engagement (see http://henceonline.org/about) was founded in 2006 in "response to the growing need to deepen, consolidate, and advance the literature, research, practice, policy, and advocacy for community engagement as a core element of higher education's role in society." The organization's membership includes a wide range of associations and individual institutions committed to working individually and together to advance civic and community engagement across higher education.

Several smaller higher education organizations whose membership consists of institutions of a particular type have a special interest in civic engagement. Project Pericles, an organization founded in 2001 by philanthropist Eugene M. Lang, has the specific goal of promoting civic engagement among college students. Each of the twenty-two colleges and universities participating in the project has found novel ways to connect traditional academic learning with social issues (Project Pericles, 2006).

Two additional examples are the Associated New American Colleges (see http://www.anac.org)—whose mission combines liberal arts, professional studies, and civic engagement—and The Research University Civic Engagement Network, a group of Carnegie Foundation–defined very high research institutions that work together to strengthen and advance civic and community engagement at research universities and nationally (see http://www.compact.org/initiatives/research_universities).

Foundations

Foundations, which can significantly influence the direction of higher education through the programs they initiate and support, are also evidencing great interest in civic engagement. In 2002, the Kellogg Foundation sponsored a series of national dialogues among more than two hundred campus and community leaders to define and further commitment and public support for a multifaceted civic mission for higher education. The report of the National Forum on Higher Education and the Public Good (formerly the Kellogg Forum) that followed the dialogues identifies an agenda for higher education institutions and practical steps toward reengaging students, including promoting student activism and leadership, making community-based learning integral to the curriculum, fostering a campus culture of dialogue and debate, and encouraging continued commitment to public service and social responsibility after graduation by providing a range of public service and nonprofit career choices (National Forum on Higher Education and the Public Good, 2003).

Since the early 1990s, the Kettering Foundation has been working to strengthen democracy. The primary question it addresses is "What does it take to make democracy work as it should?" (see http://www.kettering.org). As such, it has a strong interest in higher education's role in preparing college students for democratic citizenship. While it does not make grants, it partners with organizations with similar interests and produces excellent publications that promote the civic mission of higher education, including *Connections* and the *Higher Education Exchange,* both available free in print and online through Kettering's Web site.

The Bonner Foundation's Bonner Scholars Program supports four-year community service scholarships for students attending twenty-seven colleges and universities. Bonner programs at approximately fifty additional institutions provide a range of civic engagement opportunities. The foundation's Web site also offers substantial resources for planning and implementing civic engagement programs (see http://www.bonner.org).

The Carnegie Foundation for the Advancement of Teaching has done substantial work in both educating students for civic engagement and encouraging institutional civic responsibility. In 2003, the foundation and Jossey-Bass published *Educating Citizens: Preparing America's Undergraduates for Lives of Moral and Civic Responsibility* (Colby, Ehrlich, Beaumont, and Stephens). This volume provides examples of how different types of institutions are preparing their students to be thoughtful, committed, and responsible citizens. Following *Educating Citizens,* Carnegie initiated the Political Engagement Project, which examines and assesses the impact of twenty-one undergraduate courses and cocurricular programs designed to foster informed political engagement. The project and its implications are described in *Educating for Democracy: Preparing Undergraduates for Political Engagement* (Colby, Beaumont, Ehrlich, and Corngold, 2007).

INSTITUTIONAL CLASSIFICATION AND ACCREDITATION

When the Carnegie Foundation redesigned its classification system for higher education institutions, in 2006, it released a new elective classification for community engagement. Community engagement describes "the collaboration between institutions of higher education and their larger communities (local, regional/state, national, global) for the mutually beneficial exchange of knowledge and resources in a context of partnership and reciprocity" (Carnegie Foundation for the Advancement of Teaching, 2007). The classification includes three categories: curricular engagement, outreach and partnerships, and a combination of the first two. Of most relevance to the topic of this book, curricular engagement recognizes institutions "where teaching, learning and scholarship engage faculty, students, and community in mutually beneficial and respectful collaboration" (Carnegie Foundation for the Advancement of Teaching, 2007).

In the area of accreditation of higher education institutions, the North Central Association's Higher Learning Commission includes an accreditation criterion for engagement and service. The commission asserts, "If colleges and universities have erred in the past century, it has been in marginalizing the importance of their engagement in serving the common good" (North Central Association, Higher Learning Commission, 2003, p. 56). It is expected that other regional accrediting associations will follow North Central's lead in establishing criteria regarding civic engagement and assessing institutions based on those criteria.

RESEARCH ON CIVIC ENGAGEMENT

In this decade, a growing body of research and literature informs the development of civic engagement efforts on college campuses. The Center for Information & Research on Civic Learning & Engagement (CIRCLE) conducts and funds research specifically on the civic and political engagement of Americans between the ages of fifteen and twenty-five. CIRCLE's Web site (http://www.civicyouth.org) provides a wealth of useful resources on a range of topics regarding college and noncollege youth, including demographics, voting, community participation, attitudes and beliefs, and civic education. Campus Compact, the Higher Education Research Institute, and the Corporation for National and Community Service conduct annual surveys of college students that provide valuable information on their civic engagement. The Jonathan M. Tisch College of Citizenship and Public Service at Tufts University and Harvard University's Institute of Politics also conduct studies on multiple aspects of youth civic engagement. The International Association for Research on Service-Learning and Community Engagement was launched in 2005 to support the development and dissemination of research that promotes civic engagement across the educational spectrum (see http://www.researchslce.org). Chapter 2 further discusses research on college student civic engagement.

In addition, several studies address the issues of college students' lack of civic knowledge and skills. The Intercollegiate Studies Institute reports that a majority of college graduates are no better off than when they arrived in terms of acquiring the knowledge necessary for informed democracy and global citizenship. Entitled *Failing Our Students, Failing America: Holding Colleges Accountable for*

Teaching America's History and Institutions, the report states that senior scores are actually lower than freshman scores at some of the nation's most prestigious institutions (see http://www.americancivicliteracy. org). Equally sobering are the results of the 2004 study conducted by AAC&U that asked college juniors and college-bound high school juniors to pick the college outcomes they considered most and least important. In each of the six groups of students who participated in the study, "civic engagement and leadership" was selected by students as the least or second-least important college learning outcome. The students overwhelmingly believed that college was a time to prepare for a job and take responsibility for themselves and their own obligations (Humphreys and Davenport, 2005).

INDIVIDUAL INSTITUTIONAL EFFORTS

In addition to well-established efforts at such institutions as the University of Pennsylvania, the University of Minnesota, Portland State University, and Trinity College in Hartford, Connecticut, the first decade of the twenty-first century has witnessed several individual institutions create major initiatives to advance civic engagement in undergraduate education, in some cases with the support of foundations. The Jonathan M. Tisch College of Citizenship and Public Service (n.d.) at Tufts University is a university-wide initiative founded in 2000 to make the values and skills of active citizenship a hallmark of a Tufts education. The goal of the UCLA in LA initiative of the University of California at Los Angeles is to nurture and develop partnerships between community groups and the university to improve the quality of life for local residents, mainly in the areas of children, youth, and families; economic development; and arts and culture. The Center for Community Learning, the undergraduate curricular arm of the initiative, offers courses, internships with a civic engagement focus, and a civic engagement minor (UCLA in LA, 2007). With the support of the Duke Foundation and the Bill & Melinda Gates Foundation, Duke University launched DukeEngage in 2007, a new program that provides full funding and faculty and administrative support to all undergraduates "who want to stretch beyond the classroom by tackling societal issues at home and abroad, and, in turn, learning from those real-world experiences" (DukeEngage, n.d.). The Office of the

Vice Chancellor for Public Service was created at the University of North Carolina at Chapel Hill in 2007 to build and strengthen relationships between the university and communities across the state. Its programs and activities include identifying and addressing the state's most pressing needs, encouraging faculty members' engaged scholarship, and supporting student civic engagement and service work (L. Robbins, personal communication, November 28, 2007). A wide range of institutional initiatives of varying sizes, scopes, and desired outcomes are profiled throughout the remaining chapters of this volume.

International Initiatives

Following eight years of work to define concepts, policies, and strategies to promote good practice in the area of education for democratic citizenship, the Council of Europe declared 2005 as the European Year of Citizenship through Education. In 2006, it released *Higher Education and Democratic Culture: Citizenship, Human Rights and Civic Responsibility*, a statement by higher education leaders and policy makers that affirms their commitment to "democratic principles and practice; [their] conviction that higher education has an essential role in furthering democratic culture; and [their] responsibility to educate each successive generation to renew and develop the attitudes, values and skills needed for this to become a reality."

Also, in 2005, Tufts University sponsored its fourth international conference at its center in Talloires, France. This one focused on strengthening the civic roles and social responsibilities of higher education. It produced a declaration in which the signatories, presidents of universities around the world, agreed to expand civic engagement and social responsibility programs; foster partnerships between universities, communities, schools, and government; and create institutional frameworks for the encouragement, reward, and recognition of good practice (Talloires Network, 2005).

In addition to a number of American associations, a wide range of international higher education organizations partnered with Tufts and the Council of Europe in these ongoing efforts, including Innovations in Civic Participation; Association of Commonwealth Universities; the International Consortium for Higher Education, Civic Responsibility, and Democracy; and the Inter-American Organization for Higher Education.

THE CIVIC RENEWAL MOVEMENT

Scholars are heralding the emergence of a civic renewal movement to revitalize democracy in the United States over the past decade (Sirianni and Friedland, 2005). Alternatively called the "democracy movement," "community-building movement," "civil-society movement," or "communities movement," it entails "investing in civic skills and organizational capacities for public problem solving on a wide scale and designing policy at every level of the federal system to enhance the ability of citizens to do the everyday work of the republic" (Sirianni and Friedland, 2005, p. 1). Carmen Sirianni and Lewis A. Friedland (2005) describe several approaches that fall under the umbrella of the civic renewal movement, including community organizing and development, civic environmentalism, the engaged campus, community youth development and K–12 civic education, healthy communities, and public journalism and civic communications. In their view, the civic renewal movement attempts to "weave these various movements and innovations into a larger tapestry that can enable democratic work to become broader and deeper, as well as more complementary and sustainable" (p. 4).

If, in fact, civic engagement in higher education is part of a broad civic renewal movement, there is hope that it will provide the rising tide that will raise all boats, effectively creating a whole that is greater than the sum of its parts. Indeed, Sirianni and Friedland hope that the various aspects of the movement will nourish one another. In the case of higher education, robust civic education in K–12 schools and in communities would encourage and support collegiate civic engagement efforts. Likewise, providing substantive opportunities for college students to learn about and practice civic engagement will prepare them to take on the deeper problems in the professions, education, government, and in all areas of our civic infrastructure (Sirianni and Friedland, 2005).

CONCLUSION

This chapter has provided an overview of educating students for civic engagement in contemporary higher education. It reviewed the difficulties in defining civic engagement and put forth a working definition. Following a brief history of civic engagement in higher education, it highlighted major current initiatives in associations, foundations, and higher education institutions. It offered perspectives from research, international efforts, and the broad civic renewal movement. The remaining chapters of this book address the challenges confronting civic engagement in higher education. These include defining what students need to know and be able to do as civically engaged citizens, scholars, and leaders on the local, national, and global levels and changing the practices of higher education to move civic engagement from the margins to the center of the curriculum and the cocurriculum. The chapter authors explore how educators can integrate opportunities for students to learn about and practice civic engagement across the college experience and, at the same time, to make vital contributions to the public good.

References

American Association of Community Colleges. "Horizons Service Learning Project." http://www.aacc.nche.edu/Content/NavigationMenu/ResourceCenter/Projects_Partnerships/Current/HorizonsServiceLearningProject/HorizonsServiceLearningProject.htm, 2006.

Association of American Colleges and Universities. *Greater Expectations: A New Vision for Learning as a Nation Goes to College.* Washington, DC: Association of American Colleges and Universities, 2002.

Association of American Colleges and Universities. "Resources on Civic Engagement." http://www.aacu.org/resources/civicengagement, n.d.

Battistoni, R. *Civic Engagement across the Curriculum.* Providence, RI: Campus Compact, 2002.

Bellah, R. N., Madsen, R., Sullivan, W. M., Swidler, A., and Tipton, S. M. *Habits of the Heart: Individualism and Commitment in American Life.* New York: Harper & Row, 1985.

Boyer, E. L. *Scholarship Reconsidered: Priorities of the Professoriate.* Princeton, NJ: Carnegie Foundation for the Advancement of Teaching, 1990.

Boyer, E. L. "Creating the New American College." *Chronicle of Higher Education,* March 9, 1994, p. 48.

Boyte, H., and Hollander, E. *Wingspread Declaration on the Civic Responsibilities of Research Universities.* Providence, RI: Campus Compact, 1999.

Bringing Theory to Practice. "Request for Proposals: Engaged Learning, Student Well-Being, and Student Civic Development." http:// www.aacu.org/bringing_theory/documents/BTP_RFP_2007. pdf, 2007.

Butin, D. "Focusing Our Aim: Strengthening Faculty Commitment to Community Engagement." *Change,* November/December 2007, 34–37.

Campus Compact. "About Us." http://www.compact.org/about, n.d.

Carnegie Foundation for the Advancement of Teaching. "Community Engagement Elective Classification." http://www.carnegiefoundation. org/classifications/index.asp?key=1213, 2007.

Checkoway, B. "Renewing the Civic Mission of the American Research University." *Journal of Higher Education,* 2001, 72(2), 125–147.

Coalition for Civic Engagement and Leadership. "About Us: Definitions." http://www.terpimpact.umd.edu/content2.asp?cid=7&sid=41, November 2007.

Colby, A., Beaumont, E., Ehrlich, T., and Corngold, J. *Educating for Democracy: Preparing Undergraduates for Political Engagement.* San Francisco: Jossey-Bass, 2007.

Colby, A., Ehrlich, T., Beaumont, E., and Stephens, J. *Educating Citizens: Preparing America's Undergraduates for Lives of Moral and Civic Responsibility.* San Francisco: Jossey-Bass, 2003.

Community-Campus Partnerships for Health. "Community-Campus Partnerships for Health: Transforming Communities & Higher Education." http://www.futurehealth.ucsf.edu/ccph.html, n.d.

Cone, R. E., Kiesa, A., and Longo, N. V. *Raise Your Voice: A Student Guide to Positive Social Change.* Providence, RI: Campus Compact, 2006.

Corporation for National and Community Service. "Our History and Legislation." http://www.nationalservice.org/about/role_impact/ history.asp, n.d.

Council of Europe. "Higher Education and Democratic Culture: Citizenship, Human Rights and Civic Responsibility." http://dc.ecml. at/index.asp?Page=Declaration, 2006.

DukeEngage. "Duke University Launches $30 Million Initiative to Make Civic Engagement an Integral Part of Undergraduate Education." http://www.dukenews.duke.edu/engage/release.html, n.d.

Gibson, C. M. *New Times Demand New Scholarship: Research Universities and Civic Engagement.* Medford, MA: Tufts University and Campus Compact, 2006.

Harkavy, I. "The University and Social Sciences in the Social Order: An Historical Overview and 'Where Do We Go from Here?'" *Virginia Social Science Journal*, 1992, *27*, 1–25.

Harkavy, I., and Puckett, J. L. "Lessons from Hull House for the Contemporary Urban University." *Social Service Review*, 1994, *68*(3), 299–321.

Humphreys, D., and Davenport, A. *"What Really Matters in College: How Students View and Value Liberal Education."* *Liberal Education*, Summer/Fall 2005, 1–6.

Jacoby, B. "Service-Learning in Today's Higher Education." In B. Jacoby (Ed.), *Service-Learning in Higher Education: Concepts and Practices*. San Francisco: Jossey-Bass, 1996.

Jacoby, B. "Fundamentals of Service-Learning Partnerships." In B. Jacoby (Ed.), *Building Partnerships for Service-Learning*. San Francisco: Jossey-Bass, 2003.

Jonathan M. Tisch College of Citizenship and Public Service, Tufts University. "About Tisch College." http://activecitizen.tufts.edu/?pid=1, n.d.

Kezar, A. J., Chambers, T. C., and Burkhardt, J. C. *Higher Education for the Public Good: Emerging Voices from a National Movement*. San Francisco: Jossey-Bass, 2005.

Lawry, S., Laurison, D. L., and VanAntwerpen, J. *Liberal Education and Civic Engagement: A Project of the Ford Foundation's Knowledge, Creativity and Freedom Program*. http://www.fordfound.org/elibrary/documents/5029/toc.cfm, 2006.

Lester, J., and Salle, M. "Review of Service-Learning Research." Los Angeles: University of Southern California Civic Engagement Initiative, 2006.

Levine, P. *The Future of American Democracy: Developing the Next Generation of American Citizens*. Medford, MA: Tufts University Press, 2007.

London, S. *Higher Education and Public Life: Restoring the Bond*. Dayton, OH: Kettering Foundation, 2001.

Meade, E., and Weaver, S. (Eds.). *Toolkit for Teaching in a Democratic Academy*. Allentown, PA: Cedar Crest College, 2004.

Morrill, R. L. "Educating for Democratic Values." *Liberal Education*, 1982, *68*(4), 365–376.

Morton, K., and Battistoni, R. "Service and Citizenship: Are They Connected?" *Wingspread Journal*, 1995, *17*, 17–19.

Musil, C. M., Wathington, H., Battistoni, R., Calderón, J., Trementozzi, M., Fluker, W. E., et al. *The Civic Learning Spiral: Education for Participation in a Diverse Democracy*. Washington, DC: Association of American Colleges and Universities, in press.

National Forum on Higher Education and the Public Good. *Higher Education for the Public Good*. Ann Arbor, MI: National Forum on Higher Education and the Public Good, 2003.

National Leadership Council for Liberal Education and America's Promise. *College Learning for the New Global Century*. Washington, DC: Association of American Colleges and Universities, 2007.

North Central Association, Higher Learning Commission. *Handbook of Accreditation* (3rd ed.). Chicago: North Central Association, 2003.

O'Meara, K. *Rewarding Faculty Professional Service*. (Working Paper No. 19). Boston: New England Resource Center for Higher Education, 1997.

O'Meara, K. *Graduate Education and Civic Engagement*. Boston: New England Research Center for Higher Education, February 2007.

O'Meara, K., and Rice, R. E. *Faculty Rewards Reconsidered: Rewarding Multiple Forms of Scholarship*. San Francisco: Jossey-Bass, 2005.

Project Pericles. "Project Pericles: Claiming the Legacy of Pericles." http://projectpericles.org/?q=node/7, 2006.

Putnam, R. D. "Bowling Alone: America's Declining Social Capital." *Journal of Democracy*, 1995, *6*(1), 65–78.

Saltmarsh, J. "The Civic Promise of Service Learning." *Liberal Education*, 2005, *91*(2), 50–55.

Sirianni, C., and Friedland, L. A. *The Civic Renewal Movement: Community Building and Democracy in the U.S.* Dayton, OH: Charles F. Kettering Foundation, 2005.

Smith, M. W. "Issues in Integrating Service-Learning into the Higher Education Curriculum." In Youth Service America (Ed.), *Effective Learning, Effective Teaching, Effective Service*. Washington, DC: Youth Service America, 1994.

Soska, T. M., and Johnson Butterfield, A. K. *University-Community Partnerships: Universities in Civic Engagement*. Binghamton, NY: Haworth Press, 2004.

Stanton, T. K., Giles, D. E., Jr., and Cruz. N. I. *Service-Learning: A Movement's Pioneers Reflect on Its Origins, Practice, and Future*. San Francisco: Jossey-Bass, 1999.

Stanton, T. K., and Wagner, J. *Educating for Democratic Citizenship: Renewing the Civic Mission of Graduate and Professional Education at Research Universities*. San Francisco: California Campus Compact, 2006.

Talloires Network. "The Talloires Declaration on the Civic Roles and Social Responsibilities of Higher Education." http://www.tufts.edu/talloiresnetwork/?pid=17&c=7, 2005.

UCLA in LA. "Center for Community Learning." http://www.ugeducation.ucla.edu/communitylearning, 2007.

Zlotkowski, E. "The Disciplines and the Public Good." In A. J. Kezar, T. C. Chambers, and J. C. Burkhardt (Eds.), *Higher Education for the Public Good: Emerging Voices from a National Movement.* San Francisco: Jossey-Bass, 2005.

Zlotkowski, E., Longo, N. V., and Williams, J. R. *Students as Colleagues: Expanding the Circle of Service-Learning Leadership.* Providence, RI: Campus Compact, 2006.

CHAPTER TWO

WHAT WE KNOW ABOUT CIVIC ENGAGEMENT AMONG COLLEGE STUDENTS

Mark Hugo Lopez and Abby Kiesa

Authors' Note: We thank Peter Levine and Karlo Marcelo for comments on this chapter. We also thank Alex Orlowski for excellent research assistance. All errors in fact or interpretation are our own.

As the previous chapter revealed, many scholars have argued that higher education has the potential as well as the responsibility to prepare students for their roles as active citizens. Historically, colleges and universities have played an important role in developing civic knowledge and skills in undergraduates, but that role declined in priority during most of the twentieth century (Talcott, 2005). In recent years, however, many higher education institutions have recommitted to their public purpose and are offering more opportunities for students to learn about and practice civic engagement (Levine, 2007).

Not all young people are enrolled in college. In the fall of 2005, according to our analysis of data from the 2005 *Current Population Survey Education Supplement,* approximately 27 percent of young people ages eighteen to twenty-five were enrolled in a postsecondary institution. An additional one-quarter of young people ages eighteen to twenty-five had some college experience but were not currently enrolled. And at least 11 percent had completed a bachelor's degree (U.S. Bureau of the Census and U.S. Department of Labor, 2006).

Recent evidence suggests that young people currently enrolled in college and those who have attended college are among the most engaged of all young people, despite declines in engagement over the past thirty years among all young people. For example, according to the 2006 Civic and Political Health of the Nation Survey (CPHS) published by the Center for Information & Research on Civic Learning & Engagement (CIRCLE), 23 percent of college students and 28 percent of college graduates ages eighteen to twenty-five were active group members (Lopez and Brown, 2006). In contrast, using the 2006 CPHS, Mark Hugo Lopez and Brent Elrod (2006b) find that only 20 percent of unenrolled young people with some college experience and 13 percent of young people with no college experience were active members of a group. College attendance also appears to produce lasting effects on civic engagement after college, although most differences between those who attended college and those who did not persist decades after attending college (Nie and Hillygus, 2001; Pascarella and Terenzini, 2005; Verba, Schlozman, and Brady, 1995).

There are several possible reasons why young people with college experience are among the most engaged. First, college may impart a positive effect on civic engagement. This could be the result of programs in colleges and universities designed to encourage engagement or the number of engagement opportunities and resources available to students when compared to the opportunities available to those who are not in college or who have not attended college.

Second, colleges through their admissions processes choose those students who are most likely to be engaged already. This civic "creaming" effect may, in essence, make colleges look better than they are at fostering civic engagement (Dee, 2004). One example of this phenomenon is the relative importance of volunteer experience in the college admissions process. According to Lewis A. Friedland and Shauna Morimoto (2005), many young people who volunteer do so to improve their chances of attending college, particularly colleges they perceive as prestigious. The Higher Education Research Institute (HERI) reports that volunteering among incoming college freshmen has been rising since the mid-1980s. Similar patterns of rising volunteerism over the past twenty years are evident in data on high school seniors from the Monitoring the Future data collection (Lopez and Marcelo, 2007). It is possible that these increases reflect the growing importance of volunteer experience in college admissions decisions.

Third, college students have opportunities to interact with many individuals who are civically engaged. Through friends, professors, and professional staff members, they gain access to networks of people who can, in turn, connect them to other networks that include potential employers and mentors.

This chapter explores recent evidence documenting the civic engagement of college students. In addition to highlighting these trends, it addresses civic engagement after college. Finally, the chapter concludes with a discussion of these findings and their implications for civic engagement efforts in higher education.

CIVIC ENGAGEMENT AND THE COLLEGE EXPERIENCE

Generally, college students are the most engaged group of young people on many, but not all, measures of civic engagement. Furthermore, civic engagement among college graduates is generally even higher than among college students or young people who have no college experience. However, there is evidence that civic engagement declines and changes in character several years after college (Vogelgesang and Astin, 2005).

Despite this evidence, there is still a common view that college students are not as engaged as expected. Two recent surveys challenge this viewpoint. According to a recent national survey conducted by Tufts University, college students are more engaged and knowledgeable than is generally believed (Portney and O'Leary, 2007). For example, 28 percent of college students reported they are involved in their communities, and two-thirds knew the name of at least one senator from their home state. Furthermore, according to HERI, 67 percent of incoming freshmen in 2006 said that "helping others who are in difficulty" was an "essential" or "very important" objective (Pryor et al., 2006). Similarly, the following section shows that young people in general and college students in particular are becoming more engaged politically (Lopez et al., 2006).

ELECTORAL PARTICIPATION OF COLLEGE STUDENTS

While voter participation increased for all groups of young people in recent elections, the voter turnout rate for college students reflects one of the largest increases. It rose three percentage points between 2002 and 2006, to 27 percent, and 12 percentage points between 2000 and 2004, to 59 percent. College graduates have the highest voter turnout rate among eighteen- to twenty-five-year-olds, at 35 percent in 2006 and 67 percent in 2004. Young people with no college experience voted at the lowest rates, 19 percent in 2006 and 34 percent in 2004 (Lopez, Kirby, Sagoff, and Herbst, 2005; Lopez, Marcelo, and Kirby, 2007). Table 2.1 provides further detail.

In the 2004 presidential election, many college students reported that they were active and mobilized (Niemi and Hanmer, 2004). Specifically, 88 percent of college students registered to vote, and more than 88 percent of these students voted. While turnout was high for all college students, those who were registered to vote at their college address were more likely to have voted. Eighty-five percent also followed the election closely, and nearly three-quarters said they discussed the election at least once a week during the campaign.

Youth voter participation in the 2008 presidential primaries was high. According to an analysis of available exit polls and vote tallies by CIRCLE, voter participation among eighteen- to twenty-year-olds in the 2008 primaries and caucuses was 17 percent, up from 9 percent in 2000, the last year with a comparable primary season (Kirby, Marcelo, Gillerman, and Linkins, 2008). Recent survey evidence suggests that college students will be very engaged in the 2008 presidential election. According to a recent poll conducted by Harvard University's Institute of Politics (2008) in the spring of 2008, 83 percent of college students in four-year colleges and universities say they are registered to vote. Furthermore, 64 percent of students at four-year institutions say they plan to participate in the presidential primaries and caucuses in 2008, and 88 percent say they will vote in the 2008 general election (Harvard University Institute of Politics, 2008). For noncollege youth, 67 percent reported they were registered to vote, 58 percent plan to vote in one of the 2008 presidential primaries or caucuses, and

TABLE 2.1: VOTER TURNOUT RATES FOR CURRENT COLLEGE STUDENTS AND OTHER YOUNG PEOPLE, 2000–2006.

	Current college students	Recent college graduates	Some college experience, not currently enrolled	No college experience
Midterm election years				
2006	27%	35%	24%	19%
2002	24%	35%	22%	17%
1998	24%	28%	23%	16%
1994	29%	41%	26%	18%
1990	30%	36%	28%	20%
1986	31%	36%	30%	22%
Presidential election years				
2004	59%	67%	55%	34%
2000	47%	61%	37%	25%
1996	47%	56%	39%	25%
1992	63%	77%	55%	34%
1988	51%	64%	50%	27%
1984	58%	72%	54%	32%

Source: Authors' tabulations using U.S. Department of Commerce, Bureau of the Census, *Current Population Survey, Voter Supplement File,* 1985, 1986, 1989, 1990, 1992, 1994, 1997, 1999, 2001, 2004, 2005, 2007.

74 percent plan to vote in the 2008 general presidential election (Harvard University Institute of Politics, 2008). It should be noted that noncollege youth in the Institute of Politics report are young people who are not in four-year colleges. Thus, those enrolled in two-year colleges are included in the "noncollege" tabulations (Harvard University Institute of Politics, 2008). If these intentions and trends translate into 2008 electoral participation for college students, it is likely that the voter turnout rate among college students will increase relative to 2004.

VIEWS OF AND PARTICIPATION IN CIVIC ENGAGEMENT

In 2006 and 2007, CIRCLE conducted a series of focus groups of college students across the nation to learn about their views of politics and civic engagement. Results from forty-seven focus groups at twelve colleges and universities suggest that college students today, in contrast to those in the early 1990s, are more active as a group on a broader array of activities, in contrast to a singular focus on volunteering, and desire to be more engaged (Kiesa et al., 2007). However, the study found that college students do not see the political system as accessible and that their views of politics, politicians, and elections are not very high. Many believe that politics are an inefficient vehicle for change and that the political system should be more accessible and realize the impact public policy can have. Further, students want to participate in the political process but do not know how to get involved.

In CIRCLE's 2006 Civic Public Health Survey, more than 1,700 young people ages fifteen to twenty-five were interviewed, together with 550 adults ages twenty-six and older. The participants were asked an extensive set of questions about nineteen civic engagement activities along three broad dimensions: electoral activities, civic activities, and political voice activities (Lopez et al., 2006). Differences in the nineteen activities measured among young people with no college experience, those who are currently in college, college graduates, and unenrolled young people with some college experience are shown in table 2.2 (Lopez and Elrod, 2006b).

Overall, young people with college experience are among the most engaged, with recent college graduates surpassing their counterparts in engagement in most activities. For example,

TABLE 2.2: College Attendance and Civic Engagement Among 18- to 25-Year-Olds.

Indicators of civic engagement	Current college students	College graduates, not enrolled	Some college experience, not currently enrolled	No college experience
Civic activities				
Community problem solving (past 12 months)	22%	26%	17%	12%
Volunteered (past 12 months)	43%	45%	24%	24%
Regular volunteer for nonpolitical groups	25%	28%	14%	8%
Active member of at least one group	23%	28%	20%	13%
Ran/walked/biked for charity (past 12 months)	22%	15%	15%	13%
Raised money for charity (past 12 months)	25%	29%	21%	20%
Electoral activities				
Regular voter (for those 20 and older)	30%	34%	26%	20%
Tried to persuade other in an election	40%	40%	35%	29%
Displayed a campaign button or sign	27%	26%	20%	19%
Donated money to a candidate or party (past 12 months)	6%	13%	8%	5%
Member of a group involved in politics	20%	32%	19%	9%

TABLE 2.2: (Continued).

Indicators of civic engagement	Current college students	College graduates, not enrolled	Some college experience, not currently enrolled	No college experience
Regular volunteer for political candidates or groups	2%	4%	1%	1%
Political voice activities (past 12 months)				
Contacted an official	12%	17%	13%	8%
Contacted the print media	7%	8%	7%	4%
Contacted the broadcast media	10%	6%	10%	7%
Protested	12%	8%	6%	12%
Signed an e-mail petition	23%	30%	11%	10%
Signed a paper petition	25%	28%	20%	12%
Boycotted	36%	39%	40%	23%
Buycotted	33%	36%	34%	23%
Canvassed	4%	8%	2%	1%
Summary				
No activities	12%	14%	17%	23%
10 or more activities	9%	11%	7%	3%

Source: Lopez and Elrod, 2006b.

45 percent of college graduates and 43 percent of current college students said they had volunteered in the year before the 2006 CPHS, while only 24 percent of unenrolled young people with college experience and 24 percent of those with no college experience had volunteered. In contrast, current college students had the greatest levels of participation in run, walk, or ride charity events at 22 percent versus 15 percent for college graduates. This may be a result of the many such events that academic programs, residence halls, student organizations, and community service offices organize on college campuses.

Young people with college experience do not always report the highest levels of participation in engagement activities. According to the 2006 CPHS, young people with no college experience reported levels of protest activity that matched their college student counterparts (at 12 percent each) and a higher level of such activities than either college graduates (8 percent) or those with some college (6 percent). According to Lopez and Marcelo (2008), many young people who protested in the year before the survey were immigrants or the children of immigrants, who indicated protest rates of 25 percent and 18 percent respectively. Many of these young people have lower levels of educational attainment and have limited college experience.

Differences in engagement by educational attainment can be summarized by two measures. First, as shown in the last two rows of table 2.2, only 12 percent of current college students are not engaged in any activities measured by the 2006 CPHS. In contrast, 23 percent of young people with no college experience are not engaged in any activities. Second, 9 percent of current college students and 11 percent of recent college graduates are engaged in ten or more of the activities measured by the 2006 CPHS compared to 3 percent of those with no college experience. These large differences likely reflect the many opportunities that are readily available on college campuses but that are not as accessible to those who are not enrolled in college. However, while college students are generally more engaged than young people with no college experience, a small but substantial number of young people with college experience are engaged in no activities. It should be noted that the 2006 CPHS employed both telephone and Internet sampling methods. Because the telephone sample was drawn using a random digit dialing methodology that relied on lists of landline telephone numbers, the increasing numbers of young people who exclusively use a cellular telephone may have been excluded.

Based on the focus groups CIRCLE conducted in 2006 and 2007 at several colleges and universities, a large majority of college students at four-year institutions indicated that they are volunteering. While there was no pattern to the type of volunteering students engaged in, there were some common threads. First, students believe that volunteering is not a substitute for political action. Looking back at their volunteer experiences, some students view volunteering as an important way to become knowledgeable about an issue. Second, most students became volunteers because of a personal connection to an issue. These connections involved personal events such as the death or disease of a family member or friend. Many students spoke of wanting to "help others" and "make a difference" and indicated that volunteering in local communities provides them with the opportunity to see their work through, see the impact of their work, and be with others while doing so (Kiesa et al., 2007).

These findings suggest that there is a positive correlation between college attendance and civic engagement. However, they also suggest that students who are enrolled in college are not the most engaged among all young people. In fact, young people who have recently graduated from college are generally more engaged than students currently enrolled in college, implying that the college experience may impart a sense of civic engagement that grows once students leave. Other researchers have suggested this important role for college education, but one must be cautious when interpreting the results presented here because it is unclear whether the positive correlation between college attendance and civic engagement is the result of attending college or other factors (Carnegie Foundation for the Advancement of Teaching and CIRCLE, 2006; Dee, 2004).

DIFFERENCES BY INSTITUTIONAL TYPE AND DEMOGRAPHIC CHARACTERISTICS

While it is generally the case that young people who attended college are more civically engaged than those who did not, differences exist based on the type of institution a student attended.

For example, among those who attended four-year colleges only, engagement was higher than among those who attended two-year institutions. Those who attended two-year institutions had higher levels of engagement than those who did not attend college. In a recent report on the civic engagement of college students by the type of institution they attended, Mark Hugo Lopez and Benjamin Brown (2006) report that volunteering was highest among those with experience at a four-year institution (52 percent in 1994 and 40 percent in 2000) shortly after college. The rate of volunteering was second highest among those who attended a two-year institution (28 percent in 1994 and 25 percent in 2000). It was lowest among those who have no college experience (20 percent in 1994 and 21 percent in 2000). Similar patterns are evident for other measures of engagement, such as voter registration (Lopez and Brown, 2006).

Lopez and Elrod (2006b) and Vogelgesang and Astin (2005) report that while there is a general pattern of greater engagement among those with college experience compared to those without, among those with college experience there are important differences in engagement by gender. For example, female college students reported volunteering at a rate of 48 percent, while recent female college graduates reported a volunteer rate of 56 percent. Their male counterparts, in contrast, reported lower levels of volunteering, at 37 percent and 29 percent respectively. Young women who have attended but not completed college are more likely to be volunteers than their male counterparts who also attended college but did not graduate (Lopez and Elrod, 2006b).

Differences in self-reported regular voting are also evident, though in a different pattern from that reported for volunteering. According to Lopez and Elrod (2006b), 40 percent of young female current college students reported they voted regularly, as did 34 percent of young women who had recently graduated from college, 19 percent of nonenrolled young women with some college experience, and 18 percent of young women with no college experience. However, among young men, differences based on educational attainment were much smaller. For current male college students, 40 percent reported being regular voters, compared with 34 percent of recent graduates, 32 percent of nonenrolled young people with college experience, and 22 percent of those with no college experience.

It is interesting to note that young males in these last two groups of lower educational attainment report that they participate more than their female counterparts (Lopez and Elrod, 2006b).

Lori J. Vogelgesang and Alexander W. Astin (2005) report that, after college, young men are more likely to engage in political activities or contact officials than young women. However, young women are more likely to volunteer or sign petitions to express their voice than young men, reflecting some of the differences observed among current college students.

As described earlier, recent college graduates are the single most civically engaged group among young people. There are nevertheless differences in civic engagement among some groups of recent college graduates. Lopez and Elrod (2006a) report some modest differences among recent college graduates from four-year institutions. First, African American and Native American graduates are more highly engaged than non-Hispanic whites. Second, graduates of private universities are more engaged than graduates of public universities. Third, verbal SAT scores positively correlate with graduates' political participation. Last, college undergraduates with degrees in areas related to law, public administration, and the humanities are more engaged than college graduates from other fields.

In contrast to the results reported earlier comparing college students to college graduates, Vogelgesang and Astin (2005) report that postcollege civic engagement among graduates from four-year institutions falls once students leave school. The sample used in the HERI study contains only young people who attended four-year institutions (Vogelgesang and Astin, 2005). In contrast, the 2006 CPHS contains those who were enrolled in any postsecondary institution, including two-year colleges and technical schools (Lopez and Brown, 2006). It is likely that this difference in the sample populations affects the contrast between the findings of these two national studies. Also, upon leaving college, graduates report changes in values. Based on a longitudinal data collection of the entering college freshman class of 1994, by 2004 (six years after college graduation) volunteering had fallen from 74 percent in the senior year of college to 68 percent. Furthermore, fewer viewed "helping others in difficulty" as important to them personally, falling from 69 percent during the senior year of college to 57 percent six years after graduation (Vogelgesang and Astin, 2005).

IMPLICATIONS FOR HIGHER EDUCATION

The future of civic engagement among college students appears very promising. College students are already among the most engaged of young people, yet they desire to become more involved. As Harvard's Institute of Politics (2008) survey found, many four-year college students are interested in participating in many ways in the upcoming presidential election. Additionally, our own focus group work suggests that there is demand among college students for more opportunities for engagement.

These findings and implications, however, do have several caveats. First, civic engagement is not uniformly high among all college students. For example, students at four-year institutions are the most engaged, with students in two-year colleges less engaged. At the very least this suggests that there is an argument to provide more opportunities for two-year college students to become engaged, either on their campus or in their community. This would help close the gap in engagement between four-year and two-year students. Second, while students want to become more involved, more opportunities will not necessarily be enough. Instead, they seek high-quality opportunities to engage with others and to learn in the process. As suggested by our focus group report, this desire for more engagement opportunities includes volunteer, political, and deliberation opportunities (Kiesa et al., 2007).

Colleges and universities already offer numerous opportunities for students to become involved. However, as evidenced by our focus groups, students sometimes do not know where to go or how to find opportunities. One way to direct students to opportunities is to make clear the access points to engagement, both on and off campus. Students also seek more reliable information and spaces where they can engage in discussions free of partisanship (Kiesa et al., 2007).

CONCLUSION

The future of civic engagement among college students appears to be promising. College students are already among the most engaged of young people, yet they desire to become more involved. The findings in this chapter suggest that there is an upsurge in college students' interest and engagement in politics and elections.

However, the rate of civic engagement is not uniformly high among all college students. For example, students at four-year institutions are more engaged than students in two-year colleges. As far as gender goes, female college students are generally more engaged than their male counterparts in civic activities like volunteering but are less engaged than their male counterparts in electoral activities both during and after college. Findings such as these suggest implications for the higher education practices that are discussed in the following chapters.

While college students seek more opportunities for engagement, just providing more opportunities will not suffice. Students seek high-quality opportunities to engage with others and to learn in the process. As suggested by CIRCLE's *Millennials Talk Politics* report, this desire for more engagement opportunities includes volunteer, political, and deliberation opportunities (Kiesa et al., 2007). In addition, the *Millennials Talk Politics* focus groups reveal that students sometimes do not know how to find opportunities. One way to direct students to opportunities is to make clear engagement access points, both on and off campus. Students also seek more reliable information and spaces where they can participate in discussions free of partisanship and rancor. Providing these spaces would be an important way that colleges can give students from diverse backgrounds opportunities to engage with one another on issues both local and global (Kiesa et al., 2007).

While the findings presented in this chapter cannot prove that more education is associated with greater engagement, they suggest a strong connection. Further research on the links between college institutional differences and later civic engagement may shed light on this question and may also offer insights into what programs work to increase (or decrease) civic engagement among college students.

References

Carnegie Foundation for the Advancement of Teaching and Center for Information & Research on Civic Learning & Engagement. *Higher Education: Civic Mission & Civic Effects.* College Park, MD: Center for Information & Research on Civic Learning & Engagement, 2006.

Dee, T. "Are There Civic Returns to Education?" *Journal of Public Economics,* 2004, *88*(9), 1697–1720.

Friedland, L. A., and Morimoto, S. *The Changing Lifeworld of Young People: Risk, Resume-Padding, and Civic Engagement.* (Working Paper No. 40). College Park, MD: Center for Information & Research on Civic Learning & Engagement, 2005.

Harvard University Institute of Politics. "Executive Summary." *The 14th Biannual Youth Survey on Politics and Public Service by Harvard's Institute of Politics.* Cambridge, MA: Harvard University Institute of Politics, 2008.

Kiesa, A., Orlowski, A. P., Levine, P. L., Both, D., Kirby, E. H., Lopez, M. H., et al. *Millennials Talk Politics: A Study of College Student Political Engagement.* College Park, MD: Center for Information & Research on Civic Learning & Engagement, 2007.

Kirby, E. H., Marcelo, K. B., Gillerman, J., and Linkins, S. *The Youth Vote in the 2008 Primaries and Caucuses.* College Park, MD: Center for Information & Research on Civic Learning & Engagement, 2008.

Levine, P. L. *The Future of Democracy: Developing the Next Generation of American Citizens.* Medford, MA: Tufts University Press, 2007.

Lopez, M. H., and Brown, B. *Civic Engagement among 2-Year and 4-Year College Students.* College Park, MD: Center for Information & Research on Civic Learning & Engagement, 2006.

Lopez, M. H., and Elrod, B. *Civic Engagement among Recent College Graduates.* College Park, MD: Center for Information & Research on Civic Learning & Engagement, 2006a.

Lopez, M. H., and Elrod, B. *College Attendance and Civic Engagement among 18 to 25 Year Olds.* College Park, MD: Center for Information & Research on Civic Learning & Engagement, 2006b.

Lopez, M. H., Kirby, E. H., Sagoff, J., and Herbst, C. *The Youth Vote 2004: With a Historical Look at Youth Voting Patterns, 1972–2004.* (Working Paper No. 35). College Park, MD: Center for Information & Research on Civic Learning & Engagement, 2005.

Lopez, M. H., Levine, P. L., Both, D., Kiesa, A., Kirby, E. H., and Marcelo, K. B. *The 2006 Civic and Political Health of the Nation: A Detailed Look at How Youth Participate in Politics and Communities.* College Park, MD: Center for Information & Research on Civic Learning & Engagement, 2006.

Lopez, M. H., and Marcelo, K. B. *Volunteering among Young People.* College Park, MD: Center for Information & Research on Civic Learning & Engagement, 2007.

Lopez, M. H., and Marcelo, K. B. "The Civic Engagement of Immigrant Youth: New Evidence from the 2006 Civic and Political Health of the Nation Survey." *Applied Developmental Science,* 2008 (Special Issue), *12*(2).

Lopez, M. H., Marcelo, K. B., and Kirby, E. H. *Youth Voter Turnout Increases in 2006.* College Park, MD: Center for Information & Research on Civic Learning & Engagement, 2007.

Nie, N., and Hillygus, D. "Education and Democratic Citizenship." In D. Ravitch and J. Viteritti (Eds.), *Making Good Citizens: Education and Civic Society.* New Haven, CT: Yale University Press, 2001.

Niemi, R., and Hanmer, M. *College Students in the 2004 Election.* College Park, MD: Center for Information & Research on Civic Learning & Engagement, 2004.

Pascarella, E. T., and Terenzini, P. T. *How College Affects Students.* Vol. 2: *A Third Decade of Research.* San Francisco: Jossey-Bass, 2005.

Portney, K. E., and O'Leary, L. *Civic and Political Engagement of America's Youth: A Report from the Tisch College "National Survey of Civic and Political Engagement of Young People."* Medford, MA: Tufts University, Jonathan M. Tisch College of Citizenship and Public Service, 2007.

Pryor, J. H., Hurtado, S., Saenz, V. B., Korn, J. S., Santos, J. L., and Korn, W. S. *The American Freshman: National Norms for Fall 2006.* Los Angeles: University of California at Los Angeles, Higher Education Research Institute, 2006.

Talcott, W. *Modern Universities, Absent Citizenship? Historical Perspectives.* (Working Paper No. 39). College Park, MD: Center for Information & Research on Civic Learning & Engagement, 2005.

U.S. Bureau of the Census and U.S. Department of Labor, Bureau of Labor Statistics. *Current Population Survey October 2005: School Enrollment.* Washington, DC: U.S. Department of Commerce, Bureau of the Census, 2006.

U.S. Department of Commerce, Bureau of the Census. *Current Population Survey: Voter Supplement File,* 1984 [Computer file]. Washington, DC: U.S. Department of Commerce, Bureau of the Census [Producer], Ann Arbor, MI: Inter-University Consortium for Political and Social Research [Distributor], 1985.

U.S. Department of Commerce, Bureau of the Census. *Current Population Survey: Voter Supplement File,* 1986 [Computer file]. Washington, DC: U.S. Department of Commerce, Bureau of the Census [Producer], Ann Arbor, MI: Inter-University Consortium for Political and Social Research [Distributor], 1986.

U.S. Department of Commerce, Bureau of the Census. *Current Population Survey: Voter Supplement File,* 1988 [Computer file]. Washington, DC: U.S. Department of Commerce, Bureau of the Census [Producer], Ann Arbor, MI: Inter-University Consortium for Political and Social Research [Distributor], 1989.

U.S. Department of Commerce, Bureau of the Census. *Current Population Survey: Voter Supplement File,* 1990 [Computer file]. Washington, DC:

U.S. Department of Commerce, Bureau of the Census [Producer], Ann Arbor, MI: Inter-University Consortium for Political and Social Research [Distributor], 1990.

U.S. Department of Commerce, Bureau of the Census. *Current Population Survey: Voter Supplement File,* 1992 [Computer file]. Washington, DC: U.S. Department of Commerce, Bureau of the Census [Producer], Ann Arbor, MI: Inter-University Consortium for Political and Social Research [Distributor], 1992.

U.S. Department of Commerce, Bureau of the Census. *Current Population Survey: Voter Supplement File,* 1994 [Computer file]. Washington, DC: U.S. Department of Commerce, Bureau of the Census [Producer], Ann Arbor, MI: Inter-University Consortium for Political and Social Research [Distributor], 1994.

U.S. Department of Commerce, Bureau of the Census. *Current Population Survey: Voter Supplement File,* 1996 [Computer file]. Washington, DC: U.S. Department of Commerce, Bureau of the Census [Producer], Ann Arbor, MI: Inter-University Consortium for Political and Social Research [Distributor], 1997.

U.S. Department of Commerce, Bureau of the Census. *Current Population Survey: Voter Supplement File,* 1998 [Computer file]. Washington, DC: U.S. Department of Commerce, Bureau of the Census [Producer], Ann Arbor, MI: Inter-University Consortium for Political and Social Research [Distributor], 1999.

U.S. Department of Commerce, Bureau of the Census. *Current Population Survey: Voter Supplement File,* 2000 [Computer file]. Washington, DC: U.S. Department of Commerce, Bureau of the Census [Producer], Ann Arbor, MI: Inter-University Consortium for Political and Social Research [Distributor], 2001.

U.S. Department of Commerce, Bureau of the Census. *Current Population Survey: Voter Supplement File,* 2002 [Computer file]. Washington, DC: U.S. Department of Commerce, Bureau of the Census [Producer], Ann Arbor, MI: Inter-University Consortium for Political and Social Research [Distributor], 2004.

U.S. Department of Commerce, Bureau of the Census. *Current Population Survey: Voter Supplement File,* 2004 [Computer file]. Washington, DC: U.S. Department of Commerce, Bureau of the Census [Producer], Ann Arbor, MI: Inter-University Consortium for Political and Social Research [Distributor], 2005.

U.S. Department of Commerce, Bureau of the Census. *Current Population Survey: Voter Supplement File,* 2006 [Computer file]. Washington, DC: U.S. Department of Commerce, Bureau of the Census [Producer], Ann Arbor, MI: Inter-University Consortium for Political and Social Research [Distributor], 2007.

Verba, S., Schlozman, K. L., and Brady, H. E. *Voice and Equality: Civic Voluntarism in American Politics.* Cambridge, MA: Harvard University Press, 1995.

Vogelgesang, L. J., and Astin, A. W. *Post-College Civic Engagement among Graduates.* Los Angeles: University of California at Los Angeles, Higher Education Research Institute, 2005.

CHAPTER THREE

EDUCATING STUDENTS FOR PERSONAL AND SOCIAL RESPONSIBILITY
The Civic Learning Spiral

Caryn McTighe Musil

The students, both rising high school seniors and rising seniors in college, were puzzled by the words *civic engagement*. The focus group leader prodded them by recasting her question a number of ways. Glazed eyes looked back at her. Then students finally began to talk about providing service to those in need, but few had any other conceptual understanding of the phrase *civic engagement* or its critical connection to democratic institutions. None connected it to expectations they had for what college would or should teach them. As one of the high school students explained, "Civic responsibility and leadership are qualities that individuals are born with" (Association of American Colleges and Universities Board of Directors, 2004).

Such notions are in direct contradiction with those of Thomas Jefferson, who argued that the struggling new republic would surely founder if it did not invest in educating its citizens. Developing a strong democracy, according to Jefferson, was inextricably linked to education. For contemporary students in U.S. higher education, however, that bond has largely faded from their consciousness. In fact, in the series of focus groups sponsored by the Association of American Colleges and Universities (AAC&U) in 2004 to explore what students hoped to achieve as a result of going to college, students identified civic learning outcomes as the two least critical ones from a list of sixteen (Humphreys and Davenport, 2005). Thus, students in both groups selected among *three of the least desirable* capacities learned in college: "tolerance and respect for people of other backgrounds, races, ethnicities, and lifestyles"; "expanded cultural and global awareness and sensitivity"; and at the very bottom, "appreciation of your role as a citizen and an orientation toward public service" (Humphreys and Davenport, 2005, p. 40). Developing civic knowledge, skills, and habits are, of course, utterly dependent on all three. Without them, U.S. democracy and its concomitant responsibilities as part of a globally interdependent world are at peril.

These students did look to college to develop their *individual* aspirations of maturity, succeeding on their own, time-management skills, strong work habits, and self-discipline. But there was little sense of a heightened responsibility to others locally or globally as an important outcome of a college education. In fact, some of the students thought that service-learning, one of the more benign faces of civic engagement, threatened to interfere with what they perceived to be their primary college goals, such as preparing for a career (Humphreys and Davenport, 2005). Students have not developed their more narcissistic perspectives on their own. Higher education has accommodated them by largely abandoning its historical role in educating students for democracy. It has gladly assigned civics to high schools and rarely paid any attention to the quality of what students might have learned in those mandated courses that everyone had to take and few can remember.

A NEW EDUCATIONAL COMPACT

Happily for the future of a vibrant democracy dependent on participatory citizenship, a seismic shift is occurring that promises to disrupt this devilish compact. (Chapter 1 provides an overview of the current resurgent focus on civic engagement in higher education.) In its recent report, *College Learning for the New Global Century* (National Leadership Council for Liberal Education and America's Promise, 2007), AAC&U argues that there is consensus among colleges and universities about four broad essential learning outcomes that students will need for a world characterized by dynamic change, interdependence, destabilizing inequalities, and volatility:

- Knowledge of human cultures and the physical and natural world
    Through study in the sciences and mathematics, social sciences, humanities, histories, languages, and the arts
- Intellectual and practical skills
    Inquiry and analysis
    Critical and creative thinking
    Written and oral communication
    Quantitative literacy
    Information literacy
    Teamwork and problem solving
- Personal and social responsibility
    Civic knowledge and engagement—local and global
    Intercultural knowledge and competence
    Ethical reasoning and action
    Foundations and skills for lifelong learning
- Integrative and applied learning
    Synthesis and advanced accomplishment across general and specialized education (p. 12)

The first pair is familiar, embraced by faculty and branded as distinguishing hallmarks of U.S. higher education around the world. The second pair of essential learning outcomes expands the vision and expectations of higher education. As such, they represent a source of innovation and creativity that also promises to reinvigorate our nation's civic imagination and habits. However, the latter two also have much in common with the bottom tier of outcomes that students in the focus groups ranked so low.

The challenge is how to translate all four of these consensus outcomes into the academic and cocurricular life of students and into the everyday practices and policies of a tradition-bound academy. Success in accomplishing this will entail a radical transformation of how higher education organizes itself. But there seems to be agreement among higher education and business leaders alike that the country's economic and social future is at stake. In a national poll of business leaders, 76 percent of employers want colleges to place more emphasis on the intercultural competencies that lead to teamwork skills in diverse groups, and 72 percent want more emphasis on global knowledge (National Leadership Council for Liberal Education and America's Promise, 2007). Developing a talent pool equipped to address the challenges of the new global century requires graduates who are adept critical thinkers capable of addressing unscripted problems whose solutions require navigating through and relying on the resources of highly diverse communities. Ultimately, this leads inevitably to a new framework for excellence governing higher education. As *College Learning for the New Global Century* describes it, such a vision for learning calls "for a far-reaching shift in the focus of schooling from accumulating course credits to building real-world capabilities" (National Leadership Council for Liberal Education and America's Promise, 2007, p. 5).

CONVERGING STUDENT LEARNING REFORM MOVEMENTS

The fecundity of innovative programs about civic engagement and social responsibility that are currently lodged everywhere on campuses—from the president's office and course catalogs to campus life and facility operations—have begun to lay the scaffolding for how higher education can reassume its role of preparing graduates for their roles as informed citizens ready to engage and lead responsibly in their work and community roles. The growing breadth and depth of these myriad activities have been fueled by the convergence of three streams of educational reform movements, all of which have brought exciting possibilities at this historic juncture. While the trio use different nomenclatures, they include constellations of activities around U.S. diversity, global learning, and civic engagement.

Any learning goals for civic engagement diminish these movements' intellectual scope and capacity to seriously address social justice issues in diverse democracies if isolated from the powerful critical lenses of the other two. Far too often, however, that is exactly what has happened as civic engagement activities have taken root on college campuses. Similarly, U.S. diversity and global learning, devoid of an exploration of their responsibilities to a larger public good, reduce their power as education for democratic citizenship.

U.S. DIVERSITY

Nowhere have civic lessons been more instructive than in the very democratization of colleges and universities themselves over the past century as they moved from being exclusionary institutions to more inclusive ones. Such a change did not occur simply because time passed. It occurred because citizens at every level, especially those denied even the right to vote, acted collectively to recast the script of American democracy. They organized, marched, lobbied, used legal strategies, wrote, tapped the media, defied the laws that excluded them, and through their public actions, largely ended the most shameful aspects of apartheid systems in the United States. Higher education was largely a conspirator in this apartheid system until the civil rights movement forced it to change. Progress first appeared in the kind of student population sought and admitted, then in the campus life structures to support those students, and finally in the new areas of scholarship and teaching spurred by the greater diversity of people working and studying on college campuses. One consequence of this dramatic shift in the demographic profile of students is a concurrent commitment to engage more responsibly and deeply with diverse local and global communities.

At the beginning of the twentieth century, only 4 percent of Americans went to college (Veysey, 1965). Today 75 percent of students who complete high school go on to some kind of college (Education Trust–West, 2002). Even as late as 1976, after the civil rights movement had ended the formal apartheid educational laws and practices, only 14.5 percent of all enrolled college students were minorities (U.S. Department of Education, 2006). Today, that percentage has climbed to 28 percent, with predictions of a steady increase across all nonwhite racial groups (U.S. Department of Education, 2006). The number of female college students across all racial/ethnic groups increased from 44 percent in 1970 to 57 percent by 2005 (U.S. Department of Education, 2006), which has accelerated the readiness of higher education to address local and global issues because the students who participate in service-learning and study abroad programs are predominantly female. A disposition to reach out to underserved communities is also enhanced by the fact that by the 1989–1990 academic year, 43 percent of first-time entering students were first generation, the majority of whom were likely to be racial minorities being taught by some faculty who were themselves the first in their families to go to college (U.S. Department of Education, Office of Educational Research and Improvement, 1998).

The rich perspectives brought to the classroom, to areas of research, and to the very definition of what issues are considered urgent have been captured in the expanding body of work that illuminates how diversity, if deployed correctly, is a not just an expression of democratic opportunity but a source of educational insights and excellence. Some examples of this body of work include the following: Lawrence W. Levin, *The Opening of the American Mind: Canons, Culture, and History* (Beacon Press, 1996); Daryl G. Smith and Associates, *Diversity Works: The Emerging Picture of How Students Benefit* (AAC&U, 1997); Patricia Gurin, Eric L. Dey, Sylvia Hurtado, and Gerald Gurin, "Diversity and Higher Education: Theory and Impact on Educational Outcomes," *Harvard Educational Review*, Fall 2002; and Patricia Gurin, Jeffrey Lehman, and Earl Lewis, *Defending Diversity: Affirmative Action at the University of Michigan* (University of Michigan Press, 2004). The effort to diversify higher education is, of course, a reflection of the larger societal demands that American democracy extend its opportunities, education among them, equally to everyone. At its very heart, then, the U.S. diversity reform movement is civic work and offers deliberation across differences as an everyday encounter.

GLOBAL LEARNING

The educational reform movement of U.S. diversity has found a natural partner in the closely related reform movement centered on global learning. With an ever-sharpening awareness of the inescapable interdependency in the world, with all the asymmetries of power inherent in those relationships, higher education has recognized the necessity of incorporating global knowledge as a fundamental dimension of learning for contemporary graduates. An AAC&U project funded by the Mellon Foundation revealed that a large (and growing) number of liberal arts colleges specify in their mission statements that their graduates should be prepared to thrive in a future characterized by global interdependence (Hovland, 2005). Research universities, community colleges, and other types of higher education institutions are following suit. Preparing students to be "global citizens" is another phrase commonly sprinkled across mission statements. More than 70 percent of the respondents (Americans over age eighteen and college-bound high school seniors) in an American Council on Education (2005) study believe it is important for colleges and universities to offer international experiences and opportunities, and 83 percent believe it is important for colleges and universities to offer occasions to interact with students from other countries.

While institutions claim that global learning is an essential component for a twenty-first-century college education, the Mellon study revealed that there is little evidence that students are provided with multiple, robust, interdisciplinary learning environments at increasing levels of engagement to ensure that they acquire the global learning professed in the mission statement. As the newest of the three reform movements, such structured learning opportunities, both within the curriculum and within student life, are the least developed. However, evidence abounds that colleges are devoting more attention and resources to new programs, courses, living-learning centers, and study abroad opportunities. They are also hiring new faculty across departments with expertise in global knowledge.

Like the U.S. diversity movement, global learning is both about new knowledge and about reframing existing knowledge. Global learning also has profound civic dimensions, since it is not just about what students think but what they do as a result of what they have learned. Sharing similarities with its cousins, U.S. diversity and civic engagement, global learning is not an add-on but an essential means for academic institutions to achieve their educational and civic missions. AAC&U's *College Learning for the New Global Century* states: "Global integration is now our shared context. The potential benefits of global interdependence are extraordinary, but so too are the challenges. Wealth, income, and social power are dramatically unequal within and across international boundaries. We are reminded daily of the clash of cultures, histories, and worldviews. The globe itself is fragile and vulnerable as are our shared civic spaces. These global challenges will be with us for the foreseeable future" (National Leadership Council for Liberal Education and America's Promise, 2007, p. 21).

CIVIC ENGAGEMENT

As chapter 1 describes, civic engagement has been emerging as a focus as higher education institutions are recommitting to their public purpose. On many campuses, students have been the catalyst for a wide range of activities that serve communities in need, and structures to support that outreach are visible everywhere.

Throughout the 1990s, more and more students arrived on campus eager to continue the practice of volunteering in the community inspired by their faith communities, high school involvements, and the larger cultural focus on individual solutions for larger social problems. By 2005, over 3.3 million students arrived on college campuses having already served as volunteers (Corporation for National and Community Service, 2006). Volunteer centers, often run by nonacademic staff, became a more common fixture, and the numbers of student organizations devoted to community service grew. In many cases, presidents' offices readily took on civic engagement as a robust entrepreneurial and public relations dimension of the president's, and the institution's, role.

The last group to fall into line with the expanding civic engagement activities was the faculty. Gradually, however, they became more involved in incorporating the possibilities of community-based learning through credit-bearing service-learning courses and community-focused undergraduate research projects. Faculty teaching diversity courses had already initiated community-based internships, research, and pedagogy as a dimension of their work. From their inception, black studies and women's studies, for example, understood their academic disciplines as an aspect of larger historic and contemporary social movements for full equality. Other faculty fell under the civic engagement umbrella through their commitment to education for democratic citizenship or by embracing pedagogies of engaged civic learning.

The most recent focus of campus activity across students, faculty, administrators, and facilities' units is sustainability. Driven by a sense of environmental and economic responsibility and their link to developing viable social communities, colleges and universities have increasingly turned to "greening" their campuses, created new courses and programs in sustainability, and seen the rise of student activism. The sustainability movement locally is linked inevitably with larger global concerns, offering one more footbridge between these three reform movements, all of which are different faces of civic learning.

These various rivulets within the civic engagement movement have led to more comprehensive civic engagement initiatives or centers. Many of these are now housed within academic affairs, thus inserting themselves at the heart of student learning.

However, too often these new civic engagement initiatives or centers fail to connect with those addressing U.S. diversity and global concerns. Defining how all three share similar learning goals and work collaboratively within that larger vision can enhance the transformative civic power of all three movements.

Maximizing the Educational Capital of All Three Movements

Unfortunately, these powerful educational reform movements typically operate with different personnel, are located in different departments or divisions, use different language, and have different histories. But there is evidence of emerging efforts to capitalize on the congruencies as administrators and faculty members recognize common conceptual frameworks, complementary pedagogies, and increasingly similar student learning goals. Together they can and should form a powerful educational partnership that promises to provide students with the knowledge, commitment, and practical skills to be socially responsible citizens in a diverse democracy and increasingly interconnected world.

What was first developed to capture diversity literacy in a simple schema of five essential questions soon became equally useful in describing both civic and global learning. It is offered as additional evidence that while they may operate under different banners, all three are fundamentally about the same process. Students move from the self, to others, and finally to cooperating with others for a larger public good. The following five questions, slightly adapted from the original, suggest critical queries for students to pose that should lead them to a deeper capacity to work collectively with others toward shared social and civic ends:

Who am I? (knowledge of self)
Who are we? (communal/collective knowledge)
What does it feel like to be them? (empathetic knowledge)
How do we talk with one another? (intercultural process knowledge)
How do we improve our shared lives? (applied, engaged knowledge)
(Musil, 2006b)

When the power of each of the three educational reform movements is influenced by the special insights and distinguishing pedagogies of the others, they have greater likelihood of meeting what are shared educational goals across the trio. A way out of the conundrum of intellectual silos between the three is the creation of a kind of intellectual commons. That such a space is possible can be most clearly seen in the common aspirations across all three as they seek to help students:

- gain a deep, comparative knowledge of the world's peoples and problems;
- explore the historical legacies that have created the dynamics and tensions of their world;
- develop intercultural competencies to move across boundaries and unfamiliar territory and see the world from multiple perspectives;
- sustain difficult conversations in the face of highly emotional and perhaps uncongenial differences;
- understand—and perhaps redefine—democratic principles and practices within an intercultural and global context;
- secure opportunities to engage in practical work with fundamental issues that affect communities not yet well served by their societies; and
- believe that actions and ideas matter and can influence their world. (Hovland, 2005)

As noted earlier, AAC&U has further articulated a simple phrase that connects all three movements as well: personal and social responsibility. Defined as one of the four essential learning outcomes of a college education, personal and social responsibility also offers overarching language that encompasses U.S. diversity, global learning, and civic engagement. It, too, tenders an intellectual commons for all three. By doing so, it reflects what college campuses are gradually discovering: the interchangeable and complementary concepts and commitments of the three.

Too frequently, however, civic engagement continues to narrow its scope by excluding the expanding dimensions possible when the insights of U.S. diversity and global learning inform understanding of civic engagement, civic responsibility, and education for democracy. By contrast, in the definition of civic engagement put forth in this volume, the integration of the three is clearly articulated: civic engagement is acting on a heightened sense of responsibility to one's communities that encompasses the notions of global citizenship and interdependence, participation in building civil society, and empowering individuals as agents of positive social change to promote social justice locally and globally.

THE CIVIC LEARNING SPIRAL

As institutions struggle to move from scattered and uncoordinated activities within and across all three learning reform movements, one vehicle for creating educational coherence is to organize more intentional, developmental, and integrated student learning outcomes. As part of AAC&U's five-year initiative Greater Expectations: Goals for Learning as a Nation Goes to College, the Civic Engagement Working Group was charged with investigating whether there were pathways from K–12 through college that offered a developmental arc of civic learning that was cumulative over time and built on what had previously been learned. The members of the Civic Engagement Working Group were selected because they approached civic learning informed deeply by their expertise in U.S. diversity and global learning reform movements as well as in civic engagement.

Through a series of public forums in six cities across the country that gathered educators and nonprofit staff from all educational sectors, the Civic Engagement Working Group accumulated examples of models for civic learning and greater clarity about how educators were defining components of civic engagement. Elements of the working group's findings are captured in Andrea Leskes and Ross Miller's *Purposeful Pathways: Helping Students Achieve Key Learning Outcomes* (2006). Ultimately, the working group developed a new model of civic learning that could be applied from elementary school through college and, in the process, establish the habit of lifelong engagement as an empowered, informed, and socially responsible citizen. The group called its model the Civic Learning Spiral.

Distinguished by principles of interactivity and integration, the spiral has six elements or braids within each full turn:

1. Self
2. Communities and cultures
3. Knowledge

4. Skills
5. Values
6. Public Action (Musil et al., in press)

These six braids coexist simultaneously, indicating the connections between and among them, even if a given educational environment is designed to develop one element more than another. An introductory writing course at Rutgers University in New Brunswick, New Jersey, that uses ethno-autobiographies might have special emphasis on the self and communities and cultures, but students in that course would likely also learn something about the history of other people's ethnic groups, better understand and appreciate others' perspectives, and perhaps be more inclined to join in a public rally to support immigrants' rights because of what they might have learned from classmates in their personal writings. Living-learning programs organized around civic engagement—like those being created at the University of Delaware in Newark—offer a series of developmental outcomes for students across four years, with each year having a designated set of activities that help develop students' dialogic and deliberative skills, ethical values, and practice in public service. By contrast, a senior capstone course in general education at St. Edwards University in Austin, Texas, has a thicker braid in public action since it requires students to organize a project that addresses a social dilemma to which they apply knowledge from their major.

The Civic Engagement Working Group chose the metaphor of the spiral over the more commonly used steps and ladders because ladder advocates typically organize student learning into a series of separate and unconnected boxes instead of a fluid, integrated continuum. In contrast to a hierarchical ladder model often used to justify deferring some learning as inappropriate at lower levels, the spiral suggests that complexity and integration can be—and, in fact, should be—addressed at all levels. With each turn of the spiral, learners bring with them their recently acquired knowledge and their synthesis of the integration of the six interrelated braids of the spiral. The repetitive rhythm of the rotation of the wheel also helps foster a routine of integration that can lead to a lifelong disposition of open inquiry, dialogue across differences, and practice in public activism.

The spiral is constructed around the notion of relationships and deeply embedded interdependencies that are part of everyday life and learning. The working group argued that schools should introduce students to the core principles and dilemmas of democracy at an early age to begin the process of acquiring a sophisticated understanding of their rights and responsibilities as citizens in a diverse democracy and multicultural global society. Such learning requires repeated opportunities in high school and college to translate new knowledge, values, and skills into the practice of collective public action. As Benjamin Barber (2007) argues, "We are born free, but we are not born citizens. The difference between born free and becoming citizens is a lifetime of learning and practice, of which formal education is only a piece."

LEARNING OUTCOMES FOR THE SIX BRAIDS WITHIN THE CIVIC LEARNING SPIRAL

The Civic Engagement Working Group asserted that a series of assumptions undergirds the Civic Learning Spiral and therefore should influence the pedagogies, the nature of assignments, and the intellectual architecture of a given course or program:

- We all learn and live within an intricate web of interdependencies that are with us from childhood to old age.
- Being a learner and being a responsible citizen are continuous, lifelong, and intricately dependent upon cultivating and recognizing relationships.
- At the heart of education for civic engagement is the notion of the self in ongoing relationship with others.
- Civic engagement is dependent upon collaborative inquiry, dialogic pluralism, and negotiated collective action.
- Civic engagement needs to be informed by knowledge, rooted in values, tied to democratic aspirations, and embodied through practice.
- Given that U.S. democracy is marked as much by its failures as its aspirations, engagement in such a context implies both a promise and an undertaking. (Musil et al., in press)

Every college should examine its curriculum to be sure it provides a pathway for students to develop civic imagination, civic values, and civic habits cultivated in part by exposure to the complex struggle for democratic justice that poses both enduring and contemporary questions in human history. There is no single model. But within whatever mapping of mindful citizenship that is selected, the Civic Learning Spiral can help bring coherence and integration to the student so that this century's graduates will be informed, responsible, and civically engaged members of their globally linked societies. Following is a set of civic learning outcomes that the Civic Engagement Working Group developed for the six braids of the spiral for the purpose of integration into a wide range of courses and cocurricular experiences:

Outcomes for civic learning about the self:

- Understanding that the self is always embedded in relationships, a social location, and a specific historic moment
- Awareness of ways one's identity is connected to inherited and self-chosen communities
- Ability to express one's voice to effect change
- Disposition to become active in what a person cares about
- Capacity to stand up for oneself and one's passionate commitments

Outcomes for civic learning about communities and cultures:

- Appreciation of the rich resources and accumulated wisdom of diverse communities and cultures
- Understanding how communities can also exclude, judge, and restrict
- Curiosity to learn about the diversity of groups locally and globally
- Willingness to move from the comfort zone to the contact zone by transgressing boundaries that divide
- Capacity to describe comparative civic traditions expressed within and by different cultural groups

Outcomes for civic learning about knowledge:

- Recognition that knowledge is dynamic, changing, and consistently reevaluated
- Understanding that knowledge is socially constructed and implicated with power
- Familiarity with key historical struggles, campaigns, and social movements to achieve the full promise of democracy

- Deep knowledge about the fundamental principles of and central arguments about democracy over time as expressed in the United States and in other countries
- Ability to describe the main civic intellectual debates within one's major

Outcomes for civic learning about skills:

- Adeptness at critical thinking, conflict resolution, and cooperative methods
- Ability to listen eloquently and speak confidently
- Skills in deliberation, dialogue, and community building
- Development of a civic imagination
- Capacity to work well across multiple differences

Outcomes for civic learning about values:

- Serious exploration of and reflection about core animating personal values
- Examination of personal values in the context of promoting the public good
- Espousal of democratic aspirations of equality, opportunity, liberty, and justice for all
- Development of affective qualities of character, integrity, empathy, and hope
- Ability to negotiate traffic at the intersection where worlds collide

Outcomes for civic learning about public action:

- Understanding of, commitment to, and ability to live in communal contexts
- Disposition to create and participate in democratic governance structures of school, college, and the community
- Disciplined civic practices that lead to constructive participation in the communities in which one lives and works
- Formulation of multiple strategies for action (service, advocacy, policy change) to accomplish public ends/purposes
- Planning, carrying out, and reflecting upon public action
- Development of the moral and political courage to take risks to achieve the public good
- Determination to raise ethical issues and questions in and about public life (Musil et al., in press)

Using and Assessing the Outcomes of the Civic Learning Spiral

While this chapter can only begin to touch on some key issues related to using and assessing the outcomes of the Civic Learning Spiral, clarifying what the key civic learning goals are for each course, program, or other educational experience is the necessary starting point. An AAC&U board of directors report, *Our Students' Best Work* (2004), suggests three levels of learning to aim for that can be applied within a single course or over time in a full program of study. Those include foundational learning, milestone learning, and capstone experiences. What, for example, would be the foundational learning necessary to gain some threshold civic skills? Are there milestones that might illustrate that a student has turned the spiral one more time and developed new democratic competencies to stay in sustained dialogue despite uncongenial differences? In a capstone experience in that skill-building area, how might a community-based service project demonstrate a student's ability to negotiate the complex power differentials that typify so many campus-community partnerships? Without the inherent structure of the syllabus, attendance requirements, and grades in an academic course, it is more challenging to assess learning in cocurricular experiences.

If we examine one level of learning—the individual course—as an example, several questions arise that enable the faculty member to integrate student learning outcomes and assess the degree to which students achieve them. Are the civic components of the course clearly defined? Would a student know these are goals for the course? Is the course constructed in such a way as to give students the opportunity to achieve those goals? Has the faculty member clearly articulated to the students what success would look like related to the course goals? Are the course goals part of a larger developmental arc of more complex and long-term goals? Do the course assignments build on one another? How are students involved in assessing their gains so they might become more adept at evaluating both their own civic knowledge and skills and those of their peers?

It is important for an institution to align its overall commitment to students' civic learning at all levels. If local and global

citizenship is articulated as a goal in the institution's mission statement, how do divisions, departments, programs, courses, and campus life reinforce that goal, develop different aspects of the Civic
Learning Spiral, and assess how well a student has mastered new
competencies, values, and dispositions that serve as evidence of
civic imagination and habits?

New publications about how to assess different dimensions
of civic engagement are appearing regularly. And many have
become concerned that while students acquire elements of the
Civic Learning Spiral, most structured campus experiences fail to
foster a sense of political efficacy, and as a result, the public action
braid is underdeveloped (Musil et al., in press; Spiezio, 2002).
*Educating for Democracy: Preparing Undergraduates for Political Engage-
ment* (Colby, Beaumont, Ehrlich, and Corngold, 2007) offers new
research about what kind of courses most effectively instill in students the will, capacity, and practice to effect political change in
society. Other publications in this vein include the following: José
Z. Calderón's *Race, Poverty, and Social Justice: Multidisciplinary Perspectives through Service Learning* (Stylus, 2007); Susan A. Ostrander
and Kent E. Portney's *Acting Civically: From Urban Neighborhoods
to Higher Education* (Tufts University Press, 2007); and Lorraine
McIlrath and Iain Mac Labharainn's *Higher Education and Civic
Engagement: International Perspectives* (Ashgate Publishing, 2007). It
is also extremely important to harvest the accumulated civic learning across the range of opportunities offered to students that are
embedded in U.S. diversity and global efforts as well as in those
domains labeled "civic engagement." There is a rich set of assessment books and articles to capture institutional and student learning in diversity as well as an emerging body on assessing global
learning, all of which are also useful for assessing civic learning
(Bolen, 2007; Clayton-Pederson, Parker, Smith, Moreno, and Teraguchi, 2007; Garcia et al., 2001; and Musil, 2006a).

CONCLUSION

Adam Hochschild's *King Leopold's Ghost: A Story of Greed, Terror, and
Heroism in Colonial Africa* (1998) recounts the brutal regime of Bel-
gium's King Leopold at the end of the nineteenth century, when
he subjugated people in the Belgian Congo through systematic

murder, torture, and enslavement as he exploited the riches from that piece of Africa. His heinous operation was uncovered and forced to end in part because E. D. Morel, a lowly civil servant working as a shipping clerk in Antwerp at the time, happened to notice that something was awry. The ships coming into port from the Belgian Congo were laden with ivory, rubber, and other material goods, but the ships that were sent back offered no such exchange of goods. Instead, they were filled with soldiers, guns, machetes, and chains. Also a newspaperman, Morel documented what he saw and had the skills, courage, and will to speak up publicly about what he had discovered. The result was the emergence of a massive global human rights movement that continued until King Leopold was forced to abandon his unchecked exploitation.

At this historic juncture, higher education has the opportunity to help equip all its graduates with the civic engagement personified by E. D. Morel. To achieve such a goal, the academy needs to realign its goals and reassess its offerings to include personal and social responsibility as an inescapable dimension of every student's college experience. Students need to acquire the knowledge to see the threads that link local and global fortunes, to recognize when injustice is the normative coin of the realm, and to document the impact of the unchallenged systems that perpetuate destabilizing inequalities. They also need to cultivate civic skills to speak up and think that it matters when they do. In addition, they need to have the intercultural competencies to work in concert with others in public actions to demand that a more just society be put in place and the motivation and commitment to persist. It would take many turnings of the Civic Learning Spiral to hone such capacities, but higher education has an unprecedented opportunity to reengage with its fundamental mission to educate citizens. Higher education holds the potential to turn democracy's peril into democracy's promise.

References

American Council on Education. *Public Experience, Attitudes, and Knowledge: A Report on Two National Surveys about International Education.* Washington, DC: American Council on Education, 2005.

Association of American Colleges and Universities Board of Directors. *Our Students' Best Work.* Washington, DC: Association of American Colleges and Universities, 2004.

Barber, B. "Global Education in a World Torn between Jihad and McWorld." Paper presented at the Association of American Colleges and Universities conference, Denver, CO, October 2007.

Bolen, M. C. (Ed.). *A Guide to Outcomes Assessment in Education Abroad.* Carlisle, PA: Forum on Education Abroad, 2007.

Clayton-Pederson, A. R., Parker, S., Smith, D. G., Moreno, J. F., and Teraguchi, D. H. *Making a Real Difference with Diversity: A Guide to Institutional Change.* Washington, DC: Association of American Colleges and Universities, 2007.

Colby, A., Beaumont, E., Ehrlich, T, and Corngold, J. *Educating for Democracy: Preparing Undergraduates for Political Engagement.* San Francisco: Jossey-Bass, 2007.

Corporation for National and Community Service. *College Students Helping America.* http://www.nationalservice.gov/pdf/06_1016_RPD_college_full.pdf, September 2006.

Education Trust–West. *The High School Diploma: Making It More Than an Empty Promise.* Prepared for Senate Standing Committee on Education hearing on Senate Bill 1731, April 2002.

Garcia, M., Hudgins, C. A., Musil, C. M., Nettles, M. T., Sedlacek, W. E., and Smith, D. G. *Assessing Campus Diversity Initiatives: A Guide for Campus Practitioners.* Washington, DC: Association of American Colleges and Universities, 2001.

Hochschild, A. *King Leopold's Ghost: A Story of Greed, Terror, and Heroism in Colonial Africa.* New York: Houghton Mifflin, 1998.

Hovland, K. "Shared Futures: Global Learning and Social Responsibility." *Diversity Digest,* 2005, *8*(3), 1, 16–17.

Humphreys, D., and Davenport, A. "What Really Matters in College: How Students View and Value Liberal Education." *Liberal Education,* Summer/Fall 2005, 1–6.

Leskes, A., and Miller, R. *Purposeful Pathways: Helping Students Achieve Key Learning Outcomes.* Washington, DC: Association of American Colleges and Universities, 2006.

Musil, C. M. *Assessing Global Learning: Matching Good Intentions with Good Practice.* Washington, DC: Association of American Colleges and Universities, 2006a.

Musil, C. M. "Discovering the Streets Where We Live: Mapping the Future of Inclusion and Higher Education." Paper presented at the Association of American Colleges and Universities conference, Washington, DC, January 2006b.

Musil, C. M., Wathington, H., Battistoni, R., Calderón, J., Trementozzi, M., Fluker, W. E., et al. *The Civic Learning Spiral: Education for*

Participation in a Diverse Democracy. Washington, DC: Association of American Colleges and Universities, in press.

National Leadership Council for Liberal Education and America's Promise. *College Learning for the New Global Century.* Washington, DC: Association of American Colleges and Universities, 2007.

Spiezio, K. E. "Pedagogy and Political (Dis)Engagement." *Liberal Education,* 2002, *88*(4), 14–19.

U.S. Department of Education. *Digest of Education Statistics.* (National Center for Education Statistics No. 2006–030). Washington, DC: U.S. Government Printing Office, 2006.

U.S. Department of Education, Office of Educational Research and Improvement. *First-Generation Students: Undergraduates Whose Parents Never Enrolled in Postsecondary Education.* (Statistical Analysis Report No. 98–082). Washington, DC: National Center for Education Statistics, 1998.

Veysey, L. R. *The Emergence of the American University.* Chicago: University of Chicago Press, 1965.

CHAPTER FOUR

CIVIC ENGAGEMENT IN THE FIRST COLLEGE YEAR

Mary Stuart Hunter and Blaire L. Moody

Students coming to college campuses enter a new culture and face new challenges and opportunities. The behavior patterns of new students are set early in their college careers and often last throughout their undergraduate experience and beyond. Thus, it is critical for the first-year experience to introduce new students to the importance of civic engagement, help them understand why civic engagement is a critical element of a college education, and provide opportunities to learn about and practice civic engagement.

This chapter defines the first-year experience and first-year student success and provides a rationale for civic engagement as a key component. It then identifies and describes model programs and offers lessons learned from the first-year experience movement that can be applied to enhancing campus-based civic engagement initiatives in the first college year.

The first college year is an opportunity for unprecedented growth, development, and change for new students. As institutions of all types have implemented special initiatives to assist students as they transition into higher education, faculty and staff have asked important questions: What is the first-year experience? What should it be? The only universal answer to such questions is "it depends." It depends on students' backgrounds and educational goals as well as institutions' curricular and cocurricular focus. It is perhaps easier to articulate what the first-year experience is *not*.

It is not a single program or initiative aimed at new students. It is not the same experience for all students. It is not the same from campus to campus, institution to institution, or year to year.

It is perhaps easier and more useful to define first-year student success than to define the first-year experience itself. Outcomes that lead to student success can be more readily measured and can also be used to guide programmatic and curricular initiatives. In 2005, M. Lee Upcraft, John N. Gardner, and Betsy O. Barefoot updated an earlier, widely accepted definition of freshman success. They suggested that a narrow definition of first-year success that focused solely on successful completion of courses and continued enrollment into the second year is not sufficient. They recommend a broader definition of first-year student success that includes one or more of the following: developing intellectual and academic competence, establishing and maintaining interpersonal relationships, exploring identity development, deciding on a career path, maintaining health and wellness, considering faith and the spiritual dimensions of life, developing multicultural awareness, and developing civic responsibility.

RATIONALE FOR CIVIC ENGAGEMENT IN THE FIRST YEAR

Students are coming to college with greater interest and experience in various forms of civic engagement. Many also indicate that their interest increases over the course of their first year. According to the Higher Education Research Institute, the class of 2006 entered college with more political and civic awareness than in previous classes. Nearly 34 percent of new students reported frequently discussing politics during their senior year of high school, a significant increase over the 25.5 percent who so responded in 2004 (Pryor et al., 2006). The 2005 data reported that 83.2 percent of incoming students had volunteered at least occasionally during their high school senior year (Pryor et al., 2005). In addition, in 2005, 40.2 percent of the first-year class reported influencing social values as very important or essential, and by the end of this first year, this percentage increased to 49.4 percent (Hurtado et al., 2007). There was also an increase in students indicating a desire to help others in difficulty; in fact, 65.3 percent reported doing so as essential or very important upon college entry, and 75.0 percent so indicated at the end of their first college year (Hurtado et al., 2007).

In 2005, 49.7 percent of incoming students reported they had participated in an organized demonstration during high school, the highest percentage ever (Pryor et al., 2005). Students are also becoming more committed politically as they shift away from the center, with 28.4 percent identifying themselves as liberals, the highest since 1975 (30.7 percent), and 23.9 percent identifying themselves as conservatives, the highest in the history of the annual freshman survey (Pryor et al., 2006).

Thus, today's first-year college students remain torn, as Levine and Cureton (1998) suggest, "between doing well and doing good, that is, between having material resources and helping others" (p. 138). Although students may well be able to describe "doing well" and "doing good," "in practice students generally could not figure out how to do both at the same time" (Levine and Cureton, 1998, p. 138).

Several theoretical frameworks from retention and student success literature support the deliberate and intentional focus on civic engagement in the first college year. The early transition to college is important in that the expectations that students bring with them to college and the early behavior patterns they establish are powerful influences on their behaviors, attitudes, and experiences throughout their college years. The concept of student and institutional fit, first put forth by Vincent Tinto (1993), suggests that undergraduate students enter college with a particular background and set of characteristics that help determine their initial commitment to their education goals and their institution. The greater congruence between the student's values, goals, and attitudes and those of the institution, the more likely it is that the student will persist to graduation. Opportunities to practice civic engagement in the first year enable students to clarify their values and goals and to recognize how their attitudes affect their behaviors.

The work of George D. Kuh, Jillian Kinzie, John H. Schuh, and Elizabeth J. Whitt (2005) stresses two key factors that contribute strongly to student success: the amount of time and effort students put toward their studies and activities and the extent to which institutions direct resources and structure learning opportunities to engage students in both the curriculum and the cocurriculum. Students who find support for their learning, receive frequent feedback about their learning, and are actively involved in learning, especially with others, are more likely to learn and, in turn, more likely to stay in college (Astin, 1977; Kuh et al., 2005; Pascarella and Terenzini, 2005). Opportunities to learn about and practice civic engagement in the first year can be designed to purposefully incorporate these factors and, thus, to increase student success. The newly developed Beginning College Survey of Student Engagement (BCSSE) is a survey instrument that measures the precollege academic and cocurricular experiences of first-year students. It addresses new students' interest in and expectations for participating in educationally purposeful activities during college (see http://bcsse.iub.edu). Like the National Survey of Student Engagement, the BCSSE will provide valuable information for designing such activities with and without desired civic engagement outcomes.

Providing opportunities for first-year students to learn about and practice civic engagement can also lead to the achievement of other institutional goals for the first-year experience. Because civic engagement is fundamentally about acting on a heightened sense of responsibility to one's communities, discussion topics can include exploration of the meaning of community, self in relation to others, civility, and community standards of behavior. Participation in civic engagement activities in the communities surrounding the campus, together with structured reflection, can introduce students to the concept of the college as a responsible citizen of its community. Expectations for students to take an active role in student organizations, campus governance, and local and global communities can also be introduced to students in the context of first-year civic engagement opportunities.

INSTITUTIONAL EXAMPLES OF GOOD PRACTICE

Incorporating civic engagement into first-year experiences takes many forms. Experiences range from one-day components of the orientation process to one- or two-year intensive living-learning communities. A variety of examples is offered here to represent this range and to inspire adaptation to particular institutional settings and purposes.

Seeking to introduce civic engagement to students even before they attend summer orientation, the University of Georgia offers Classic City, one of four experiences in a program for new students called Dawg Camp. Classic City is a five-day retreat during which students live on campus and participate together in various service activities in the Athens, Georgia community, the fifth-poorest county in the nation for its size. The students serve in several different governmental, nonprofit, and social service agencies working with the elderly, children, and people who are homeless. Program goals include familiarizing students with the local area and the community organizations that serve it, enabling students to learn about the issues the community organizations address, and suggesting how students can be change agents in their own communities. To achieve these goals, the students hear from the staff members of each agency about how they work personally and professionally on the social issues that most concern them. The students are encouraged to record their reflections in personal journals as well as in a group journal. The group journal initially serves as a way to share silly stories and inside jokes. As the week progresses, it becomes a safe place where the students can vent their disappointment and anger about what is happening in their community. The group journal also becomes a powerful tool for group discussion as the students reflect on the inequalities faced by the marginalized communities they encounter, the team-building and leadership skills they have used, and what it all means for them. Following the experience, each student receives a copy of the group journal, together with information about further civic engagement opportunities on campus and in the Athens community (A. Beale, personal communication, May 7, 2007).

To ease the transition to college while also introducing new students to local communities, civic engagement can be a component of new student orientation programs. The State University of New York's College of Environmental Science and Forestry hosts the Saturday of Service during its annual welcome week in partnership with the local parks and recreation department. Approximately three hundred students engage in a daylong service project that is directly related to the institution's environmental mission (Moody,

2007). Similarly, new students at Concordia College participate in Hands for Change, a daylong service event that focuses on what it means to be a responsible citizen (Moody, 2007). Before and after the event, mayors from the local towns, the college's president, and the student body president speak about the impact of their service on the local communities and the value of service both locally and globally. At the University of Maryland in College Park, approximately a thousand new students in the College Park Scholars living-learning community participate in Service Day immediately before the first day of classes. College Park Scholars is a community of twelve living-learning programs for academically talented first- and second-year students. Each program addresses a specific theme and offers specially designed courses and experiences that relate to its theme. Service Day is an opportunity for students in each of the programs to engage in a day of service together in the local community along with group reflection activities that focus on the meaning of community and the goal of developing students as lifelong citizens, scholars, and leaders. Such activities can engage students before they even start classes and expose them to an institutional emphasis on civic responsibility.

First-year seminars offer a platform within the first-year curriculum to involve students in civic engagement. Service-learning is one civic engagement strategy frequently employed in first-year seminars. Reflective of the institutional mission at Millersville University in Pennsylvania, civic responsibility was integrated through service-learning into the first-year seminar when the seminars were implemented in 2001. The university's quantitative and qualitative assessment efforts indicate that these early collegiate experiences have both an immediate and long-term impact on student perceptions and civic participation. Students increase their roles as citizens in a diverse world through the service-learning experiences (McDowell, Phillips, and Burns, 2007).

Moving beyond service-learning alone, civic engagement in first-year seminars at Indiana University–Purdue University Indianapolis is the fulcrum of the first-year seminar entitled Discover Indianapolis. Students learn about the city and civic issues through participating in excursions into the city, engaging in service, using the local newspaper as text for a major project, and discussing civic engagement as an active collaboration that builds on the resources of the campus to improve the quality of life in communities in a manner that is consistent with the institution's mission. An assessment of the fall 2006 course indicated that a larger percentage of students agreed or strongly agreed in the posttest than in the pretest with such statements as "being a citizen of my community has a great deal of personal meaning for me," "I am knowledgeable about local socioeconomic issues and problems," and "being involved in a program to improve my community is important" (Evenbeck, Ross, and Hansen, 2007).

The core program at Antioch College in Yellow Springs, Ohio, offers topical academic seminars with a civic engagement and experiential education component to first-year students. Each multidisciplinary course is taught by four faculty members from various academic departments. The courses enable students to view social and political issues through a multidisciplinary framework while becoming involved in their community. One such course, Water Matters, incorporates civic engagement through field study that connects students to community water issues. The students travel into the local community to examine stream contamination, aging infrastructure, and wetland degradation. The course examines freshwater needs through the study of environmental chemistry, freshwater ecology, literature, and creative writing (LaBare, 2007). Students also learn about water issues around the globe, including basic sanitation, everyday drinking water, and water use and management. The students then share what they have learned with the larger Antioch community through WaterFest, a two-day program of discussions and presentations on local, regional, and global freshwater issues (LaBare, 2007). Another Antioch core course titled Citizenship focuses on citizenship in political science and history through the context of art. A goal of the seminar is to reduce political apathy among college students and to improve their knowledge of the public policy process, the rights and responsibilities of citizenship, and the American political system, including its institutions, culture, power, and challenges. Studio assignments complement required readings and written critical reflections (LaBare, 2007).

Suffolk University in Boston hosts the Media Literacy freshman seminar in which students evaluate media content for cultural, political, and social influences. The students examine the media's role as a dominant source of information and entertainment through its broad reach in print, Internet, radio broadcasting, and television sources. Course activities include readings, written assignments, class discussions, guest speakers, field trips, and community service projects. Additionally, students are required to write a public service announcement for the local nonprofit agency they work with for their community service component. Each year the Media Literacy seminar series focuses on a particular theme. For example, the fall 2005 courses were centered on the interconnected issues of poverty, homelessness, and hunger (LaBare, 2007). The students investigated news coverage on the topic and compared what they found in the media to what they experienced firsthand during their volunteer time. The students were then able to critically question media reporting and form their own views regarding homelessness and poverty and created public service announcements that aired on the university's student-run radio station. In addition to learning how the media can influence public opinion, some students continued their work as volunteers for local agencies after the course ended (LaBare, 2007).

The First-Year Interest Groups (FIGs) Program at the University of Michigan in Ann Arbor offers a variety of first-year seminars dealing with diversity and social justice issues that are taught from the perspectives of various disciplines. The objective is to expose students to social justice issues very early in their college career while also placing them in contact with persons on campus who are interested in the same issues. One such course—I, Too, Sing America: Talking about Racism and Other Difficult Topics—is taught through the Program on Intergroup Relations and is designed to allow students with varying viewpoints and backgrounds to talk openly about stereotyping, conflict, privilege, and discrimination in the United States. The course is based on dialogue. Students learn the techniques of dialogue versus those of conversation. Conflict is accepted and considered as a learning opportunity. To uphold the dialogue, the students agree to respect and listen to one another, even if they disagree with their peers' opinions, per the multicultural ground rules established during the first class. In addition to the in-class structure, the students are required to engage in experiential learning outside the classroom through cultural, religious, and other experiences that are related to their dialogues (C. Behling, personal communication, May 2, 2007).

First-year students not only learn about social issues within the classroom context but can also be profoundly affected by what they learn in their living environments. George Washington University in Washington, DC, seeks to fulfill this potential through its first-year theme houses focusing on topical areas of interest and related cocurricular activities. Each year students create their own living-learning cohorts centered around the house themes. During the 2006–2007 academic year, the students of the Politics and Public Policy House created several innovative living-learning communities related to political and social issues. Based on the novels of J. K. Rowling, Potter for President was a community in which students compare the governmental systems of the United Kingdom, the United States, and the Harry Potter wizard world. Students met biweekly to discuss how politics are portrayed in fiction and the role politics play in real-life issues. Another community, Cookies and Colbert, aimed to improve the political awareness of its residents through dissecting popular media outlets. The group viewed and discussed *The Colbert Report* to learn about the influence of comedic satire in modern news and the implications on national dialogue and political discourse. The Do It Green community was created by students who were politically invested and interested in the environment. The students engaged in outdoor activities and learned about environmental conscientiousness and healthy behavior through participation in discussions on global warming and related conferences in the District of Columbia. All the houses worked with academic and student affairs departments to structure learning opportunities to enhance in-class education. This collaboration often brought professors, academic advisers, and other staff members into the houses for various programs, activities, and discussions (C. Campbell, personal communication, May 14, 2007).

Engaging students in service-learning and other forms of experiential education outside the classroom can be a challenge for campuses that serve commuter or nontraditional students. Such students are frequently more involved in family, work, and community responsibilities than traditional, residential students. Targeting this student population, Chandler-Gilbert Community College

of Arizona implemented "See Your World" as a collegewide theme
with the goal of educating students about world issues. Over a
thousand first-year students enrolled in eighty-six courses in more
than twenty disciplines. Faculty members encouraged students
in these courses to attend events and presentations that examined the meaning of citizenship and how to act in the face of
global problems (LaBare, 2007). The students critically reflected
on and discussed what they had learned in class and in course
assignments. Topics included the rebuilding of New Orleans after
Hurricane Katrina, the impact of groundwater pumping, oil exploration, and the relationship between South American and U.S.
policies (LaBare, 2007).

These examples illustrate that opportunities to learn about
and practice multiple forms of civic engagement can successfully
be integrated into the first-year experience. They can be curricular
or cocurricular, one-time or long-term in duration, and designed
to achieve a wide range of learning outcomes.

Lessons Learned from the First-Year Experience Movement

The first-year experience movement over the past thirty-five years
has produced a set of reform strategies that have been employed
by countless institutions. Many of these are applicable to efforts
to create and implement civic engagement initiatives in first-year
experiences at institutions of all types.

Understand Students

Although data from national surveys such as that mentioned in
chapter 2 and earlier in this chapter is useful, it is also important to collect data on the characteristics and experiences of the
students at your particular institution. Enrollment management
offices and offices of institutional research and assessment are
likely to collect such data.

In addition, students' attitudes, behaviors, and experiences
are in constant flux, depending on how they have experienced
significant world and local events. The events of September 11,
2001, and subsequent terrorist activity; natural disasters, including

Hurricane Katrina and the deadly tsunami of 2004; and the war in Iraq have profoundly affected current college students and subsequent entering cohorts.

One lighthearted and useful resource is the Beloit College Mindset List. Compiled annually by faculty members at Beloit College in Wisconsin, this list describes the worldview of each incoming class of college students and distinguishes their views and experiences from the cohorts that preceded them (Nief and McBride, 2008).

Include Social and Academic Integration

Undergraduate students learn more effectively when their learning is integrated throughout the curriculum and across in-class and out-of-class experiences (Pascarella and Terenzini, 2005; Tinto, 1993). According to the Association of American Colleges and Universities and the Carnegie Foundation for the Advancement of Teaching (2004), "The undergraduate experience is often a fragmented landscape of general education, concentration, electives, co-curricular activities, and for many students 'the real world' beyond campus." Integrative learning helps students find ways to put the pieces together and develop habits of mind that prepare them to make informed judgments in a complex, fast-moving world. To participate responsibly in their local communities as well as in the global community, students must learn to be aware of complex interdependencies and be able to synthesize information from a wide variety of sources (Association of American Colleges and Universities and the Carnegie Foundation for the Advancement of Teaching, 2004). As a result, introducing students to the concept and practice of integrative learning is fundamental to the first-year experience.

Connect to Institutional Mission

Educational reform of any sort is more likely to succeed if it is consistent with the mission of the institution. Clearly articulating the connection between civic engagement initiatives and institutional mission provides a solid foundation and rationale for civic engagement in the institutional context. Robert M. Hollister,

Molly Mead, and Nancy Wilson (2006) state that in their efforts in infusing active citizenship at the Jonathan M. Tisch College of Citizenship and Public Service at Tufts University, aligning "active citizenship with the core priorities of the university" is "perhaps the most important lesson" from their experience (p. 50).

PROVIDE OPPORTUNITIES FOR FACULTY AND STAFF DEVELOPMENT

Another element central to the first-year experience movement that has direct application for the incorporation of civic engagement initiatives is deliberate and effective faculty and staff development. Traditional preparation of faculty rarely includes courses on pedagogy, much less a specific focus on civic engagement or how first-year students learn. The movement to institutionalize first-year seminars and other first-year initiatives includes a core component of faculty development. One of the characteristics of successful seminars is that "instructors are trained in basic methods of group facilitation and active learning pedagogies" and that "course process becomes as important as course content" (Barefoot and Fidler, 1996, p. 61). Faculty preparation can include workshops, curriculum development guides, and examples of in-class and out-of-class activities. Faculty development should include student characteristics, active learning pedagogies, resources on and off campus, and evaluation and assessment techniques.

ESTABLISH OUTCOMES AND ASSESS STUDENTS' DEGREE OF ACHIEVEMENT

Creating well-crafted, measurable, and attainable learning outcomes will strengthen the integration of civic engagement into first-year programming from the start. They will guide the development of appropriate learning activities and provide the basis for formative and summative assessment. Pre- and postmeasures of the degree of students' achievement of desired outcomes can be effective in providing feedback that students can then use in seeking opportunities to continue their growth in areas of civic engagement. The results of such measures should also be used by faculty and staff to refine existing initiatives and to plan new ones.

It should also be noted that it is far easier to include assessment from the beginning than it is to assess something in retrospect. Chapter 3 provides a framework for understanding potential learning outcomes for civic engagement.

CREATE PARTNERSHIPS

Many of the most successful examples of first-year seminars, learning communities, and residential colleges are based in partnerships between academic affairs and student affairs. For civic engagement initiatives, community partners should also be included, as appropriate. Clear articulation of the benefits to each partner is critical, as is clear delineation of the roles of each.

A planning committee or task force that includes individuals with varied backgrounds and perspectives is important in designing initiatives that will appeal to a wide range of diverse students. Although progress may seem slow initially, the result is likely to be stronger, more comprehensive, and well supported. It is wise to include those who are predisposed to embrace civic engagement and those who will challenge assumptions, as well as representation from all offices and programs that have a stake in enabling the new initiative to succeed. Students and individuals who have experience with campus change are also important members of project teams.

LEARN FROM OTHERS' EXPERIENCES

Networking with colleagues at other institutions who have experience with civic engagement initiatives in the first year that are similar to those under consideration is useful, as is attending conferences where civic engagement is on the agenda. Smitheram (1989) offers a step-by-step guide to creating a first-year seminar, but much of his strategy can be applied to other civic engagement efforts as well.

OPERATE WITH OPEN COMMUNICATION

It is essential to keep the campus community informed about new efforts. By circulating early drafts of a program prospectus to stakeholders and seeking suggestions and constructive criticism, the proposal can be refined to incorporate as much of this feedback as is possible and appropriate. It is also worth taking the time to learn what civic engagement opportunities exist beyond the first year so the first-year initiatives can prepare students for them. Open and wide communication will also attract potential opponents. Dealing with their issues in the early development stages is usually easier and more effective.

Start Small

It is recommended that an institution begin with a pilot project on a manageable scale, so that all components can be done well. Evaluation and assessment are also easier on a smaller scale, and results can be more easily used to inform practice. Starting small will also enable needed changes to be more easily made as the program is expanded to serve a larger proportion of students.

Conclusion

The first year is a pivotal time for student success in college. Involvement in civic engagement initiatives can assist students in this transition by providing opportunities to consider the purpose of the college experience, to assume the rights and responsibilities of membership in multiple communities, to learn about the concept of responsible citizenship, and to form relationships with peers and connections to the institution. Recent student profiles suggest that new students are more civically aware and engaged than in the past. Therefore, it is important to design and implement ways in which first-year students can begin to explore how civic engagement can and should be integral to their academic, career, and life goals.

As individual institutions and higher education at large become more invested in their public purpose, efforts to involve all first-year students in learning about and practicing civic engagement should be embraced. They should be not only curricular and cocurricular in nature but also purposefully integrated so that the student experience is seamless. Critical reflection should be a component of all civic engagement initiatives so that students have the benefit of awareness of the knowledge and skills they have acquired and feel empowered to use them for positive change in their communities. In conclusion, introducing college students to civic engagement as an institutional priority early in their undergraduate experience will engage them at a time when behavior and activity patterns are being established and has great potential to lay a solid foundation to increase their commitment to lifelong civic engagement.

References

Association of American Colleges and Universities and the Carnegie Foundation for the Advancement of Teaching. "A Statement on Integrative Learning." http://www.carnegiefoundation.org/dynamic/downloads/file_1_185.pdf, 2004.

Astin, A. W. *Four Critical Years.* San Francisco: Jossey-Bass, 1977.

Barefoot, B. O., and Fidler, P. P. *The 1994 National Survey of Freshman Seminar Programs: Continuing Innovations in the Collegiate Curriculum.* (Freshman Year Experience Monograph Series, No. 20). Columbia, SC: National Resource Center for the First-Year Experience and Students in Transition, University of South Carolina, 1996.

Evenbeck, S., Ross, F. E., and Hansen, M. J. "Integrating Civic Engagement in the First-Year Curriculum." Paper presented at the National Conference on the First-Year Experience, Addison, TX, February 2007.

Hollister, R. M., Mead, M., and Wilson, N. "Infusing Active Citizenship throughout a Research University: The Tisch College of Citizenship and Public Service at Tufts University." *Metropolitan Universities: An International Forum (Civic Engagement at Traditional Research Universities),* 2006, *17*(3), 38–55.

Hurtado, S., Sax, L. J., Saenz, V. B., Harper, C. E., Oseguera, L., Curley, J., et al. *Findings from the 2005 Administration of Your First College Year (YFCY): National Aggregates.* Los Angeles: University of California at Los Angeles, Higher Education Research Institute, 2007.

Kuh, G. D., Kinzie, J., Schuh, J. H., and Whitt, E. J. *Student Success in College: Creating Conditions That Matter.* San Francisco: Jossey-Bass, 2005.

LaBare, M. J. (Ed.). *First-Year Civic Engagement: Solid Foundations for College, Citizenship and Democracy.* New York: New York Times, 2007.

Levine, A., and Cureton, J. S. *When Hope and Fear Collide: A Portrait of Today's College Student.* San Francisco: Jossey-Bass, 1998.

McDowell, L., Phillips, C., and Burns, T. "Early Service Experiences Provide Immediate and Long-Term Impact on Civic Participation."

Paper presented at the National Conference on the First-Year Experience, Addison, TX, February 2007.

Moody, B. L. "Forming Connections: Combining Orientation and Community Service." *E-Source for College Transitions*, 2007, *4*(6).

Nief, R., and Mc Bride, T. "Beloit College Mindset List." http://www. beloit.edu/~pubaff/mindset/2011.php, 2008.

Pascarella, E. T., and Terenzini P. T. *How College Affects Students.* Vol. 2: *A Third Decade of Research.* San Francisco: Jossey-Bass, 2005.

Pryor, J. H., Hurtado, S., Saenz, V. B., Korn, J. S., Santos, J. L., and Korn, W. S. *The American Freshman: National Norms for Fall 2006.* Los Angeles: University of California at Los Angeles, Higher Education Research Institute, 2006.

Pryor, J. H., Hurtado, S., Saenz, V. B., Lindholm, J. A., Korn, W. S., and Mahoney, K. M. *The American Freshman: National Norms for Fall 2005.* Los Angeles: University of California at Los Angeles, Higher Education Research Institute, 2005.

Smitheram, V. "The Politics of Persuasion: Establishing a New Freshman Seminar with Full Academic Credit." *Journal of the Freshman Year Experience*, 1989, *1*(1), 79–94.

Tinto, V. *Leaving College: Rethinking the Causes and Cures of Student Attrition* (2nd ed.). Chicago: University of Chicago Press, 1993.

Upcraft, M. L., Gardner, J. N., and Barefoot, B. O. *Challenging and Supporting the First-Year Student: A Handbook for Improving the First Year of College.* San Francisco: Jossey-Bass, 2005.

CHAPTER FIVE

ENGAGING GENERAL EDUCATION

Kim Spiezio

In the twenty-first century the ability to promote social capital quickly has become one of the most valuable forms of human capital. For educators interested in civic engagement, this should be a welcome development because it lends a newfound sense of urgency to efforts to help students acquire the skills and aptitudes essential to the practice of engaged citizenship. Put simply, the ability to empathize, collaborate, compromise, and integrate suddenly has become as central to the marketplace as it has long been in regard to the town hall. Hence, we stand at the threshold of a perhaps unique historical moment wherein the dictates of capitalism and the requisites of democracy have converged to underscore the necessity of providing students with a civic education.

The purpose of this chapter is to present the key theoretical and organizational elements of a pedagogical framework that would enable colleges and universities to seize the opportunities inherent in this new era. The model profiled in this analysis—the Democratic Academy—is intended to serve as a guide for establishing an institutionally based, mission-driven strategy of civic education expressly dedicated to the challenge of transforming students into social entrepreneurs. Central to its design, the Democratic Academy is premised on a theory of civic education that views the classroom as a distinctive site of civic engagement that can be combined with service-learning and other pedagogies of engagement to support an evolutionary process of character education that extends over the course of a student's undergraduate career.

As such, the model suggests how educators could use the courses composing a general education curriculum to create a learning environment that will simultaneously promote engaged citizenship while also equipping students with the social intelligence to navigate the transnational knowledge networks that have become a defining characteristic of the era of globalization.

The major portion of this chapter will be dedicated to a discussion of the role that classroom engagement can play as the foundation for a comprehensive, yet flexible, approach to civic education. In addition, however, it will provide an overview of the practical steps that faculty members can take to begin transforming individual courses into democratic classrooms. Finally, the chapter also will briefly discuss the results of an empirical study of the Democratic Academy.

From 2002 to 2004, the pedagogical techniques emphasized in this model were field-tested at eight colleges and universities nationwide in an assessment study involving approximately two dozen academic disciplines and two thousand undergraduates. For purposes of this presentation, the results are significant because they suggest that it is possible to incorporate pedagogies of engagement into a sufficient number of general education courses to render this approach to civic education a viable institutional option. Moreover, the study also reveals that there are measurable and statistically significant differences between students enrolled in Democratic Academy classrooms and the general student population in terms of student learning outcomes relevant to the promotion of human and social capital. In short, the study strongly suggests that this strategy of civic education is both doable and worth doing.

Theory of Civic Education

There is an emerging consensus that in the twenty-first century sociality will be as central to student success as literacy and analytical skills. Despite their differing points of emphasis, commentators such as Thomas L. Friedman (2006) and Howard Gardner (2006), as well as professional organizations such as the Association of American Colleges and Universities and Campus Compact, have all arrived at the same basic conclusion: in the future, individuals will be expected and often required to address collective problems by pursuing collaborative initiatives within the context of increasingly diverse communities.

Given that this type of social entrepreneurship necessarily involves several of the student learning outcomes outlined in chapter 3, there are good reasons to believe that those emphasizing the importance of civic engagement are on the right track. Unfortunately, the literature on this subject is much more equivocal when it comes to specifying the causal pathways whereby educational institutions can help students acquire civic knowledge and skills. This section addresses this shortcoming by presenting a theoretical framework that serves as a guide for transforming a general education program into a civic arts curriculum.

Funded by the Teagle Foundation and Atlantic Philanthropic, the Democratic Academy is an outgrowth of a national educational initiative designed to promote greater civic engagement among college students. Officially known as the Participating in Democracy Project, the overarching purpose of this three-year, $1.2 million undertaking was to identify innovative pedagogical strategies and instructional techniques that could be used to promote student engagement "both in courses for majors and in general and honors education" (Blaney, 2001, p. 9). The colleges and universities participating in the study were Cedar Crest College, St. Thomas Aquinas College, Lesley University, Heidelberg College, Pacific Lutheran University, Notre Dame College, Seton Hill University, and the College of Notre Dame of Maryland. Cedar Crest College was the lead institution for the initiative, and the author was the academic director of the project.

From the outset, the Democracy Project approached the challenge of civic disengagement from an institutional perspective. In essence, the project started with the premise that the beliefs, perceptions, and behaviors of individuals are conditioned by the institutional environments within which they live, work, and learn. Hence, if institutions are not based on democratic principles, one should not expect the individuals in these institutional environments to become socialized to democratic practices. Seen from this perspective, the problem of student disengagement should not be attributed solely to the characteristics of the current generation of students. Rather, these behavioral traits should be viewed, in part, as a structural effect of specific institutional values.

As a consequence, to address the problem of civic disengagement among students, attention must be directed to the nature of the institutions in which they learn how to participate in society.

The intellectual framework guiding the Democracy Project was based on a theory of participatory democracy developed by Carole Pateman (1970). The theory specifies the causal relationships that link institutions, individuals, and democratic practice, while also suggesting practical steps that can be taken to promote engaged citizenship. Pateman's model draws heavily on sociological insights derived from the work of Jean-Jacques Rousseau and John Stuart Mill. The result is a theoretical framework outlining the important role that classroom engagement can play in regard to civic education and how classroom engagement relates to other forms of community and political engagement.

In *The Social Contract*, Rousseau hypothesizes that participation in a democratically oriented decision-making process can have a profound effect on the development of individual character. This is attributed to the fact that democratic systems are rooted in the principle of intrinsic equality. This means that none are entitled to lead and none are obligated to follow. Procedurally, the principle of intrinsic equality also means "that each citizen would be powerless to do anything without the co-operation of all the others, or of the majority" (Pateman, 1970, p. 23). In light of this, Rousseau contends that participating in a democratic process will nurture a sense of both empathy and efficacy in individuals.

Empathy emerges as a consequence of the fact that an individual must take more into consideration than immediate self-interest if the support of others is to be secured. In short, participating in a democratically oriented decision-making process teaches an individual to take the interests of others into account, thereby nurturing an appreciation of the linkage between public and private as well as a sense of responsibility to a broader community.

Efficacy emerges as a consequence of the fact that democracy is fundamentally a deliberative phenomenon driven by the need for voluntary cooperation among sovereign equals. Participation promotes a sense of efficacy because the deliberative process is essentially a process of negotiation designed to mediate conflicts of interest such that a majority can arrive at an agreement. Given that consent must be socially constructed within the context of a democracy, each individual is presented with an opportunity to participate in and influence the decision-making process. Hence, Rousseau concludes that participating in a democratic process will promote "a sense of general, personal effectiveness" in the individual because this institutional environment systematically encourages and rewards individuals for their participation (Pateman, 1970, p. 46).

On the basis of this analysis, Pateman deduces a key proposition that can serve as the foundation for any institutionally based strategy of civic education: "[Democracy] is self-sustaining through the educative impact of the participatory process. Participation develops and fosters the very qualities necessary for it; the more individuals participate, the better able they become to do so" (Pateman, 1970, pp. 42–43). This insight also underscores the importance of reconsidering the role that the classroom might play as a distinctive site of civic engagement in its own right and how student engagement in this arena might better prepare students to participate in their local communities and the political process.

THE UN(DEMOCRATIC) CLASSROOM

The literature on political socialization identifies a number of institutions that are central to the formative experiences of children when it comes to the subject of citizenship (Gimpel, Lay, and Schuknecht, 2003). Among these, educational institutions play an especially prominent role. Indeed, a recent empirical study suggests that the impact of educational institutions on political participation may now exceed the influence exerted by family and religious institutions in America (Verba, Schlozman, and Brady, 1995, pp. 416–450).

From the standpoint of a civic education, however, educational institutions are problematic because they traditionally have emphasized hierarchy and discipline at the expense of equality and consent. Put differently, the culture of schooling in America is suspect because the traditional approach to student learning attaches little value to the type of sociality that Rousseau and others would regard as the defining characteristic of an authentic democratic system. For these theorists, democracy is fundamentally a social phenomenon that prescribes how individuals should relate to, and interact with, one another. Hence, an education that aspires to truly prepare students for citizenship in a democratic society must do more than simply prepare students to read critically, write persuasively, and think creatively. Students also must learn how to relate to others in ways that are consistent with democratic principles. This argument highlights the importance of evaluating institutional practices in regard to their consistency with the foundational principles of a democratic society. Within the context of education, such an analysis necessarily must begin with a reconsideration of the classroom as a site for civic engagement, since this is the primary organizational setting devoted to student learning.

While educators tend to view the classroom as primarily a learning environment, it also functions as a social and a political system. In regard to the latter, classrooms historically have been highly stratified and generally undemocratic, with instructors firmly entrenched at the apex of this structure (Caspary, 1996; Freire, 1990). The lecture, of course, stands as the most conspicuous manifestation of this phenomenon. However, in practice, social and political inequality historically has pervaded virtually every aspect of course administration—from the preparation of syllabi to the selection of assignments and the determination of grades. Viewed from the perspective of a civic education, this is a relatively inhospitable environment for the promotion of engaged citizenship because it implicitly conditions students to accept a decidedly passive approach to class participation (Herman, 1996). Traditionally, educational institutions have systematically taught students to leave the task of governance to those who know better. Compounding the problem, students are repeatedly exposed to this type of learning experience during the most formative years of their lives. Given the theory of civic education outlined earlier, the role of the traditional classroom as a foundation for civic education is inherently questionable.

To address this concern, the Democracy Project embraced classroom engagement techniques explicitly designed to encourage students to participate directly in the governance of a course and, in the process, to redefine the relations of power and authority that have characterized the classroom as a social and political system. Students are provided with authentic opportunities to participate collectively in decision-making processes relating to the administration of a course, including syllabus construction, assessment procedures, and the specification of classroom protocols that both students and faculty are expected to observe (Meade and Weaver, 2004).

From the standpoint of engaged citizenship, classroom engagement techniques are designed to help students take personal
responsibility for their learning and appreciate the value of participating in the life of a community, while also developing a sense
of self-confidence, empowerment, and efficacy. In the literature on
civic education, this pedagogical approach commonly is referred
to as the "democratic classroom" (Becker and Couto, 1996).

Building a Democratic Classroom

To encourage faculty to begin transforming courses into democratic classrooms, the Democracy Project has published the *Toolkit
for Teaching in a Democratic Academy* (Meade and Weaver, 2004),
which discusses a range of practical techniques that instructors can
use to promote student engagement in their classes. A copy of the
toolkit can be obtained from the project's Web site (http://www
.cedarcrest.edu/Redesign/democracy/framework.html). Given
that the toolkit goes into considerable detail about the steps faculty can take to construct a democratic classroom, this section will
outline the two essential principles that serve as the foundation
for this pedagogy of engagement.

The first principle of the democratic classroom is to create a
social environment consistent with the principle of intrinsic equality (Meade and Weaver, 2004). To that end, faculty can engage
students in a number of socially meaningful activities, ranging
from the simple act of introducing themselves to the much more
demanding challenge of establishing rules that will guide how the
members of the class (including the instructor) should relate to
and interact with one another. The overarching purpose of such
exercises is to help create an environment wherein students routinely build social capital through the application of democratic
principles. In short, these pedagogical techniques enable "the
classroom [to] become a model of a community devoted to participatory democracy" (Meade and Weaver, 2004, p. 22).

The second key principle is to create a classroom environment that will encourage students to take personal responsibility for their own learning (Meade and Weaver, 2004). To achieve
this goal, faculty can engage students in several different types of
activities relating to the governance of the class, ranging from the

construction of the course syllabus to the selection of the types of assignments to be required. Students also may be permitted to participate in various aspects of the assessment process via peer evaluations and self-evaluations. Learning agreements, in which students articulate their learning goals for the course and outline an action plan for achieving those goals, represent yet another way of empowering students and nurturing their sense of efficacy.

The attractiveness of the democratic classroom as a pedagogy of engagement lies in its flexibility. Ultimately, faculty are free to use as many—or as few—of the techniques as they deem appropriate, given the content of the course and their own comfort level with democratizing the "heretofore walled-in Realm of Pedagogy" (Zahorski and Cognard, 1999, p. 4). Even if the level of student engagement in a given course seems minimal, it still represents an important step forward in terms of tapping the classroom's potential as a site for civic education because any meaningful opportunity for students to participate in the building of social capital is better than none. Nor is class size an insurmountable obstacle. Just as instructors use group-based exercises to help students acquire academic content, so too can faculty employ small groups to promote sociality. In essence, the democratic classroom is simply another form of experiential learning, although in this case, the pedagogy is explicitly aligned with the purposes of a civic education. Based on the experiences of faculty who participated in the Democracy Project, using the techniques outlined in this section, "[a] professor should find that she has a better relationship with her students; that the students have gotten to know each other and formed a more respectful relationship with each other; that students have been more engaged in the course, both in terms of class participation and in self-governance; [and] that students have assumed more responsibility for their learning and grades" (Meade and Weaver, 2004, p. 22).

Toward a Democratic Academy

As the fundamental element of an institutional strategy of civic education, the democratic classroom can serve as the basis for transforming a college's general education curriculum into a Democratic Academy. Two considerations underlie this claim.

First, the instructional techniques associated with the democratic classroom can be incorporated into courses and disciplines across the curriculum. This is an especially important consideration because the theory of civic education outlined earlier suggests that engaged citizenship is a summative effect of the mutually reinforcing educational experiences that individuals have over the course of their lives and especially during their most formative years. In fact, Pateman's theory of participatory democracy suggests that no single academic experience will be capable of accomplishing the learning objectives highlighted in this volume's working definition of civic engagement. Thus, colleges and universities need a means to provide students with opportunities to learn about and practice civic engagement throughout their college experience. Given that the instructional techniques associated with the democratic classroom are fungible across academic disciplines, institutions can use this pedagogy as part of a broader institutional effort to reform the curriculum to promote civic engagement.

As a result, the skills and aptitudes that students acquire in democratic classrooms can serve as the foundation for student civic engagement in other venues, including their local communities and the political process. More specifically, the human capital that students develop in democratic classrooms will better prepare them to participate in, and benefit from, community and political engagement.

Service-learning has emerged as the most widely used pedagogy of engagement in higher education (Colby, Ehrlich, Beaumont, and Stephens, 2003). Despite its prominence, however, most students have a limited number of opportunities to take service-learning courses. Moreover, students typically enroll in service-learning classes with little practical experience in applying the principles that serve as the foundation of a democratic society. In practice these constraints conspire to limit the potential of service-learning as a tool for the promotion of engaged citizenship. As John Stuart Mill (1963) observed, random acts of civic engagement are an inadequate foundation for a lifetime of engaged citizenship: "A political act, to be done only once in a few years, and for which nothing in the daily habits of the citizen has prepared him, leaves his intellect and his moral predispositions very much as it found them. . . . We do not learn to read or write, to ride or swim, by being merely told how to do it, but by doing it, so it is only by practising [*sic*] popular government on a limited scale, that the people will ever learn how to exercise it on a larger" (p. 229). Viewed from this perspective, democratic classrooms present students with repeated opportunities to develop the habits that will enrich the learning experiences that can unfold within the context of service-learning courses when students are prepared to take advantage of them.

Indeed, the internal architecture of the Democratic Academy is predicated on an explicit linkage between the classroom and the community as distinct, yet mutually reinforcing, sites of civic engagement: "The Democratic Academy is comprised of three stages, reflecting the journey from passive learner in an ivory tower, to active participant in the broader world. The three stages are centered around nurturing three different types of engagement: classroom, community and political. We believe that there is a progressive relationship among these different forms of engagement—that being engaged in the classroom can both model and lead to a deeper engagement in one's community, and that a deep engagement in one's community can lead to deeper engagement in the political process and the political life of a community" (Meade and Weaver, 2004, pp. 11–12).

As this formulation suggests, the design of the Democratic Academy is based on the implicit claim that each site of student engagement (the classroom, local communities, and the political process itself) makes a unique, but mutually reinforcing, contribution to the process of civic education. One of the benefits of this model is that it challenges higher education institutions to reconsider their current piecemeal approaches to civic education.

It also presents an opportunity for educators to think more creatively about the contribution that service-learning can make to the promotion of engaged citizenship (Spiezio, 2002). Within the context of the Democracy Project, for example, the pedagogy of service-learning was used as a form of differentiated instruction to promote two distinct types of student learning outcomes. For faculty emphasizing community engagement as a way of promoting moral and civic development, service-learning was used to place students in nonprofit organizations in local communities where they had the opportunity to acquire a sense of personal responsibility for the well-being of those communities and to affirm the importance of public service as a basic responsibility of citizens.

For faculty emphasizing political engagement as a way of promoting an individual's sense of efficacy as an agent of social change, students did their service-learning activities with political and other organizations where they could learn about the techniques that citizens can use to reconcile contending normative values and diverse interests within the context of a democratic process operating under the constraints of limited public resources. From the standpoint of engaged citizenship, such placements were designed to help students appreciate the intrinsic importance of political engagement and to promote their acquisition of skills essential to the art of political participation.

Taken as a whole, the Democratic Academy constitutes an integrated educational framework that promotes civic engagement in courses and disciplines across the curriculum through the application of pedagogical techniques emphasizing engaged and experiential learning over the course of a student's undergraduate career. As such, the Democratic Academy is a guide that educators can use to create a general education curriculum that becomes the academic foundation for an institutionally based, mission-driven commitment to civic engagement.

ASSESSING THE DEMOCRATIC ACADEMY

Between 2002 and 2004, the key theoretical and organizational claims underlying the design of the Democratic Academy were field-tested at several institutions nationwide, ranging from relatively small liberal arts colleges to significantly larger universities. Over the course of the study, nearly a hundred faculty members incorporated democratic classroom techniques and service-learning into dozens of courses encompassing academic disciplines as diverse as art, business, education, English, history, international studies, nursing, political science, psychology, religious studies, social work, and sociology. Unfortunately, natural science faculty members opted not to participate; they were reluctant to incorporate pedagogies of engagement for fear that such approaches would interfere with the delivery of academic content. (It should be noted, however, that successful models of science, technology, engineering, and mathematics [STEM] courses that explicitly connect these disciplines to critical civic issues exist. The SENCER approach to building civic capacity through general education courses in the STEM disciplines is described in chapter 1.) Overall, approximately two thousand undergraduate students ultimately participated in the research (Spiezio, Baker, and Boland, 2006). Within the context of the present discussion, the study is noteworthy for two reasons.

As an empirical test of the organizational design underlying the Democratic Academy, the study demonstrates that the pedagogies of engagement emphasized in this framework can be incorporated into most of the academic disciplines found on a typical college campus. Hence, in principle, the study suggests that it would be administratively feasible for colleges and universities to use democratic classroom and service-learning pedagogies in the context of a general education curriculum expressly dedicated to the promotion of civic engagement. However, the study also revealed that if such an initiative is to succeed, key administrators must provide sustained academic leadership. More specifically, the research indicates that there is a direct relationship between the level of support that presidents and chief academic officers exhibit for civic education and the number of service-learning and democratic classroom courses offered at an institution. In the absence of such support, faculty interest in initiatives such as the Democratic Academy will be difficult to mobilize and maintain (Spiezio et al., 2006).

As an assessment of student learning outcomes in courses employing either service-learning or democratic classroom techniques, the study found that there were measurable and statistically significant differences between students enrolled in Democratic Academy courses and the general student population when it came to their attitudes toward engaged citizenship. More specifically, the major findings of the study suggest that the pedagogies of engagement tend to do the following: increase the value and significance that students attach to the principle of civic engagement; enhance the sense of confidence that students express in regard to their ability to serve as agents of social and political change; increase the level of civility that students exhibit when it comes to the way they relate to, and interact with, other members of the community; and increase the degree of confidence that students express in regard to their problem-solving and leadership skills (Spiezio et al., 2006).

In essence, the assessment results provide compelling empirical evidence in support of the key educational claim underlying the Democracy Project. When instructors use pedagogical strategies expressly dedicated to the promotion of civic engagement, they can have a significant effect on the development of students' values, behaviors, efficacy, and commitment to engaged citizenship.

CONCLUSION

The purpose of this chapter has been to suggest how colleges and universities can develop a general education curriculum that will promote engaged citizenship among students while also preparing them for the challenges and opportunities they will encounter working and living in the global society of this century. This should be of interest to all types of institutions as their leaders seek to explain how a liberal education remains relevant at a time when college is increasingly valued by the public for the role it plays in preparing people for a financially rewarding career.

As chapter 3 clearly demonstrates, employers and the general public expect that higher education will prepare students with the knowledge and skills of civic engagement that are critical for effective participation in the global workplace and society. For reasons suggested in this chapter, civic education can make a critical contribution to this effort. For these outcomes to be achieved, however, institutions should integrate the pedagogies of the democratic classroom and service-learning into both new and existing courses across disciplines. Ultimately, the Democratic Academy enables institutions to weave together the disciplines composing the liberal arts so that they serve as an interdisciplinary learning environment explicitly dedicated to the promotion of the human and social capital essential to the practice of engaged citizenship. By doing so, the Democratic Academy also is intended to make a modest contribution to preserving the very intellectual and humanistic traditions of liberal learning on which the survival of democracy itself depends.

References

Becker, T. L., and Couto, R. A. (Eds.). *Teaching Democracy by Being Democratic.* Westport, CT: Praeger, 1996.

Blaney, D. G. *Introduction to Participating in Democracy*, Vol. 1. Allentown, PA: Cedar Crest College, 2001.

Caspary, W. R. "Students in Charge." In T. L. Becker and R. A. Couto (Eds.), *Teaching Democracy by Being Democratic.* Westport, CT: Praeger, 1996.

Colby, A., Ehrlich, T., Beaumont, E., and Stephens, J. *Educating Citizens: Preparing America's Undergraduates for Lives of Moral and Civic Responsibility.* San Francisco: Jossey-Bass, 2003.

Freire, P. *Pedagogy of the Oppressed.* New York: Continuum Publishing, 1990.

Friedman, T. L. *The World Is Flat: A Brief History of the Twenty-First Century.* New York: Farrar, Straus and Giroux, 2006.

Gardner, H. *Five Minds for the Future.* Boston: Harvard Business School Press, 2006.

Gimpel, J. G., Lay, J. C., and Schuknecht, J. E. *Cultivating Democracy: Civic Engagement and Political Socialization in America.* Washington, DC: Brookings Institution Press, 2003.

Herman, L. "Personal Empowerment." In T. L. Becker and R.A. Couto (Eds.), *Teaching Democracy by Being Democratic.* Westport, CT: Praeger, 1996.

Meade, E., and Weaver, S. (Eds.). *Toolkit for Teaching in a Democratic Academy.* Allentown, PA: Cedar Crest College, 2004.

Mill, J. S. *Essays on Politics and Culture.* G. Himmelfarb (Ed.). Garden City, NJ: Anchor Books, 1963.

Pateman, C. *Participation and Democratic Theory.* Cambridge: Cambridge University Press, 1970.

Spiezio, K. "Pedagogy and Political (Dis)Engagement." *Liberal Education,* 2002, *88*(4), 14–19.

Spiezio, K., Baker, K. Q., and Boland, K. "General Education and Civic Engagement: An Empirical Analysis of Pedagogical Possibilities." *Journal of General Education,* 2006, *54*(4), 273–293.

Verba, S., Schlozman, K. L., and Brady, H. *Voice and Equality: Civic Voluntarism in American Politics.* Cambridge, MA: Harvard University Press, 1995.

Zahorski, K. J., and Cognard, R. *Reconsidering Faculty Roles and Rewards: Promising Practices for Institutional Transformation and Enhanced Learning.* Washington, DC: Council of Independent Colleges, 1999.

CHAPTER SIX

THE INFLUENCE OF INTEGRATIVE AND INTERDISCIPLINARY LEARNING ON CIVIC ENGAGEMENT

Nance Lucas

> *It is time to reclaim the moral imperative of liberal education. To this end, we must revitalize liberal education for the twenty-first century by grounding it in a clear purpose: to prepare productive citizen-leaders. . . . It is our greatest hope for a good society. (Harrington, 2003, p. 51)*

A movement to transform higher education is well under way with progress to report in establishing robust and innovative interdisciplinary and integrative studies curricula. The arguments have been made, the experiments have been conducted, and the student learning gains have been tallied. More than a decade ago, early reformers of this movement to revitalize higher education made compelling arguments to move the academy away from silos of traditional disciplinary knowledge toward an integration of learning across disciplines and experiences. Simultaneously, higher education is seeing a rise in academic programs that include civic engagement and social responsibility at the core of the curriculum. While some believe this growth is both long over-due and does not go far enough, the movement has tipped, thanks to bold institutional and faculty leaders, risk-taking propositions, new approaches to teaching and learning, and the securing of internal and external resources. As a result, institutional leaders have transformed how students learn, how faculty teach, and how academic programs are constructed to prepare students to live and act responsibly in local and global communities.

Years later, while the agenda remains unfinished, innovative leadership and those early experiments have led to sustained inter-disciplinary programs, including learning communities, interdis-ciplinary majors and minors, living-learning programs, and entire interdisciplinary and integrative studies colleges. Because single disciplines in isolation cannot effectively address and solve today's complex societal problems, the integrative studies movement has produced academic programs at a number of colleges and uni-versities that deepen students' awareness and understanding of societal issues through the acquisition of diverse, yet coherent, dis-ciplinary and interdisciplinary knowledge combined with practical experiences. Anne Colby, Thomas Ehrlich, Elizabeth Beaumont, and Jason Stephens (2003) claim that "moral and civic learning is strengthened by educational experiences that are integrative and cumulative" (p. 195). These programs typically are embedded in the context of a liberal education.

The Association of American Colleges and Universities (AAC&U) has provided intellectual leadership in the interdisci-plinary education movement in higher education, calling for the renewal of liberal education with a focus on civic learning and engagement. AAC&U's seminal 2002 publication, *Greater Expecta-tions: A New Vision for Learning as a Nation Goes to College,* inspired national conversations about the renewal of liberal education for the twenty-first century. The report called for American higher education to promote learning that prepares students to live and work in a just democracy and a diverse society. Specifically, the association calls on the academy to educate students to become "responsible for their personal actions and for civic values" (AAC&U, 2002, p. 15). *Greater Expectations* successfully promoted an agenda that challenged colleges and universities to reconsider the principles of a revitalized liberal education with a commitment to civic engagement at the institutional and individual—including student, faculty, and staff—levels.

Building on this momentum, AAC&U (n.d.) announced a further call to action in 2007 with its national initiative *Core Commitments: Educating Students for Personal and Social Responsibility. Core Commitments* challenges higher education to provide learning opportunities along five key dimensions: striving for excellence, cultivating personal and academic integrity, contributing to a larger community, taking seriously the perspectives of others, and refining ethical and moral reasoning. Further, this initiative emphasizes the importance of documenting where and how students gain knowledge and develop competencies related to personal and social responsibility. *Greater Expectations* and *Core Commitments* place integrative and interdisciplinary learning at the center of educational experiences that are responsive to the compelling and changing needs of today's society. As a result, numerous academic programs reformed their curriculum and cocurricular offerings to better prepare students for the responsibilities of contributing to a just society.

This chapter provides an overview of interdisciplinary and integrative education. It offers models that are well positioned to deliver on the promises and expectations of preparing students for personal and social responsibility. It describes how these programs are designed to enhance students' understanding of, and commitment to, civic engagement and outlines their strengths and challenges.

OVERVIEW OF INTERDISCIPLINARY AND INTEGRATIVE LEARNING

The traditions and principles of liberal education paved the way for the growth of interdisciplinary and integrative learning over the past few decades. The original premise of liberal education was the preparation of active and responsible citizens and the education of the whole student (Pascarella, Wolniak, Seifert, Cruce, and Blaich, 2005). For the purposes of this chapter, liberal education will be defined broadly, combining the historical view of Robert Hutchins with that of Colby et al. According to Hutchins, "Liberal education should involve a core of content and precepts that transcends any particular discipline and is best reflected in the great books" (Colby et al., 2003, p. 24). Colby et al. (2003) add that a liberal education includes "the full range of efforts that pursue some version of the overarching goal of preparing students for lives that provide personal satisfaction and promote the common good, regardless of particular approaches or institutional arrangements" (p. 24). While many agree that the great books should not be the focus of a liberal arts education, Hutchins's idea that the curriculum transcends a single discipline supports multidisciplinary and interdisciplinary approaches to contemporary liberal education.

Integrative studies is defined as a curriculum that "motivates and develops learners' powers to perceive and create new relationships for themselves . . . and to construct their own meanings in order to make sense of the world of knowledge" (Smith, MacGregor, Matthew, and Gabelnick, 2004, p. 112). *Interdisciplinary studies* is defined "as inquiries which critically draw upon two or more disciplines and which lead to an integration of disciplinary insights" (Wentworth and Davis, 2002, p. 17). To achieve integrative thought and higher-order thinking, tension must exist between two or more disciplines, where integration of methods and insights is forged (Sill, 1996). Others have added that the goal of interdisciplinarity is synthesis and not simply integrated knowledge. As such, Schneider (2003) further describes integrative learning as including "the various forms of interdisciplinary learning. But it should also lead students to connect and integrate the different parts of their overall education, to connect their learning with the world beyond the academy, and, above all, to translate their education to new contexts, new problems, new responsibilities" (pp. 1–2).

While numerous distinctions have been made between integrative and interdisciplinary learning as well as arguments over which concept is preferred, the two share the desired outcome of deep interdisciplinary understanding. *Interdisciplinary understanding* is "the capacity to integrate knowledge and modes of thinking in two or more disciplines to produce a cognitive advancement—e.g., explaining a phenomenon, solving a problem, creating a product, raising a new question—in ways that would have been unlikely through single disciplinary means" (Mansilla, 2004, p. 4). According to Veronica Boix Mansilla, William C. Miller, and Howard Gardner (2000), students demonstrate interdisciplinary understanding when they integrate knowledge and modes of thinking from two or more disciplines to create products, solve problems, and offer explanations of the world around them.

Matthew Miller and Mansilla (2004) offer an additional approach for integrating disciplinary contributions in applied fields that requires *bridging the explanation-action gap.* This strategy calls for an integration of disciplinary knowledge to define a problem while drawing from other domains that can lead to interventions and solutions. The concept of bridging the explanation-action gap has given rise to the development of interdisciplinary and integrative learning models that incorporate civic engagement experiences. The approach is intentional in bringing thought and action together using multiple disciplinary perspectives "when explanations and actions are considered in dynamic relationship to one another" (Miller and Mansilla, 2004, p. 13). Some domain knowledge might provide more in-depth insights into a particular problem, while other disciplinary lenses can offer technical solutions to resolve the issue. For example, students in a conservation studies program can explore the bigger questions of sustainability by synthesizing knowledge from diverse disciplines—such as ecology, biology, public policy, economics, sociology, and leadership studies—and applying that knowledge to issues in a local community.

Despite the varied definitions and tensions surrounding the terms, pioneers of integrative and interdisciplinary education have long embedded experiential learning into the curriculum, often using service-learning approaches, as a way to deepen students' awareness and knowledge of societal issues and challenges. When providing opportunities for students to connect academic knowledge to real-world experiences, Kimberly K. Eby (2001) asserts that integrative knowledge "prepares students for citizenship in a diverse democracy, where issues are complex and interests are in competition" (p. 31). Many educators argue that a true integrative learning program not only provides students with opportunities to enhance essential critical-thinking and intellectual judgment competencies but also leads to a heightened sense of social responsibility and civic engagement:

> Integrative learning is . . . an essential element in the goal of helping students develop a strong sense of social responsibility and civic

engagement. For too long, our campuses have made civic engagement and social responsibility an extracurricular activity, the realm
of student affairs and off-campus life. Today, however, we see abundant efforts to tie the educational experience to "big questions"
that matter both to students and [to] the health of our communities. Here too, successful integration of learning is surely the key
to success. The more students transfer knowledge and skill from
the classroom to the community and then back again, the better
prepared they will be to take responsibility for their lifelong roles as
citizens and human beings. (Schneider, 2003, p. 5)

Whether comprehensive in scope, such as integrative studies
programs, or in single courses designed for interdisciplinary learning, curricular programs that infuse civic engagement and social
responsibility offer the most compelling way to reach the majority
of students (Colby et al., 2003).

In summary, the revitalization of liberal education through innovative integrative and interdisciplinary education programs has led to
new ways of thinking about learning and learning outcomes. These
efforts consistently focus on preparing students for social responsibility and civic engagement as a priority. According to Bruce Kimball,
such efforts "make a commitment to multiculturalism, elevate general education and integration rather than specialization, promote
the commonwealth and citizenship, regard all levels of education
as belonging to a common enterprise and working together, recon-
ceive the purpose of teaching as stimulating learning and inquiry,
promote the formation of values and the practice of service, and
employ assessment" (Smith et al., 2004, pp. 133–134).

However, it is important to recognize that not everyone agrees
with the tenets of liberal education, and there is less consensus
on the value of interdisciplinary and integrative studies programs
and degrees. A number of faculty members from traditional academic disciplines are suspicious, at best, about the legitimacy of
these programs. The importance of educating the whole student
typically is embraced by student affairs professionals on college
campuses. While college mission statements purport to prepare
students for the responsibilities of citizenship and leadership, this
mandate has traditionally been relegated to nonacademic units.

The good news is that learning communities, integrative studies programs, and interdisciplinary education are showing gains in

student enrollment, student learning, and faculty engagement. At more and more institutions, integrative and interdisciplinary learning are embedded firmly in the curriculum and the cocurriculum. Professional associations dedicated to integrative and interdisciplinary programs have emerged to support them, including the Association for Integrative Studies, the Atlantic Center for Learning Communities, the National Learning Communities Project, and the Consortium for Innovative Environments in Learning.

MODELS OF INTEGRATIVE AND INTERDISCIPLINARY PROGRAMS THAT EMPHASIZE CIVIC ENGAGEMENT

Innovative curricular approaches that prepare students to think critically while drawing on diverse and integrated sources of knowledge to address society's pressing problems and to assume leadership responsibilities in their professions and communities are growing in higher education institutions of all types (Smith et al., 2006). This section provides a few examples that highlight the diversity and breadth of these programs and the benefits and challenges of the different models.

KENNESAW STATE UNIVERSITY: THE MAYA HERITAGE COMMUNITY PROJECT

Kennesaw State University, just outside Atlanta, Georgia, offers an innovative program that unites the institution's academic mission with the economic and social interests of the state of Georgia and the human rights of the Maya community. Established by students and faculty in 2001, the Maya Heritage Community Project embodies the principles of service-learning and civic engagement using an interdisciplinary learning model. A compelling feature of this project is its reciprocal approach. While students and faculty work in the local community, the Maya engage in classroom learning with students and faculty and in other activities on campus. Faculty sponsor research projects that benefit the community, while students participate in internships and service-learning projects. Students' learning is informed by multiple disciplines, including economics, history, and anthropology. Members of the Maya community benefit through learning about health education, laws, and customs of the United States. In turn, the Maya contribute to students' learning about ancient and modern Maya cultures. Faculty from disciplines—including nursing, history, political science, art, and education—have participated in research or service projects that further the goals of the Maya Heritage Community Project. Recently, the university approved tuition benefits and stipends for returning Peace Corps volunteers who commit to participate in project-related community service (see http://www.kennesaw.edu/peacecorpsfellows). The benefits of this model are numerous, including the learning communities formed by students, faculty, and local Maya residents that are supported by collaborative research activities. Students and faculty have developed public policy recommendations concerning health, education, undocumented workers' issues, and the historical forces behind illegal immigration. These experiences prepare students for employment in fields such as health, law, and human services.

A unique challenge of the project is that few Maya speak English. Almost half of the Maya women affiliated with the project speak neither English nor Spanish, resulting in their isolation from the program. On the other hand, the recruitment of faculty and students has been fairly easy, resulting in an increase in mentoring and other interactions between faculty and students. Because the program gained popularity in a short time, the demand from students and faculty wishing to participate exceeded the program's infrastructure, making it difficult to include all interested students and faculty. The inclusion of adequate university resources at the onset of the project, such as secretarial and administrative support, would have enabled more rapid growth of the program. In another lesson learned, the program's leadership discovered a gap between the program's necessarily limited outcomes and the high needs and expectations of the Maya community members.

Mars Hill College: Civic Engagement Certificate

Mars Hill College in Mars Hill, North Carolina, offers a cocurricular civic engagement certificate that is connected to the college's general education curriculum (Dotson, 2007). The cocurricular

LifeWorks certificate program thematically follows a sequence of six core curriculum courses called "The Commons." Themes associated with the Commons include challenges, character, civic life, critique, and creativity (Dotson, 2007). LifeWorks provides opportunities for students to engage in increasingly challenging community-based experiences as they move through six stages: exploration, direct service, project management, advocacy, resource development, and demonstration (assessment and evaluation). These experiences accompany the six courses in the Commons curriculum and conclude with a capstone experience that corresponds to a senior capstone course and allows students to reflect on their learning, experiences, and personal growth. Certificate courses draw from the humanities, the arts, and the sciences (Dotson, 2007).

One of the strengths of the Mars Hill civic engagement certificate is the ease in which connections are made between formal learning inside the classroom and cocurricular experiential activities. Because faculty everywhere are challenged to find the time to design, implement, and assess civic engagement projects tied to their academic courses, the staff of the LifeWorks office at Mars Hill work closely with the faculty in the certificate program to design and implement the service and civic engagement activities. The courses have reflection components that allow students to integrate the materials from texts and formal knowledge with their out-of-class experiences. LifeWorks staff facilitate weekly cocurricular seminars where students write reflective essays.

A challenge associated with this academic certificate is the uneven participation of students in the cocurricular civic engagement components. It is also challenging for LifeWorks staff to keep faculty regularly informed about the civic engagement activities in which students participate related to the certificate program.

The LifeWorks staff members who work directly with the certificate program have learned the value of conducting audits of the courses that are tied to the cocurricular civic engagement activities in which certificate students are involved. The cocurricular program can benefit from knowing which texts and materials are being used by faculty in the design of students' reflective learning activities and critical analysis of their civic engagement experiences. In addition, LifeWorks staff members believe that faculty would, in turn, benefit from asking students at the beginning of each semester how they are involved in campus and community activities so the faculty can integrate those experiences into the curriculum.

UNIVERSITY OF WISCONSIN–MILWAUKEE: CULTURES AND COMMUNITIES CERTIFICATE PROGRAM

At the University of Wisconsin–Milwaukee, faculty created the new Institute for Service Learning and the Cultures and Communities Certificate Program, which allows undergraduates to fulfill their general education requirements with a set of courses that integrate civic engagement and diversity (Adams and Ajirotutu, 2007). Courses draw on the arts, science and technology, and U.S. and global studies, and they include a required service-learning course. Students in the certificate program take courses from five disciplinary areas while addressing common issues—multiculturalism and diversity, race and ethnicity, globalization and cultural diaspora, and community and citizenship. One core course is offered by six different academic departments. Faculty members from these disciplines meet to design the core courses and shape the syllabi, assignments, and conceptual frameworks. As a result, certificate students experience a coherent and integrated set of standardized general education courses.

The Institute for Service Learning provides faculty development workshops and assistance on developing course syllabi and pedagogies that facilitate civic learning and engagement experiences. The certificate program and institute facilitate relationships between students, faculty, and the community agencies and residents in metropolitan Milwaukee. They also sponsor faculty research in race, urban education, cultural identity, and innovative pedagogy (University of Wisconsin–Milwaukee, 2005). Among the program's ten learning goals, the following describe what students should be able to do in the area of civic engagement: reflecting critically on their own cultural identity and background to connect personal history to larger social and historical forces; describing how nations interact socially, politically, and culturally; demonstrating a multicultural understanding and appreciating works from different cultures and traditions; presenting examples of the interplay of cultural or community factors in the sciences, technology, and health care; collaborating productively with people from diverse backgrounds; and articulating principles and methods for community service in a pluralistic society (University of Wisconsin–Milwaukee, 2005).

The philosophical underpinning of this certificate program combines civic and multicultural education by enhancing student awareness of structural inequality and issues of oppression (Adams and Ajirotutu, 2007). One of the required interdisciplinary courses involves a collaboration with local community members, faculty, and students to facilitate residents' oral histories, document life and culture in the neighborhood, and examine the historical roots of race relations and urban change.

The certificate program includes the assessment of learning outcomes through precourse and postcourse surveys that examine students' values, beliefs, and knowledge over time. The assessment of program outcomes indicates that student learning about civic engagement and multiculturalism increased after taking the program's interdisciplinary courses and engaging in related practical experiences. For example, students reported a deeper understanding of academic content through the integration of service-learning activities in their courses. In addition to the outcomes assessment, students also participate in an exit survey when they complete the certificate. Recently, the university awarded a grant to the program to allow faculty to analyze the achievement of learning goals and outcomes through the assessment of course assignments and projects, as well as through interviews with faculty.

Rising student enrollment in the certificate program has produced a high demand for additional courses and faculty. Given that the certificate program transcends traditional disciplinary boundaries, new faculty find that it supports their interdisciplinary teaching interests. The university rewards the certificate faculty by funding professional travel, faculty development, and other activities that benefit the program. Thus, the Cultures and Communities Certificate faculty are recognized for their collaborative teaching and interdisciplinary work in a way that is often overlooked at large, public research universities.

The certificate program receives an unusual level of support from the well-staffed Institute for Service Learning and the nearly one hundred community agencies available to work with students. Community involvement is encouraged through grants for university-community collaborations. The University of Wisconsin faces a challenge typical at research universities, where research and scholarly activities are valued over teaching and community involvement. The institute is investigating ways to support faculty research and publications that are tied to themes related to service-learning and civic engagement. Another challenge of the certificate program is the enlistment of senior faculty to teach its lower-division general education courses. Like most large public universities, much of the lower-level instruction is relegated to graduate teaching assistants and lecturers.

The institute staff has gleaned from their experiences the importance of identifying the assets and activities that already exist at the university that relate to the themes of the certificate program. The program has benefited from first identifying projected areas of study and knowledge competencies and then moving on to interdisciplinary learning models that bring together faculty with diverse disciplinary interests and expertise.

University of Michigan: Michigan Community Scholars Program

The Michigan Community Scholars Program (MCSP) at the University of Michigan in Ann Arbor is one of several thematic living-learning programs characterized by integrative learning and civic engagement. "MCSP brings together students and faculty who have a commitment to community service, social justice, and academic study. Through small courses, service projects, leadership opportunities, social programs, study groups and tutors, students strive to model an ideal community in terms of friendship, responsibility, diversity, celebration, collaboration and caring" (University of Michigan, n.d.).

MCSP students enroll in common experiences that include first-year experience seminars, service-learning courses, and specially designed English and mathematics courses, taught by faculty from multiple disciplines. Faculty and students engage in service-learning experiences in the local community. At the beginning of new students' college careers, MCSP offers them the opportunity to form a meaningful affiliation with their institution by participating in an engaging learning community. Given that half of the student population is from diverse ethnic and cultural backgrounds, first-year students participate in intergroup and intercultural dialogues in their residential and classroom learning environments. The program also exposes students early to a wide range of civic engagement and leadership experiences that many sustain throughout their college years. MCSP has witnessed success with a 95 percent retention rate for all students after one year of college and a 100 percent retention for students in traditionally underrepresented groups (Schoem, 2005).

Unlike the faculty of the University of Wisconsin's certificate program, MCSP faculty receive little recognition or reward from the institution for their involvement. The priorities of the faculty members' academic department take precedence over teaching in MCSP. Faculty are drawn to the program by shared interests with their colleagues across disciplines related to the themes of social justice, civic engagement, diverse democracy, and intergroup relations. MCSP faculty sponsor monthly seminars on these program themes, work collaboratively on grant projects, and coauthor publications.

An insight gained from MCSP faculty and staff is the importance of consistent and sustained programmatic leadership supported by administrative and faculty advocates. This type of interdisciplinary learning community model also requires intense collaborations across units and with the local community. In spite of the lack of recognition and reward, the program has succeeded in attracting faculty committed to innovation and creativity by facilitating scholarship, teaching, and learning across traditional disciplinary lines.

New Century College: Integrative Studies Degree Program

Founded in 1995 at George Mason University in Fairfax, Virginia, New Century College (NCC) is an integrative studies degree program with a competency-based curriculum. With its motto of "Connecting the Classroom to the World," NCC requires students to complete twelve credits of experiential learning. NCC's degree program draws on classroom-based integrated learning from a wide range of disciplines combined with practical experiences in the local community. NCC's first-year program, which includes a living-learning component, offers an alternative general education curriculum based on four themes: community of learners, the natural world, the social world, and self as citizen (NCC, 2007).

Faculty integrate experiential learning into their upper-division learning communities, often providing opportunities for students to participate in service-learning activities that are tied to academic course content and themes. Several learning community courses include experiential learning credits that require students to engage in local communities and to observe, reflect on, and analyze how their formal learning contributes to their community-based activities. For example, in a violence and gender course, students integrate their formal learning—drawing from research, oral histories, case studies, literature, and nonfiction texts—with experiential learning in community settings, such as women's shelters and other nonprofit agencies that address issues related to the course topic.

NCC houses two centers that sponsor programs and courses for students, faculty, and staff on civic responsibility, service-learning, community service, field studies, leadership development, and volunteer opportunities—the Center for Field Studies (CFS) and the Center for Leadership and Community Engagement. "The goal of site-specific field research is so CFS, NCC, and Mason can develop a relationship with the local community based on the values of a sustained relationship, reciprocal learning, and community involvement in field research. CFS operates from the premise that its field experiences respect and integrate local community culture, values, and needs" (NCC, 2008). CFS works closely with faculty and students to coordinate local and global field-based research and experiences that allow students and faculty to study the cultural, political, socioeconomic, environmental, historical, and artistic contexts of a community. In return, students and faculty engage together in projects to enhance the welfare of the local community. The Center for Leadership and Community Engagement (CLCE) provides consultation to faculty across campus on designing service-learning activities in academic courses and offers faculty development workshops on curricular innovations in service-learning and civic engagement. CLCE offers numerous leadership courses and a wide range of service and volunteer activities for students, faculty, and staff. Through New Century College's commitment to promoting learning related to civic engagement and social justice, it offers interdisciplinary minors in nonprofit studies and leadership studies to all undergraduate students at the university.

New Century College has experienced both challenges and successes in its degree program and in its mission to provide learning experiences centered on social justice and civic engagement principles through its integrative studies curriculum. With its emphasis on integrative and collaborative learning, NCC faculty are committed to collaborative teaching, which is costly and often viewed by administrators as inefficient. In addition, faculty report spending twice the effort on their service-learning and other experiential courses compared to regular course offerings. Another challenge is sustaining the service-learning movement across campus. Although NCC's Center for Leadership and Community Engagement offers resources to all campus faculty members to support service-learning, there is still only a small number of faculty willing to incorporate these activities in their courses.

Among New Century College's successes, the nimbleness of its learner-centered pedagogy and competency-based curriculum has allowed the college to respond to the changing needs of local, national, and global communities. Assessment reports also indicate that NCC students excel in critical thinking, communication, problem solving, and cultural competencies. Graduates of New Century College frequently cite how well an integrative studies degree prepared them for their careers and leadership responsibilities, as well as for the rigors of graduate school. Faculty from various academic departments are encouraged by their deans and department chairs to teach in NCC for a semester to expose them to its innovations in teaching and learning.

CONCLUSION

What a difference a decade can make! Many institutions have developed integrative and interdisciplinary programs, like the ones described in the previous section, that offer innovative and enriching opportunities for students to learn about and practice civic engagement in the context of a liberal education. These programs have been successful in educating the whole student and preparing students for responsible democratic citizenship and leadership.

While these programs have enjoyed numerous successes, several common challenges exist. In an environment where the traditional trilogy of research, teaching, and service is honored, it is often difficult for faculty to focus on interdisciplinary teaching and civic engagement when their institutions do not recognize and reward such efforts. In the tenure and promotion process, faculty who teach in interdisciplinary programs or who teach individual interdisciplinary courses are often evaluated by colleagues who use traditional disciplinary criteria. The tension between advocates of disciplinary versus interdisciplinary learning sometimes gives rise to questions about the legitimacy of nontraditional educational programs. Engaged scholarship and teaching for civic learning are frequently not valued as highly as traditional research and teaching by tenure and promotion committees.

Another challenge is the resources required by these programs. Exemplary interdisciplinary teaching and learning models cost more than single disciplinary courses to deliver and sustain. A high degree of interdisciplinarity and providing opportunities for student civic engagement increase the costs in terms of both human and fiscal resources. Failures of these efforts often result from a short-term infusion of resources in the early stages of program development followed by an expectation of sustainability without a financial commitment from institutions. Innovations in curricular and cocurricular programs require sustainability plans with requisite financial resources for long-term viability. Integrative and interdisciplinary programs often lack such plans, making it difficult for faculty and program administrators to fully achieve their stated outcomes and goals. This problem is compounded in programs that involve civic engagement because of the importance of sustaining partnerships with local and global communities.

Given the intensity of these programs and the significant time commitment required of students, it is frequently difficult for students who must work to participate in programs that combine formal classroom learning with civic engagement experiences. Providing financial support to student participants is becoming increasingly important and is being included as a priority in institutional capital campaigns.

Regardless of the challenges and costs, integrative and inter-disciplinary learning have taken root in the academy. If American higher education is serious about preparing students to be civically engaged citizens, scholars, and leaders in local and global communities, integrative and interdisciplinary education that embeds civic engagement is one of the most promising means of achieving this important goal. If the past decade has been an indication, innovative leaders of higher education will continue to transform how faculty teach, how students learn, and how institutions of higher education serve as responsible members of local and global communities through integrative and interdisciplinary programs.

References

Adams, S., and Ajirotutu, C. "Service Learning, Multicultural Education, and the Core Curriculum: A Model for Institutional Change." *Diversity Digest*, 2007, *10*(2), 9–11.

Association of American Colleges and Universities. *Greater Expectations: A New Vision for Learning as a Nation Goes to College.* Washington, DC: Association of American Colleges and Universities, 2002.

Association of American Colleges and Universities. "Core Commitments: Educating Students for Personal and Social Responsibility." http://www.aacu.org/core_commitments/dimensions.cfm, n.d.

Colby, A., Ehrlich, T., Beaumont, E., and Stephens, J. *Educating Citizens: Preparing America's Undergraduates for Lives of Moral and Civic Responsibility,* San Francisco: Jossey-Bass, 2003.

Dotson, S. D. "Alignment for Life." *Liberal Education,* 2007, *93*(3), 40–45.

Eby, K. K. "Teaching and Learning from an Interdisciplinary Perspective." *Peer Review,* Summer/Fall 2001, 28–31.

Harrington, L. K. "To Seek a Newer World: Revitalizing Liberal Education for the 21st Century." *Liberal Education,* 2003, *89*(2), 46–51.

Mansilla, V. B. "Assessing Student Work at the Disciplinary Crossroads." (GoodWork Project Report Series, No. 33). http://www.evergreen.edu/washcenter/resources/upload/GoodWork33.pdf, 2004.

Mansilla, V. B., Miller, W. C., and Gardner, H. "On Disciplinary Lenses and Interdisciplinary Work." In S. Wineburg and P. Grossman (Eds.), *Interdisciplinary Curriculum: Challenges to Implementation.* New York: Teachers College Press, 2000.

Miller, M., and Mansilla, V. B. "Thinking across Perspectives and Disciplines." http://pzweb.harvard.edu/eBookstore/PDFs/GoodWork27.pdf, 2004.

New Century College. "The First-Year Curriculum." http://ncc.gmu
.edu/curriculum/division1.html, 2007.

New Century College. "Experiential Learning in New Century College."
http://ncc.gmu.edu/exlearn, 2008.

Pascarella, E. T., Wolniak, G. C., Seifert, T.A.D., Cruce, T. M, and Blaich,
C. F. *Liberal Arts Colleges and Liberal Arts Education: New Evidence and
Impacts.* ASHE Higher Education Report, 2005, *31*(3).

Schneider, C. G. "Liberal Education and Integrative Learning." *Issues in
Integrative Studies,* 2003, *21,* 1–8.

Schoem, D. "Modeling a Diverse and Democratic America: The Michigan
Community Scholars Program." *About Campus,* 2005, *10*(5), 18–23.

Sill, D. J. "Integrative Thinking, Synthesis, and Creativity in Interdisciplinary Studies." *Journal of General Education,* 1996, *50*(4), 129–151.

Smith, B. L., Eby, K. K., Jeffers, R., Kjellman, J., Koestler, G., Olson, T.,
et al. "Emerging Trends in Learning Community Development."
Washington Center News, Winter 2006.

Smith, B. L., MacGregor, J., Matthew, R. S., and Gabelnick, F. *Learning
Communities: Reforming Undergraduate Education.* San Francisco:
Jossey-Bass, 2004.

University of Michigan. "Michigan Community Scholars Program." http://
www.lsa.umich.edu/mcs/aboutWho.htm#programInfo, n.d.

University of Wisconsin–Milwaukee. "The Milwaukee Idea." http://
www4.uwm.edu/milwaukeeidea, 2005.

Wentworth, J., and Davis, J. R. "Enhancing Interdisciplinarity through
Team Teaching." In C. Haynes (Ed.), *Innovations in Interdisciplin-
ary Teaching.* Westport, CT: American Council on Education/Oryx
Press, 2002.

CHAPTER SEVEN

CAPSTONE EXPERIENCES

Kevin Kecskes and Seanna Kerrigan

We gratefully acknowledge the contribution of undergraduate research specialist Nick Walden for research assistance with this chapter.

Capstone courses, sometimes referred to as "senior-year seminars," have taken hold in higher education. In the mid-1970s, Arthur Levine (1978) found that fewer than one in twenty institutions of higher education offered these culminating experiences for undergraduate students. However, by the turn of the century, the National Resource Center for the First-Year Experience and Students in Transition noted that over 75 percent of American colleges and universities offered at least one capstone course or other type of senior-year specialized learning opportunity (Henscheid, 2000).

Today undergraduates can expect to have one or more opportunities to integrate formerly disconnected pieces of their disciplinary learning into a more coherent whole (Heinemann, 1997). Although the numbers are increasing, relatively few students are required to consider and apply their knowledge in *interdisciplinary* culminating experiences (Oddo, Rosenak, Reilley, and Dunn, 2002; Rennie-Hill and Toth, 1999). This trend to integrate capstone experiences into curricula has grown in community colleges (Jensen and Wenzel, 2001) as well as in graduate education (Brown and Benson, 2005). While we know that this exponential growth of capstones is undoubtedly improving student learning experiences overall (Gardner and Van der Veer, 1998), this chapter explores how these formal culminating experiences can specifically foster civic engagement.

This chapter discusses the current terrain of capstone courses nationally and four major models for capstones. It then moves from models to exemplars and analyzes the strengths and challenges of each approach to fostering civic engagement. It describes best practices related to student learning outcomes for civic engagement in capstone courses. Finally, it offers lessons learned from the experiences of the authors at Portland State University regarding assessment and faculty development related to capstone courses.

Capstone Courses in the National Landscape

During the 2006–2007 academic year, the Center for Academic Excellence at Portland State University, in Portland, Oregon, conducted research to better understand the range of senior culminating experiences and to determine whether there were discernible capstone models extant in the United States. This study, while not exhaustive, focused on four sources of information: current and past literature on capstone courses, analysis of the seventy-six institutions that were selected in 2006 by the Carnegie Foundation for the Advancement of Teaching for its new Community Engagement Classification, thematic analysis of the twenty-nine capstone programs nationally acknowledged by *U.S. News and World Report* in 2006, and our knowledge and awareness of additional exemplary programs across the nation.

The analysis found that four primary models exist nationally to implement a culminating experiential course in the senior year: departmental (or discipline-based) capstones, interdisciplinary (or integrative) capstones, independent study capstones, and honors thesis capstones. The most prevalent model is the departmental or discipline-based capstone, which accounted for approximately 85 percent of the capstone courses studied.

Departmental Capstones

Departmental capstones include programs in which individual academic departments create their own themed, senior-level course, usually based on departmental learning goals. Generally, all students within a major are required to complete the capstone course as a graduation requirement. Such courses are frequently found in schools of engineering across the nation because these programs have strict accreditation standards that demand demonstration of applied expertise learned in the major to a real design project. Indeed, capstone offerings in engineering have increased to the point that the first national conference focusing exclusively on engineering capstone design was held in the summer of 2007. (More information can be found at the National Capstone Conference Web site at http://www.capstoneconf.org.) Engineering capstones range from projects like the design of a car powered by solar energy that can be done within the university (without requiring a community partnership) to engagement with external partners, such as the collaborative development of a sustainable irrigation system for a community agriculture center in Latin America. Departmental capstones are also quite prevalent in business and communication departments, among others. The primary emphasis in this form of capstone is the demonstration of disciplinary expertise that can be specified and tested for accuracy and assessed on the quality of outputs and project management. Disciplinary capstones are also becoming a key issue in accreditation. In engineering, for example, capstone design courses have become an important factor in receiving accreditation by ABET, the recognized accreditor for higher education programs in applied science, computing, engineering, and technology (National Capstone Conference, 2006).

INTERDISCIPLINARY CAPSTONES

Interdisciplinary or integrative capstones typically are senior-level courses that require the expertise of multiple disciplines to address a complex issue and produce a final product. These courses tend to emerge from institutional general education initiatives rather than from individual departments. Interdisciplinary capstones are usually theme-based rather than discipline-specific, and they require a collaborative, team-based approach to problem solving. When interdisciplinary courses address a social issue, which can be local or global, they are often a feature of an institution-wide civic engagement initiative. A hallmark of interdisciplinary capstones that are designed to foster civic engagement is an intentional focus on public problem solving and broad learning outcomes associated with one or more of the following: engaged citizenship, public service, community development, collaboration and team-work, working across differences, lifelong learning, critical inquiry, and interdisciplinary communication.

Independent Study Capstones

Independent study capstones include programs in which individual students develop an idea for an intellectual or creative project and work one-on-one with a faculty mentor. These capstone experiences are generally elective credit-bearing experiences rather than required for an entire discipline or student body. In most of these courses, students take the initiative to launch an academic research endeavor that connects directly with an issue or area of particular intellectual interest for the student and may or may not directly focus on a public issue or community need. Some programs encourage students to engage in direct service work with a not-for-profit agency and then tie the community-based work to larger social issues and public policy analysis.

Honors Thesis Capstones

Honors thesis capstones are generally senior research projects, usually involving an in-depth exploration associated with the student's academic discipline and may be required or optional, depending on the institution or department. Similar to the independent capstone, these credit-bearing courses require students to work in close collaboration with a faculty mentor. Students typically conduct original research on a topic of interest, write an individual paper rooted in their disciplines, and present findings. The thesis may or may not connect directly with a public issue.

Connecting Capstone Models to Civic Engagement: Strengths and Challenges

To understand the role of capstone courses, Robert Heinemann's use of the metaphors of "dome" and "spire" (1997) is helpful. His experience is based largely on teaching departmental capstones in the discipline of communication. Heinemann proposed that capstones serve two central purposes. One is to synthesize, integrate, and apply the vast material that students learn in their major and thus give closure to what they have learned (dome as the metaphor). The second is to prepare students to launch into new endeavors, to work on complex interdisciplinary societal issues that lead to additional questions and future exploration (spire as the metaphor). Using these metaphors can help articulate the various strengths and potential challenges of the four capstone models.

This section provides short vignettes of exemplary programs from each of the four capstone models. It elucidates some design issues and then discusses the challenges and opportunities of connecting each model to learning outcomes for civic engagement.

Wagner College: Departmental Capstones

At Wagner College in Staten Island, New York, all seventeen undergraduate departments offer senior capstones as an integral part of a three-year learning community program. The plan requires students to participate in three learning communities: the First-Year Program Learning Community, the Intermediate Learning Community in their sophomore or junior year, and the Senior Learning Community in their major. The Senior Learning Community consists of a capstone course and a reflective tutorial. The tutorial includes a hundred hours of experiential learning and a senior research paper (Wagner College, n.d.).

Each department shapes the Senior Learning Community to be a summative and reflective experience for the approximately 375 graduating seniors each year. The overall goal of the program is for all senior students to bring together the breadth of their liberal education and the depth of their specialized knowledge into real-world applied practice. The critical question for each student becomes this: what does it mean to practice this discipline in a reflective and responsible manner in a pluralistic society?

The following example of a senior capstone and reflective tutorial in the business department displays how the Senior Learning Communities provide students with a foundation for active social and civic involvement within the context of their field. Six business classes worked in partnership with the Staten Island Economic Development Corporation to address issues in the St. George neighborhood of Staten Island. These students collaboratively developed an eighteen-item questionnaire and personally interviewed more than sixty members of the community, including local public officials, government leaders, workers, property and business owners, school personnel, and residents of the area. Operating as business consultants, the students' goal was to identify the economic, social, and civic issues in the area and to collectively develop a needs-assessment plan with recommendations. The project, the St. George Action Plan, included short- and long-term solutions and identified the specific agencies that should be responsible for the implementation of each component. The students held a press conference and made two formal presentations of their findings (Wagner College, n.d.).

All the learning community classes are administered through the Office of Experiential Learning by the Dean of Learning Communities and Experiential Learning. The faculty members of the senior program meet monthly during the semester and elect a faculty coordinator to facilitate the meetings and oversee assessment and evaluation. Individual departments evaluate learning community classes based on a collegewide assessment plan. The college has developed a course evaluation tool that is used for every course and faculty evaluation, including capstones (Wagner College, n.d.).

Returning to the metalevel while keeping the Wagner College exemplar in mind, one can see that well-constructed departmental capstones can achieve Heinemann's first objective (1997): to synthesize and apply the stated learning objectives within a major. An advantage of this model is that departments create and assess clear learning objectives that each senior must demonstrate. The curriculum can thus provide uniform expectations of graduates within a major. A challenge of this model could be the potential difficulty of providing students with an experience that requires them to consider multiple approaches to complex problem solving. This model may unwittingly (or intentionally) reinforce a discipline-specific approach to engagement, thus potentially diminishing opportunities for students to connect disciplinary approaches with multidisciplinary or community-based strategies.

PORTLAND STATE UNIVERSITY: INTERDISCIPLINARY CAPSTONES

In 1994, after an institution-wide general education reform effort at Portland State University in Portland, Oregon, the six-credit senior capstone course requirement became the culminating general education requirement of the undergraduate curriculum. The faculty-led reform effort requires each undergraduate student to complete a capstone course. Annually, over three thousand seniors enroll in capstone courses at Portland State. The four primary goals of Portland State's interdisciplinary capstone are the following: to provide an opportunity for students to apply the expertise they learned in their overall undergraduate studies to address a real issue or problem in the community, to give students experience working in a team context that necessitates collaboration with persons from different fields of specialization, to provide the opportunity for students to become actively involved in the community, and to empower students to create a final product that is relevant to the community. Portland State University offers over 230 capstone courses annually, each enrolling about fifteen to eighteen students (Portland State University, n.d.). This program includes participation from every school, college, and major at the university. Each capstone course must address Portland State's university-wide general education learning outcomes: communication, critical thinking, appreciation of human diversity, and social responsibility. A current list of Portland State's capstone course offerings may be found at http://www.pdx.edu/unst/capstone.html.

One of the most popular capstones is Grant Writing for Social Change. In this course, the class of sixteen students breaks into four teams to write real grant proposals for community-based organizations, such as the Multnomah County Education Service District Outdoor School. The Outdoor School provides an opportunity for thousands of sixth graders throughout Portland and other regional school districts to go to an environmental education camp during the school year. The youth are away from their families for a week, often for the first time in their lives, and learn about field studies in the sciences in cooperative learning settings. Each team of university students researches potential funders for their community partner's projects, learns the requirements of the grant submission, writes the grant, obtains the organization's approval, and submits it to the funder. Other popular capstone courses include Environmental Sustainability, Business/Marketing Plans for Nonprofits, Civic Leadership, and Immigrant-Refugee Resettlement. Despite the broad range of capstone courses offered at Portland State, the program maintains consistency in quality in four primary ways: intentional partnership development work and targeted resource dissemination, including separate capstone handbooks for faculty, students, and community partners collaboratively developed and maintained by the Office of University Studies and the Center for Academic Excellence; ongoing faculty development efforts; centralized course evaluations and ongoing faculty teaching assessment and interventions based on those assessments; and a rigorous course proposal process (Portland State University, n.d.). The course proposal process requires that each faculty member document the community issues or needs to be addressed, the student learning outcomes, a list of academic literature, a description of the final product, a description of the development of the community partnership, a narrative on how the course will include the expertise of multiple majors, and a detailed account of how the faculty will incorporate the use of reflection to address the four stated learning objectives of Portland State's general education program: communication, critical thinking, social responsibility, and appreciation of diversity.

Interdisciplinary capstones are generally designed to achieve Heinemann's second goal (1997): teaching students how to work collaboratively in multidisciplinary environments requiring collaborative problem solving, cooperative decision making, and communication across multiple fields of study. Instead of addressing specific aspects of narrowly situated problems, student teams tackle high-level, complex issues. These courses allow students to critically analyze difficult community issues using the diverse talents of multiple fields of specialization. Challenges of this model include finding and training faculty to teach effectively in community-based settings from a multidisciplinary perspective. Also, it can be quite challenging to ensure the demonstration of discipline-specific knowledge in any uniform manner, thus making it difficult to assess student learning in the major.

BROWN UNIVERSITY: INDEPENDENT STUDY CAPSTONES

At Brown University in Providence, Rhode Island, the Swearer Center for Public Service provides the administrative leadership for sixty independent study capstone projects. Students may apply for fellowships that provide funding for the exploration and implementation of new ideas in the civic sector. The Swearer Center's view (n.d.) of the fellowships is that they are not only a means to accomplish specific goals but are also an investment in the future of the individuals who serve as fellows. The proposals represent diverse disciplinary perspectives and support research, advocacy, and direct service.

A foundational component of Brown's capstone program is the interview process in which students must conduct a series of interviews with representative members of diverse populations. This component ensures that capstone students consider multiple perspectives on their particular topic of study.

Students routinely report that the fellowship experience was the most significant experience they had while at Brown. They describe how the opportunity to engage in well-supported practice resulted in a reordering of knowledge or new ways of considering the public use of disciplinary knowledge. Moreover, students state that spending a year in a series of conversations with other students, with faculty, and often with individuals from the community, while approaching an issue from a range of disciplinary perspectives, was a profound experience. As a result of the conversations, fellows often begin to question distinctions between types and sources of knowledge, such as academic knowledge versus folk knowledge. Perhaps the most obvious outcome is the opportunity for highly motivated and intelligent students to negotiate the boundary between knowledge and its public use. Fellows must commit to producing knowledge that is accessible to a wide range of individuals.

One example of a Swearer Center fellowship is the Society of Royce Fellows. Through this program students receive an award of four thousand dollars to support a proposed research, curricular development, creative expression, or direct service project. Applicants must articulate the public usefulness of the proposal and be sponsored by a Brown faculty member. If selected, fellows participate in a yearlong series of conversations and seminars with peers and a group of faculty fellows. The center awards approximately twenty fellowships per year. A specific example is Jessica Beckerman, class of 2006, who used Royce funding to organize and coordinate a team of Brown students, alumni, and Malian students to work on the Mousso Ladamoule Project. The project's mission is to pioneer lasting social change and economic development in resource-poor communities in Mali, Africa, by using a women's peer education model. The program has been quite successful and graduated over 130 women in the first year. Graduates disperse into their communities and work in the area of health education on such projects as making oral rehydration fluids and organizing the distribution of mosquito nets. They also coordinate revenue-generating activities, including mud cloth painting and cloth-dying collectives. The project supports the graduates as they form neighborhood associations of women who, in turn, organize additional health and literacy initiatives. Other fellowships for advanced undergraduate students at Brown are described at http://www.brown.edu/Departments/Swearer_Center/whatwedo/fellowships.html.

Like the interdisciplinary capstones discussed previously, independent study capstones can also be designed to teach students to synthesize and apply knowledge well, Heinemann's second goal (1997). Advantages to this model include deep student learning based on a student's keen interest in a topic and an increased sense of self-efficacy that can be achieved when students learn how they can individually make a difference in the world. This model can also inspire interdisciplinary approaches to public problem solving. However, the independent nature of the projects in this model may not necessitate students' development of collaborative problem-solving and community-building skills. Additionally, the administration of this type of program can be cumbersome and costly in terms of funding for fellowships and individualized supervision.

STANFORD UNIVERSITY: HONORS THESIS CAPSTONES

At Stanford University in Palo Alto, California, approximately 350 of the senior-level students (20 percent) engage in a departmental honors thesis annually. The Haas Center for Public Service provides the leadership for a smaller subset of these students to become Public Service Scholars (PSS). The Public Service Scholars complete all the requirements of the traditional honors thesis in their respective academic units and, in addition, connect their research to a specific public issue or community organization. The students design a study, implement it, establish a relationship with a public audience, present their data, and consider the implications of their research for this audience—in addition to meeting the standards of academic rigor in their discipline. Public Service Scholars participate concurrently in the honors program in their department (including working individually with a faculty adviser) and in a credit-bearing yearlong seminar with PSS peers. In the seminar, students reflect on their community-based research projects, make meaning of their intellectual efforts, write an op-ed piece for publication based on their research to raise awareness of the issues they have investigated, and present findings and recommendations to a mock community board composed of real community decision makers. In the mock board meeting, students receive feedback on how an actual community board would react to their data, proposed conclusions, and recommendations.

Examples of recent honors thesis capstones from Stanford demonstrate their breadth and depth. Naree Chan, a public policy major, studied alternative vaccine strategies for Hepatitis B in Cambodia. The research consisted of a cost-effectiveness analysis of alternative vaccine strategies to increase delivery of doses to newborns. Another student, Catherine Baylin, a history and political science major, focused on the question of whether a systematic relationship existed between democratization and changes in the rate of extreme poverty in the 1980s and 1990s. Another public policy major, Neepa Acharya, analyzed why a large proportion of Alaska Natives who qualify for public assistance and welfare programs are not enrolling in the programs by studying the economic incentives that affect their decisions (Haas Center, n.d.).

Honors thesis capstones generally achieve Heinemann's first goal (1997) quite well in that students have many opportunities to integrate and provide clear evidence of their specific learning in their major. Students in these capstones study a topic in depth, frequently for an entire academic year, and see the tangible results of their individual efforts. The assessment of student learning in the major can be clearly evaluated based on an established departmental learning rubric. A challenge with this model could be that of developing students' collaboration and other necessary civic skills as well as an appreciation of interdisciplinary perspectives. However, the Stanford University model of the Public Service Scholars serves as a creative, applied alternative to the traditional senior thesis and overcomes many of these challenges. The PSS students are enrolled in the interdisciplinary seminar where they regularly hear and debate a wide variety of perspectives on various topics. The students also complete specific public-impact assignments intentionally designed to develop civic imagination and to overcome what otherwise might be considered a weakness in this capstone model design.

BEST PRACTICES FOR ENHANCING STUDENTS' CIVIC ENGAGEMENT THROUGH CAPSTONE EXPERIENCES

In their excellent book on learner-centered education, Amy Driscoll and Swarup Wood (2007) remind readers of one of the most basic and important insights concerning curriculum development: student learning outcomes are directly related to course learning objectives and are facilitated by specific teaching methodologies. It follows, then, that the capstone course model alone only partially affects students' achievement of civic engagement outcomes. While an institution's capstone model may accentuate the development of certain civic engagement outcomes, the faculty member's specific course objectives and teaching methodologies are of equal, or greater, importance. Each of the exemplars discussed in this chapter intentionally used teaching practices to enhance students' civic education.

To understand the role of capstone courses in enhancing students' civic engagement perspective, the Civic Learning Spiral, discussed in depth in chapter 3, offers a useful analytical lens. This model is constructed around the notion of relationships and deeply embedded interdependencies that are part of everyday life and learning. Distinguished by principles of interactivity and integration, the spiral, whose origins are in the learner, has six elements, or braids, within each full turn: self, communities and cultures, knowledge, skills, values, and public action. An institution or department that implements capstones for the purpose of increasing students' civic learning may wish to use the Civic Learning Spiral to ensure that the capstone experiences incorporate these essential aspects of civic education (Musil et al., in press).

Before we discuss specific resources and practices to enhance each of the essential elements of civic learning, it is helpful to revisit the model briefly here. There are six essential learning elements:

1. Self: focuses on relationships, identity, agency, disposition toward action, and commitment
2. Communities and cultures: considers appreciation of diversity and alternative sources of wisdom; encourages curiosity, transgressing boundaries, and exploring comparative civic traditions
3. Knowledge: includes deliberations on the implications of power, social movements, democracy, social construction, and civic intellectual debates
4. Skills: includes critical thinking, conflict resolution, communication, deliberation, community building, and civic imagination
5. Values: focuses on the relation of personal to public good, equality, opportunity, liberty, justice, and character
6. Public action: explores democratic governance, communal living, public participation, strategic thinking and action, risk taking, and raising ethical questions (Musil et al., in press)

Again, it is the *combination* of course design (in this case, a particular model for a senior seminar or capstone course) along with the specific, stated student learning outcomes and teaching methodologies that affect the level of student achievement of civic learning outcomes. Ideally, every institution, program, and faculty member would, regardless of curricular model, thoughtfully consider incorporating into capstone courses all six civic learning elements noted by Musil et al. The purpose of the following sections is to introduce best practices and resources for institutions, programs, and individual faculty for addressing each of the elements of civic learning.

FACILITATING STUDENTS' LEARNING OF SELF

Throughout our research we found that the most influential factor that allowed exemplar capstone programs to address the element of self was the formation and use of learning communities within the capstone experience. Throughout each program of distinction was a required seminar or course that asked students to reflect on their relationship with the community, their identity, their efficacy, and their commitment. Each institution reported that peer-to-peer learning was a vital element in program design. This was true regardless of the model used to implement the capstone. Those interested in learning more about facilitating the growth of self may wish to consult *A Social Change Model of Leadership Development* (Higher Education Research Institute, 1996). Readers interested in exploring in-class exercises that address the many facets of self might consult those described by Vicki L. Reitenauer (2005).

FACILITATING STUDENTS' UNDERSTANDING OF COMMUNITY AND CULTURES

Exemplar capstone programs enhanced students' understanding of communities and cultures by intentionally designing courses that involve students in culturally diverse communities and by providing preparation and reflection to effectively enter, engage, and exit the community. Many effective capstones have been specifically (re)designed to be delivered in an international setting, and/or they were (re)created to intentionally explore academic and community-based elements that have particular social, economic, or political importance.

A traditional discipline-based business capstone course that focuses primarily on knowledge and skills acquisition, for example, could be transformed by having business students provide technical support to local immigrant or refugee business owners. This could offer an opportunity in the curriculum to incorporate readings, written assignments, reflections, and guest speakers to address issues of diversity, alternative forms and sources of knowledge, the crossing of cultural boundaries, and comparison of civic and business traditions. This could also allow students to engage with persons from diverse cultural communities.

Resources that can help faculty enhance students' appreciation of diverse communities are plentiful. Providing an exhaustive list is beyond the scope of this chapter; we suggest exploring *Creating Cultural Connections: Navigating Difference, Investigating Power, and Unpacking Privilege* (Reitenauer, Cress, and Bennett, 2005). The authors offer key concepts, issues, and exercises for faculty and students.

Broadening Students' Understanding of Knowledge

Exemplar institutions intentionally examined the notion of knowledge and how knowledge was constructed and presented in capstone courses. Faculty from these institutions often used guest speakers from the community to capitalize on expert, community-based knowledge that represented diverse backgrounds. In most cases, capstone course final projects were formally presented directly to the population they were designed to inform. This strategy places representatives of the population in the place of authority and requests that they assess the project's usefulness and accuracy. In the most effective cases, students were required to solicit community feedback to inform their research; this activity can help place the power of knowledge in multiple sources. Exemplar programs frequently used the teaching strategy of interviewing multiple community partners to ensure that students understood the dynamic nature of knowledge as well as considered knowledge that was achieved through lived experiences. *Community-Based Research in Higher Education: Principles and Practices* (Strand, Cutforth, Stoecker, Marullo, and Donohue, 2003) offers detailed information and strategies on community-based research as a pedagogy to develop students' civic knowledge.

Enhancing Students' Civic Skills

Exemplar capstone programs ensure that the acquisition of civic engagement skills is an explicit learning objective in every course. Syllabi explicitly state how the course will require students to demonstrate civic skills such as critical thinking, communication, conflict resolution, deliberation, and civic imagination. In many capstone courses, these process skills are developed and assessed in association with the development of students' final community project. For example, if the intent of a graphic design capstone is to create a logo for a local mentoring program, then the learning objectives will include critical analysis of the role of a mentor in a child's life and the most effective ways to communicate the importance of mentoring. Also, the skills gained in making collaborative decisions in the logo-creation process align with the acquisition of such general community engagement skills as building consensus and working across differences. Institutions and individual faculty have successfully used *The Civically Engaged Reader* (Davis and Lynn, 2006) to deepen students' reflections on the notion of civic imagination.

HELPING STUDENTS CLARIFY VALUES

Institutions reviewed in the preparation of this chapter explicitly addressed the issue of values clarification through readings, classroom activities, discussions, and reflective writing assignments. The element of values is informed by the other elements of self, culture, socially constructed knowledge, civic imagination, and public action, among others. Each capstone faculty member chooses to address the area of values clarification in his or her own style, but a common means is through readings that provoke students to deeply investigate their own values. For example, courses that address immigrant and refugee issues expose students to social research on the topic; in addition, some faculty choose to accompany that research with novels of personal accounts of immigrants and their experience in the U.S. education or health care system. *A Practitioner's Guild to Reflection* (Eyler, Giles, and Schmiede, 1996) provides extensive suggestions of ways to enhance students' reflection on values.

ENCOURAGING STUDENTS TO TAKE PUBLIC ACTION

One of the principal strengths of each exemplar capstone program is the fact that they require and support students to take some form of public action. These actions have many forms—individually initiated or collaboratively accomplished—yet all have in common the intention to move students beyond the fear of public engagement and into public action. The seminars implemented at each institution allow students to express the fears, concerns, and challenges that can arise when they enter into the fray of community problem solving. Exemplar institutions encouraged and intentionally facilitated reflection on democracy, public participation, risk taking, and ethical issues. Many faculty in exemplar programs work with local community organizers and advocates to reinforce the importance of taking public action; others develop unique readers, with articles that explore the stories of people making a difference in their community. Also, some faculty members specifically adopt proven and provocative texts, such as *The Impossible Will Take a Little While: A Citizen's Guide to Hope in a Time of Fear* (Loeb, 2004), to inform class discussions on the importance of public participation. All exemplary programs recognize the importance of deepening and supporting students' commitment to take public action.

In conclusion, the exemplars discussed in this chapter enhance students' civic learning by carefully designing capstone courses that explicitly address all six of the essential civic learning elements discussed earlier. These capstone course experiences require students to learn, demonstrate, and apply the skills and attitudes associated with effective civic engagement as part of the curriculum. To create and sustain such capstone courses, three essential programmatic efforts should be employed: intentionality in curricular design based on the best practices discussed, ongoing assessment, and regular faculty development efforts. The final two sections of this chapter explore best practices in assessment and faculty development.

ASSESSMENT OF CAPSTONE COURSES

There are many assessment methods appropriate for capstones that are available to faculty and program directors. Regardless of method, however, assessment must be embedded into the course or program design and employed early and regularly. Portland State University has been using three formal assessment strategies consistently to evaluate capstone courses since 1995 (Kerrigan and Jhaj, 2007). First, midterm qualitative course assessments are completed by professional staff in randomly selected capstone courses (20 percent of the total) to gather formative data for faculty. Second, students complete an end-of-term quantitative course evaluation that assesses the pedagogical methods employed in the course, how well their course addressed the general education goals, the congruence between community engagement and course content, and the quality of the instruction. Finally, a qualitative section of the end-of-term evaluation invites students to state their most important learning achievements and their ideas for improving the course. Insights borne from these assessment activities strongly suggest that regular faculty development is critical for program success.

What does the data tell us about capstones? Through triangulation of all three sets of data, we know that students affirm that capstone courses help them apply theoretical academic knowledge to address real issues in the community, to provide a sense of efficacy concerning their positive contributions to their communities, to deepen understanding of diverse populations, to develop abilities to work in a collaborative effort, to improve critical-thinking skills, and to enhance communication skills. Students also regularly report that the following factors specifically helped them achieve these outcomes: effective instructors who were approachable, responsive, enthusiastic, engaging, knowledgeable, experienced, and strong facilitators; engaging class discussions that created a safe learning community, happened frequently, and connected their readings and the service; the use of readings that related to their service work and were thought provoking; depth of connection with the community and diverse populations through agency tours, meaningful service opportunities, and guest speakers who could add new perspectives to course content.

The data also suggests challenges that students face in capstone courses. Students reported four main challenges. They believe that they need more explicit timelines to complete these large community-based projects and more explicit grading criteria, since these projects were significantly different from anything they had attempted previously. They also cited as challenges the lack of time to coordinate all their other responsibilities with the requirements of the community project and issues related to transportation and logistics.

Such assessment data confirmed the best practices of using active pedagogies, such as designing capstones as learning communities, involving students in engaging discussions, and facilitating students' connections between academic coursework and their community work through reflective assignments and discussions. The challenge areas suggest the need for improving faculty teaching to include more exercises that assist students in their acquisition of project management skills, providing clearer grading rubrics associated with the quality of the community-based project, and assisting students as they consider personal time management and general logistics issues that are necessarily associated with all community-based projects.

FACULTY DEVELOPMENT FOR CAPSTONE COURSES

At Portland State, course evaluation data is broadly shared with capstone faculty through an e-mail Listserv and meetings. The assessment process documents the common strengths and challenges in the capstone courses and encourages dialogue and the exchange of ideas among faculty. In the case of community-based courses, the data demonstrates the importance of working with newer faculty on developing, organizing, and integrating the community partnership experience within the course structure. In addition to working with new faculty, faculty development efforts target instructors with extensive teaching experience but less experience in structuring community collaborations and those with extensive community knowledge but less experience in designing and delivering courses.

Since the late 1990s, Portland State's University Studies Program and the Center for Academic Excellence have employed innovative faculty learning community models to enhance teaching and learning (Cress, Kerrigan, and Reitenauer, 2003; Kecskes, Collier, and Balshem, 2006). The center supports faculty through minigrants for the integration of civic engagement outcomes into courses and assists faculty in furthering their community-engaged scholarly agendas.

The key objective of faculty seminars and workshops at Portland State is the integration of specific civic skill development into curricula so that faculty improve their course design, develop new strategies to encourage students to become civically engaged, add civic engagement pedagogies to their teaching toolboxes, and learn how to better develop and maintain constructive university-community partnerships. To nurture a lasting and dynamic culture of civic engagement among faculty, students, and the community, the Office of University Studies and the Center for Academic Excellence invite faculty to create an interactive, collaborative, and democratic space where the exploration of concerns and successes benefits the broader group. Seminars are led by a neutral facilitator and attended by both seasoned and new faculty members, who consider the different dimensions of their courses and the practice of civic engagement. By sharing a wealth of personal experiences in an egalitarian setting, faculty are able to deepen and broaden their strategies for the design and improvement of capstone and other community-based learning courses related to civic engagement (Kecskes and White, in press). Portland State has assessed courses taught by faculty after participating in these civic learning seminars and have documented that student outcomes are enhanced by this form of faculty development (Cress et al., 2003). In assessment of these faculty learning communities over the past decade, faculty members have consistently reported that their teaching and scholarship have improved, their connections to others within the university community as well as to diverse external communities have increased, and their understanding of the sources and respectful use of community-based wisdom have been significantly augmented (Kecskes et al., 2006).

CONCLUSION

Clearly, capstone courses and other types of senior-seminar-style educational experiences have taken root in higher education in the United States. This educational approach is improving and extending student learning in both private and public institutions through four primary capstone course models: disciplinary, interdisciplinary, independent study, and honors thesis. Each model has inherent strengths and potential challenges, yet the institutional examples discussed in this chapter have become exemplars by effectively integrating specific civic learning outcomes into the formal curriculum. The best capstone course experiences require students to learn, demonstrate, and apply essential skills and attitudes associated with effective civic engagement as part of the curriculum. To ensure continuous course- and program-level improvement, ongoing assessment and regular faculty development efforts are essential.

In an ideal world, institutions of higher education would consistently develop and require educational experiences for students to test and demonstrate disciplinary expertise as well as civic engagement knowledge and skills within a culminating course. Alternatively, colleges and universities could require an upper-division experience within the major—perhaps in the junior year—as well as require a separate senior-level, community-based, general education capstone course that focuses on further developing and applying skills of engaged citizenship through social action in interdisciplinary settings. Adopting one of the four capstone program design models explored in this chapter—along with intentional curricular revision, assessment, and faculty development—will increase students' ability to become increasingly more aware and effective civic leaders in the decades to come.

References

Brown, A. H., and Benson, B. "Making Sense of the Capstone Process: Reflections from the Front Line." *Education*, 2005, *125*(4), 674–692.

Cress, C. M., Kerrigan, S. M., and Reitenauer, V. L. "Making Community-Based Learning Meaningful: Faculty Efforts to Increase Student Civic Engagement Skills." *Transformations: The Journal of Inclusive Scholarship and Pedagogy, XIV*, 2003.

Davis, A., and Lynn, E. *The Civically Engaged Reader: A Collection of Short Provocative Readings on Civic Activity.* Chicago: Great Books Foundation, 2006.

Driscoll, A., and Wood, S. *Developing Outcomes-Based Assessment for Learner-Centered Education.* Sterling, VA: Stylus, 2007.

Eyler, J., Giles, D. E., and Schmiede, A. A. *A Practitioner's Guide to Reflection in Service-Learning: Student Voices and Reflections.* Nashville, TN: Vanderbilt University, 1996.

Gardner, J. N., and Van der Veer, G. *The Senior Year Experience: Facilitating Reflection, Integration, Closure, and Transition.* San Francisco: Jossey-Bass, 1998.

Haas Center. "Public Service Scholars Program." http://haas.stanford.edu/index.php/item/384, n.d.

Heinemann, R. *The Senior Capstone, Dome or Spire?* Grantham, PA: Messiah College, 1997.

Henscheid, J. M. *Professing the Disciplines: An Analysis of Senior Seminars and Capstone Courses.* Columbia, SC: National Resource Center for the First-Year Experience and Students in Transition, 2000.

Higher Education Research Institute. *A Social Change Model of Leadership Development.* Los Angeles: University of California at Los Angeles, 1996.

Jensen, V., and Wenzel, A. *Creating a Sophomore Capstone Experience in the Community College.* Freeport, IL: Highland Community College, 2001.

Kecskes, K., Collier, P., and Balshem, M. "Engaging Scholars in the Scholarship of Engagement." In K. McKnight Casey, G. Davidson, S. Billig, and N. C. Springer (Eds.), *Advancing Knowledge in Service-Learning: Research to Transform the Field.* Greenwich, CT: Information Age Publishing, 2006.

Kecskes, K., and White, R. *Engagement at the Edge: Portland State University and New Leadership for the 21st Century.* Portland, OR: Portland State University/Oregon Campus Compact Monograph Series on Civic Learning, in press.

Kerrigan, S., and Jhaj, S. "Assessing General Education Capstone Courses: An In-Depth Look at a Nationally Recognized Capstone Assessment Model." *Peer Review,* 2007, *9*(2), 13–16.

Levine, A. *Handbook of Undergraduate Curriculum.* San Francisco: Jossey-Bass, 1978.

Loeb, P. R. *The Impossible Will Take a Little While: A Citizen's Guide to Hope in a Time of Fear.* New York: Basic Books, 2004.

Musil, C. M., Wathington, H., Battistoni, R., Calderón, J., Trementozzi, M., Fluker, W. E., et al. *The Civic Learning Spiral: Education for Participation in a Diverse Democracy.* Washington, DC: Association of American Colleges and Universities, in press.

National Capstone Conference. "Welcome to the National Capstone Conference Website." http://www.capstoneconf.org, 2006.

Oddo, L., Rosenak, D. S., Reilley, L. F., and Dunn, C. "Using an Interdisciplinary Capstone to Promote Cultural Preservation." *Metropolitan Universities,* 2002, *3*(1), 33–40.

Portland State University. "Capstone Resources." http://www.pdx.edu/cae/capstone_resources.html, n.d.

Reitenauer, V. L. *"Becoming Community: Moving from I to We."* In C. M. Cress, P. J. Collier, and V. L. Reitenauer (Eds.), *Learning through Serving: A Student Guidebook for Service-Learning across the Disciplines.* Sterling, VA: Stylus, 2005.

Reitenauer, V. L., Cress, C. M., and Bennett, J. "Creating Cultural Connections: Navigating Difference, Investigating Power, Unpacking

Privilege." In C. M. Cress, P. J. Collier, and V. L. Reitenauer (Eds.), *Learning through Serving: A Student Guidebook for Service-Learning across the Disciplines.* Sterling, VA: Stylus, 2005.

Rennie-Hill, L., and Toth, M. A. "The Portland State University Studies Initiative: General Education for the New Century (Part 1)." *Journal of General Education*, 1999, *48*(2), 65–136.

Strand, K. J., Cutforth, N., Stoecker, R., Marullo, S., and Donohue, P. *Community-Based Research and Higher Education: Principles and Practices.* San Francisco: Jossey-Bass, 2003.

Swearer Center for Public Service, Brown University. "Royce Fellowship." http://www.brown.edu/Departments/Swearer_Center/whatwedo/fellowships-royce.html, n.d.

Wagner College. "Experiential Learning Program." http://www.wagner.edu/experiential_learning, n.d.

ENHANCING INTERCULTURAL COMPETENCE THROUGH CIVIC ENGAGEMENT

Michelle R. Dunlap and Nicole Webster

Civic engagement requires working collaboratively and productively with others who may be different from ourselves to address common issues and to achieve common purposes. Intercultural competence encompasses awareness of multiple differences and commonalities, understanding of issues that may arise when working across differences, and skills that build our capacity to accomplish our shared goals. In this chapter, we argue that high-quality opportunities for students to work in environments outside their comfort zones can be an effective means of developing intercultural competence. However, creating such opportunities presents several challenges for educators, both in the curricular and cocurricular arenas.

Human differences exist along many dimensions. These differences are not just among groups; they are also complicated by a myriad of *intragroup* differences. A wide range of historical, cultural, social, and economic factors characterize any community in which students engage. Also, both students and community members will be at various levels of identity development and intercultural understanding and skills. Developing and sustaining the trust of community partners presents several challenges in itself. This chapter offers five recommendations for addressing these challenges and designing opportunities for students to develop intercultural competence in community contexts.

Recommendation 1: Provide a Thorough Introduction to the Community

It is essential that we begin our civic engagement work with students in community settings by facilitating their development of an understanding of the historical, racial, economic, and social factors that have an impact on the communities with which they will engage. A good way to start is for the students to simply spend some time in the community, informally visiting its shops, public buildings, parks, churches, and residential neighborhoods. It is also important to supplement this firsthand experience by reading local government documents, exploring relevant Web sites, and examining census data. Talking with government officials, political leaders, community activists, and residents adds a human dimension to the initial research. With this background, it is appropriate for students to initiate contact with the community-based organization or local government office where they will be working. On-site training by community leaders, in addition to campus-based preparation, is critical. For example, in one project, the students were part of a community engagement luncheon. The purpose of the luncheon was to introduce students to the local community politicians, give them a close-up view of the cultural nuances that take place in community meetings, learn about community issues directly from community members, and see how local issues are addressed. As a result of attending the meeting, students gained a clearer vision of the potential impact of their project and how a community's culture and history must influence the design of its projects and programs.

Other less personal but also potentially meaningful ways to introduce students to new communities are through readings, documentaries, and films (Dunlap, 2000). At Connecticut College in New London, Connecticut, one of the authors prepares students in her course Children and Families in a Multicultural Society by viewing clips from films such as *Once Upon a Time When We Were Colored, Crooklyn, Mi Familia,* and *The Joy Luck Club.* Following the clips, class discussions enable students to explore and critically analyze possible cultural similarities and differences as well as inaccurate stereotypes. This process helps students assess and interact more successfully in real-life community environments.

Recommendation 2: Work to Dispel Myths and Negative, Inaccurate Stereotypes

In addition to a thorough introduction to the historical, economic, social, and racial factors that affect the community, civic engagement educators must address students' misperceptions and stereotypes, sometimes deeply rooted, about the community and its members. When designing community engagement programs, facilitators should provide a solid foundation of reflection and learning to help students dispel myths and negative stereotypes and to help create a healthy experience.

Research and theoretical models concerning racial identity suggest that individuals travel through various developmental stages of thinking about, and working through issues related to, racial and/or cultural differences (Dunlap, Scoggin, Green, and Davi, 2007; Helms, 1990; Tatum, 1992). The authors of this chapter liken these stages to Elizabeth Kubler-Ross's model of death and dying (1970). In Kubler-Ross's terminology, individuals may begin their journey related to a particular struggle with which they are faced at the far extreme of "denial." At the opposite end of the continuum, they may be at the extreme of total "acceptance." Or they may be anywhere along the continuum, between the extremes. In terms of racial and cultural differences, some people are in fear and denial and are not ready to deal effectively with others who come from backgrounds that are different from their own, while others have been working on effectively understanding both the differences and similarities that exist among groups of individuals for a long time.

When designing civic engagement experiences for students that will take place in the community, facilitators need to be aware that students will be at various stages in the racial identity development process. It is essential to work with those at the initial stage to help dispel myths and negative stereotypes before they come in contact with community members. If this does not occur, students' negative reactions and interactions at the community site can jeopardize the entire experience, damage the institution's relationship with the community, and reaffirm any negative biases the students may have. Numerous tools exist to facilitate reflection about human differences and commonalities and can aid civic engagement educators (Dunlap, 2000; Dunlap et al., 2007; Eyler, Giles, and Schmiede, 1996; Webster and Ingram, 2007). Structured reflection combined with working with others in a community setting can encourage progress through the racial identity development process and can increase intercultural competence (Dunlap et al., 2007; McIntosh, 1990; Tatum, 1992).

The civic engagement experience in a course about how adolescents develop as leaders in their families and communities at Pennsylvania State University illustrates how initially addressing students' discomfort level and biases can lead to gains in intercultural competence. As a group of twenty-five white university students began to prepare for a semester-long project in an urban African American community, they stated that, among other things, they did not want to be caught in the service site after dark. After some prompting, it became clear that the students had some deeply rooted stereotypes about the nature of the community. They had heard rumors that they would be robbed or even offered drugs because they were white. When asked about their expectations, some students had expressed images such as "Everyone walks around high on crack and with gold chains and teeth."

On the other hand, some students were comfortable with the concept of working with the community and saw the service project as a learning experience that would challenge them to move outside their comfort zones. Several students were from areas of the country with substantial minority populations or had been involved in diversity experiences that made them feel more comfortable around individuals from other racial or cultural groups. Still others fell somewhere between these two extremes. Among these, some who came from isolated, predominantly white communities felt apprehensive but also recognized that the project was a way to help them prepare for the real world. Some students expressed that they would check their stereotypes at the door and enter the project with an open mind, while others held steadily on to their obviously inaccurate stereotypes until those stereotypes were reinforced.

The project goals attempted to engage both the predominantly black community partners and the white college students during a number of orientation and planning sessions throughout the semester. At each session, the coordinator saw some of the students retreat back into their comfort zones, sitting only with their white counterparts and not engaging in conversations with their community partners. Some of the students appeared to wrestle to understand why their negative stereotypes were not ringing true as indicated by comments such as "Let's go to the *real* part of the city" and "Let's wait 'til dark; that's when the *other* people come out." Comments such as these reinforced the notion that the students were still holding on to stereotypical beliefs and were expecting these beliefs to be reinforced. As the project continued throughout the semester, even the most reserved students began to open up and appeared to feel more comfortable with the community partners. All the students talked more with the community members and engaged in more deeply reflective conversations with them. Through time, experience, and patience, the most skeptical students realized they had a lot to gain from their community partners. The danger of clinging to stereotypes became clear to both the students and the community members as both groups continued to build on their relationships over the course of the semester. Some of these relationships continued beyond the semester and led to other community partnerships and joint endeavors.

As this example illustrates, community-based projects, even brief ones, can create a template for developing deeper relationships and understandings. They can be effective if followed up quickly and regularly with support and activities to further develop intercultural competence and community engagement (Dunlap, 2000; Dunlap et al., 2007). These activities may include written and oral reflection, regular meetings with facilitators and community partners, and readings and resource materials about the community and the community engagement process (Webster and Ingram, 2007). However, in-depth learning about diversity as well as the accomplishment of cultural competence cannot occur within the scope of a one-time project.

RECOMMENDATION 3: CONSIDER THE MULTIDIMENSIONALITY OF THE SOCIAL FACTORS AND SYSTEMIC ISSUES AFFECTING THE COMMUNITY

The systems surrounding the community environment need to be studied and attended to as much as the circumstances of the people within it. Systemic challenges include decreases in available jobs, discriminatory hiring or housing policies, and lack of crime prevention and effective educational programs. It is important for students to understand that the concept of a fair and equally accessible meritocracy does not extend to all communities and individuals and that systemic issues like these can disproportionately affect minorities and poor people. As a result, students will encounter community partners who have not had access to the highest quality of life. If community issues such as poverty, fair housing, and educational inequality are not addressed in a truthful historical context, students can be left with naive, skewed perceptions about why people live in inadequate conditions.

To illustrate how to address systemic factors, the following example engaged a group of first- and second-year predominantly white college students at Michigan State University in East Lansing in a housing project in a low-income, inner-city community. Based on course readings—including *Migration, Transnationalization, and Race in a Changing New York* (Cordero-Guzman, Smith, and Grosfoguel, 2001) and *Understanding Poverty* (Danziger and Haveman, 2002)—they found themselves quickly asking questions about the source of poverty and economic deprivation in the community. In addition, the instructor organized panel discussions with local community officials and board members about economic issues in the area. As a result, students began to grapple with how bureaucratic policies can limit the development of people in a community. Through readings and community engagement, students were able to reflect deeply about the extent to which existing conditions were and were not due to the community members themselves, politics, bureaucracy, or a combination of all three. It has been the authors' experience that using readings in combination with interacting with community members brings the community's realities to life for the students. An added bonus of early and ongoing interaction with community members is that it also allows students to see that the community is fully engaged and invested in the project.

Recommendation 4: Take into Account the Intragroup Diversity That Exists between the Community and Those Engaged with the Community

Critical race theory (Delgado and Stefancic, 2001) and similar models suggest that most people do not fit neatly into socially constructed categories such as black and white, male and female, rich and poor, and so forth. Rather, they exist along multilayered, multidimensional, interdependent continuums that combine into complex lived experiences and identities that cannot be articulated using only one category. While theoretical knowledge about particular categories is helpful, it obviously is not fixed and immutable. To begin to understand how the identities of students and community participants in community engagement activities consist of unique and rich combinations of categories, deep and ongoing interaction and reflection are required. The community engagement experiences of minority students and partners reveal that such experiences may not have the same meaning for everyone (Evans, Taylor, Dunlap, and Miller, in press). Even though students are from the same racial or ethnic group, their individual identities reflect a great deal of diversity within the same or similar groups. Thus, they are likely to bring a diversity of perspectives and opinions to the community and project in which they are engaged.

To offer an example from Pennsylvania State University, during the development of a weeklong study-away experience in Belize City, Belize (which experiences issues and dynamics similar to those of U.S. inner-city communities) with a group of predominantly black students, several students began to reflect on and discuss the meaning of community and engagement. While the purpose of the study-away project was to focus on increasing the technological infrastructures in an elementary school in a low-income neighborhood, the students found themselves struggling with how to think about themselves as a part of the larger context of service to a community composed of individuals of their own race. During one of the ten weekly preparation meetings for the project, the coordinator initiated a discussion with the students about expectations for service within the local culture and what service meant specifically to her as a black woman with Caribbean heritage. She shared that, from her cultural perspective, service was giving back, or helping those in need, like what is familiarly taught in many churches. The coordinator's comments generated much discussion among the group, with a student expressing that she felt that rather than being about giving back, service was more of an uplifting and empowering act for the one providing the service. The student went on to relate her expectations for community engagement to the service contributions of W. E. B. DuBois and George Washington Carver.

On the other hand, unlike many of her classmates, another student, who was brought up in an inner-city environment, challenged the need or desire to go back to work in economically struggling inner-city communities. She strongly iterated that she did not want to go back. She felt it was better to move ahead and not focus on those "who cannot be helped." Although she was a product of an environment similar to the one about which she was speaking, she did not want to return to it even for the community engagement project. For her, the community environment was a painful one that she would prefer to avoid to whatever extent possible. Realizing that the majority of the students did not share her views, she made her point by citing incorrect statistics about the health and human welfare in urban cities. Some of the other African American and Caribbean students judgmentally perceived her as distancing herself because, in their opinion, she was not only ashamed of being from an urban, inner-city community but also was "ashamed to be black."

Thus, while all the students considered themselves to be black, racially speaking, they all had different perspectives about their blackness, their responsibility to the community, and their purposes for engaging in it. These differences seemed to be connected to one degree or another with their socioeconomic status, gender, sexual orientation, and experiences associated with being a member of such categories. Their different perspectives translated into very different motivations and reasons for engaging in service and different outlooks on, and opinions about, the community.

Diversity of intragroup experiences and opinions may manifest itself in different ways as students engage in their community projects. It is vital for facilitators to reflect on and discuss their own feelings and to work intentionally and continuously with students to reflect on theirs. For example, project facilitators were active participants in reflection exercises and shared their thoughts and feelings pertaining to the project, the group dynamics, and their own experiences. The facilitators also kept a journal with the students and periodically shared readings in group discussions. Sometimes their entries were used as the starting points of dialogue during the reflection time. Facilitators can also brainstorm with students and point them to diversity-related resources and supports that may be helpful to them (see Dunlap et al., 2007).

RECOMMENDATION 5: ATTEMPT TO DEVELOP TRUST GRADUALLY AND OVER AN EXTENDED PERIOD OF TIME

In terms of engaging in the community, trust must be established and developed slowly, incrementally, and carefully. It is wise for those who desire to engage with the community to be sensitive to where people of diverse racial, ethnic, and cultural backgrounds are in terms of their trust levels. It is important to the trust-building process to include both campus and community stakeholders in all aspects of the community project. This encourages stakeholders to help identify problems and to creatively solve them. The development of trust is a key element that often is overlooked, yet without it, little progress can be made (Dunlap, 2000; Webster and Ingram, 2007). The following examples illustrate the painstaking, time-consuming process of bringing groups together for community engagement in an atmosphere of trust. The first example explores trust building among student participants in community engagement; the second focuses on developing the trust of community partners in the context of students' community experiences.

At Pennsylvania State University, one of the authors received a copy of a national organization's newsletter in her mailbox that discussed the need for student groups within the agricultural sciences to work together. This article was based on preliminary findings from agriculturally based organizations regarding the lack of tolerance and diversity in the workplace. Attention was drawn to two specific organizations: Future Farmers of America (FFA) and Minorities in Agriculture, Natural Resources, and Related Sciences (MANRRS). Both national organizations have a strong history in the agricultural field, both are housed on many land-grant university campuses, and both are typically racially segregated. FFA's membership is predominantly white and from rural or suburban areas. The members of MANRRS are predominantly black and from suburban-to-urban and urban neighborhoods. Like many organizations, the racial segregation stems from the history of and access, or lack of access, to both groups. These groups had never worked together, although the students saw each other in classes and perhaps at campuswide meetings. As the author continued to reflect on the article, she approached a colleague to discuss the idea of bringing together the two groups on her campus. After much discussion, she received a grant from her institution to create a collaborative community engagement project for the groups.

The project goals, developed by representatives of both groups, were twofold: to engage members of the two segregated organizations in a needed community project and to build intellectual and emotional bridges of understanding across the two racial groups. A diverse mix of forty-seven students took part in a weekend urban environmental project at a community center in Philadelphia. The project was also connected to a youth development course in which over one-third of the participants were enrolled.

The coordinators struggled to determine the most appropriate location for the collaborative planning meetings before the weekend project because of the racial makeup of both campus groups and of the community partners. The coordinators did not want to create an undesirable situation for either group but knew they needed to push students outside their comfort zone. Therefore, they opted to have the students meet in the economically challenged urban area where the community partners were located for both the planning and the project itself. During the weekend retreat, the partners cleaned and repaired the center and spent time meeting with community members and touring historical sites with residents of the city. To prevent the students from falling into self-selected, racially segregated groups, the project coordinators purposefully placed them in racially mixed groups for work, reflection, and social activities throughout the weekend.

Despite some students' reluctance about the project's location and mixed-group activities, the overall goals were met as indicated in focus group reflections and surveys. Relationships were fostered during the retreat that carried over into interactions between FFA and MANRRS long after the retreat, and the students returned even more motivated to build on their weekend of success. For instance, upon returning to campus, the presidents of both groups planned an outing that would enable members from each group to build on their new relationships. This has become an annual event that has carried over into additional cosponsored events between the organizations throughout subsequent academic years. To facilitate the team-building process, project coordinators assisted students in scheduling meetings, locating rooms, securing money for events, and creating a plan of action. In addition to these activities, the project coordinators worked with the executive boards of the student groups to create a cadre of students who were willing to meet informally to discuss how to continue similar projects. Students from both groups were selected for collegewide activities that enabled continuous interaction and the ability to further develop relationships over time. Trust also was built through group interactions on class projects and other campus activities (Webster and Hoover, 2006).

A second example of building trust slowly and over time concerns a group of predominantly white students in a three-credit class on positive youth development at Pennsylvania State University. One of the first comments the students heard upon arriving in the socioeconomically challenged, predominantly black and

Latino community was "Who are you to come into my community and tell me what is wrong and right?" Most of the students had never expected to be greeted with the backlash that several community members described as "white privilege" (McIntosh, 1990). Some community members expressed that these well-to-do college students were going to come in and tell them "how to fix problems that had been inherent in this community for years" and then go back to "their side of the tracks, sip their tea, and tell their friends they had helped those poor minorities over in *that* community." This was the first time some of the students had interacted with a community that was both of a lower socio-economic class and of color and, consequently, confronted their whiteness head-on.

The students were shocked because they were unprepared for the reactions from the community partners. They had been preparing for a community project that would engage them in a "different" community and allow them to use the skills and knowledge they had recently acquired through the course in work with a group of "needy" individuals. Instead, they found the community members to be strong, empowered, articulate, and opinionated, sometimes expressing deeply rooted feelings about their disgust when "white folks come in and tell us what is wrong with our community, instead of trying to learn what is right." At one meeting, a community member passionately expressed, "It is not so much about what is wrong; rather, it should be about learning what we have to offer and, perhaps, what happened to put people in these kinds of conditions." Her concern, which sometimes was perceived as anger, resulted from several other failed projects that brought in predominantly white college students who appeared to be there to monitor the community and its issues in what felt like an objectifying, even patronizing, manner.

Through the critical reflection process, the students began to shed their initial idealism and to realize that they had to address the community members' feelings and concerns. Through their readings and facilitated reflection, they questioned how their whiteness had, would, and could, affect their relationship with the community and, ultimately, the success of the project. As one student said, "I knew this was going to be different, but I didn't expect all of this [resistance and emotional work]." The students

were emotionally moved by the candor of the community partners and began to openly explore their "knapsack" of privileges
(McIntosh, 1990). Over the course of the project, the students
carefully maneuvered their position within the community and
learned how to make the project one with more shared owner-
ship. Continued conversations with community members revealed
that some partners would never accept "others" coming into their
community, while some would. One less accepting partner indicated that she may have shown up to participate, but deep down
she wished she could have seen more students "who looked like
the members of her community" and perhaps better understood
their challenges.

Over time, the community members and students participated
in joint reflection sessions, discussing the issues of race, privilege,
whiteness, and access. These frank discussions led to collaborative
workshops to promote greater understanding.

CONCLUSION

This chapter provided five recommendations, together with
related examples and challenges, for enhancing intercultural
competency through civic engagement. These recommendations
and challenges are by no means exhaustive, nor are they mutually
exclusive. Rather, they highlight a few of the challenges and strategies that the authors have encountered in their many years of
teaching and facilitating the community engagement process.

Attention first must be paid to establishing rapport because,
as in any relationship, without rapport, little can be accomplished.
It also is critical to recognize and value differences within and
between communities (Dunlap, 2000). Webster and Ingram (2007)
and other scholars have stressed the importance of communication, as well as encouraging community stakeholding in the community engagement process. We also should avoid the missionary
mentality, or what some call the "white horse syndrome" (Dunlap
et al., 2007; Webster and Ingram, 2007). We hope that our colleagues who facilitate civic engagement experiences for students
will feel all the more encouraged, engaged, and equipped in the
ongoing journey of intercultural learning, with its many hills and
valleys, that can and should last over the course of a lifetime.

References

Cordero-Guzman, H., Smith, R., and Grosfoguel, R. *Migration, Transnationalization, and Race in a Changing New York.* Philadelphia: Temple University Press, 2001.

Danziger, S., and Haveman, R. *Understanding Poverty.* Cambridge, MA: Harvard University Press, 2002.

Delgado, R., and Stefancic, J. *Critical Race Theory: An Introduction.* New York: New York University Press, 2001.

Dunlap, M. *Reaching Out to Children and Families: Students Model Effective Community Service.* Lanham, MD: Rowman & Littlefield, 2000.

Dunlap, M., Scoggin, J., Green, P., and Davi, A. "White Students' Experiences of Privilege and Socioeconomic Disparities: Toward a Theoretical Model." *Michigan Journal of Community Service Learning,* 2007, *13*(2), 19–30.

Evans, S. Y., Taylor, C., Dunlap, M., and Miller, D. *African Americans and Community Engagement in Higher Education.* New York: SUNY Press, in press.

Eyler, J., Giles, D., and Schmiede, A. *A Practitioner's Guide to Reflection in Service-Learning: Student Voices and Reflections.* Nashville, TN: Vanderbilt University, 1996.

Helms, J. E. *Black and White Racial Identity: Theory, Research and Practice.* Westport, CT: Greenwood Press, 1990.

Kubler-Ross, E. *On Death and Dying.* New York: Macmillan, 1970.

McIntosh, P. "White Privilege: Unpacking the Invisible Knapsack." *Independent School,* 1990, *49*(2), 31–39.

Tatum, B. "Talking about Race: The Application of Racial Identity Development Theory in the Classroom." *Harvard Educational Review,* 1992, *62*(1), 1–24.

Webster, N., and Hoover, T. "Impact of an Urban Service Learning Experience on Agricultural Education Students." *Journal of Agricultural Education,* 2006, *47*(4), 91–101.

Webster, N., and Ingram, P. "Exploring the Challenges for Extension Educators Working in Urban Communities." *Journal of Extension,* July 2007, *45*(3). http://www.joe.org/joe/2007june/iw3.shtml.

CHAPTER NINE

LEADERSHIP EDUCATION AND THE REVITALIZATION OF PUBLIC LIFE

Nicholas V. Longo and Marguerite S. Shaffer

> *It is time for citizens to strike out in new directions and refashion our ideas about community leadership. We need some leadership in changing our concept of leadership.*
> —David Mathews (1996, p. 17)

> *In the beginning, I had a very narrow view of a leader as an individualistic, in-charge person who pulled or pushed others along with them. Having a better understanding of the way communities are structured and function, I now see that leaders do not necessarily have to be out in front of an issue, but rather need only to stand by their own convictions and often will work mutually with other leaders in their efforts.*
> —Miami University Wilks Scholar

In an age of divisive, zero-sum politics and global consumer culture, it is difficult to imagine a vibrant democratic public, let alone publicly empowered citizen leadership. Our students make this painfully clear. Having come of age in a culture of increased privatization and renewed individualism, they have been socialized to think of themselves as consumers and measure their accomplishments according to marketplace standards. As William Galston (2004) has noted, today's young adults "have confidence in personalized acts with consequences they can see for themselves; they have less confidence in collective actions (especially those undertaken through public institutions), whose consequences they see as remote, opaque, and impossible to control" (p. 263).

It also seems abundantly clear, given the problems confronting us—among them intractable global poverty, pervasive educational inequity, the spread of HIV/AIDS, and the decline in civic participation—that the dominant model of the "heroic" or "charismatic" person with authority leading a cadre of followers is no longer acceptable (Heifetz, 1994). Likewise, the established model of teaching and learning in higher education, in which students are filled up with knowledge and credentialed by scholarly experts, is ineffective in preparing students to address these problems. Higher education cannot simply be a site for the creation and acquisition of knowledge for its own sake, nor can our nation's colleges and universities operate under an efficiency-driven, customer service model that views preparing students for the workforce as its top priority.

Rather, colleges and universities must be engaged in leadership for the diverse democracy of the twenty-first century. In fact, higher education is perhaps the single most important catalyst not only for educating the next generation for a new kind of leadership but also for mobilizing institutional resources to engage in the type of collaborative problem solving necessary to address difficult public issues. Thus, leadership education needs to be relational, collaborative, community based, and perhaps most important, public. It also must be integrally connected to the kind of learning that asks students to see themselves as creators and agents actively shaping local and global communities, rather than as passive consumers of their education and the broader culture.

This chapter begins with an overview of models of leadership development. After describing the leadership efforts of the Highlander Folk School during the civil rights movement, to give some historical context to the theory and practice of leadership education on college campuses today, the core of this chapter presents an emerging program for putting this conception of leadership into practice at one institution of higher education. It describes the Harry T. Wilks Leadership Institute at Miami University in Oxford, Ohio, as a case study of the development of a national model for public leadership that connects leadership education with civic engagement through curricular and cocurricular initiatives in southwest Ohio. The Wilks Institute and, more specifically, an interdisciplinary think tank in American studies called Acting Locally serve as promising examples for thinking differently about leadership education for democracy. Building from these examples, the chapter concludes by offering recommendations for connecting leadership education with civic engagement that are applicable to all types of institutions.

COUNTERING THE DOMINANT MODEL OF LEADERSHIP DEVELOPMENT

The tensions between individualism and community and between private and public goods have a long and deep history in the United States. From its earliest days, ideals of biblical mission and republican virtue have vied with the realities of frontier self-reliance and liberal individualism (Bellah, Madsen, Sullivan, Swidler, and Tipton, 1985). Although the ideal of the independent, successful individual embodied in Benjamin Franklin's model for personal success and Ralph Waldo Emerson's notion of self-reliance has been dominant in American culture, our history is marked with moments from the abolitionist movement to the Progressive Era, from the New Deal to the civil rights movement, in which civic engagement and commitment to community have sought to turn individual self-interest toward the larger public good. We believe that American culture is currently in the midst of another one of these moments. An understanding of these trends, especially in the context of higher education, is important for designing leadership education programs that create opportunities for students to act as engaged citizens.

The past thirty years have witnessed a dramatic shift away from investing in the public good toward individual interests and private concerns. The election of Ronald Reagan in 1980 solidified the turn away from issues of civil rights and social justice that defined the culture of the 1960s. Reagan's presidency ushered in an era of policy that promoted small government, deregulation of public utilities, and supply-side economics. The emerging culture of conservatism cast big government as a villain, pilloried the welfare system, and demonized all forms of taxation. Government, politicians, and the public became suspect, while the ideal of the private individual, the self-made man, and the free market resurged. As the private sphere flourished, consumer values of therapeutic self-fulfillment and expressive individualism recast public culture in terms of the marketplace. Historian Lizbeth Cohen (2003) has extensively documented this "consumerization of the Republic" in which citizens have become shoppers and public institutions have become an extension of the marketplace (p. 369). "The market," according to Galston (2004), "has become more pervasive during the past generation as organizing metaphor and as daily experience, [and] the range of opportunities to develop non-market skills and dispositions has narrowed" (p. 263).

The loss of public life is reflected in the predominant model of leadership that promotes individual accomplishment and personal success. This idea of leadership can be seen everywhere. For example, in American politics, candidates are treated like celebrities, while citizens are treated like spectators. Equally alarming is the suggestion that arose after the events of September 11, 2001, that the best way for ordinary Americans to respond to the attacks against the United States was to "go shopping" (Pelligrini, 2007).

On a more hopeful note, the individualistic, consumer-driven model is being called into question by rising concerns over the decline in civic life. There are countertrends emerging where "citizens are at the center," as Harry Boyte (2004), Cynthia Gibson (2006), Peter Levine (2006), and others have argued. This citizen-centered approach has taken many forms and is rooted in the ideals of republicanism, with its grounding in classical ideals of civic virtue and in the theory and practice of John Dewey, Jane Addams, Ella Baker, and Myles Horton. Although too often seen as outside the domain of leadership education in higher education, these developments inform some of the earliest efforts to transform the nature of leadership education. For instance, David Mathews (1996) describes the importance of "leaderful communities," which make leadership "the responsibility of the many" (p. 9). Drawing on the research of the Kettering Foundation, Mathews finds that the challenges we face require a new conception of leadership that includes people from every facet of a community contributing their talents. Likewise, Benjamin Barber (1998) argues that in a strong democracy there is a need for strong citizens, not strong leaders. Barber's point is that when leadership is defined by charismatic individuals, the result is disempowered citizens.

More engaged and relational models have emerged over the past four decades from leadership scholars and practitioners as well (Goethals and Sorenson, 2006; Roberts, 2007). These models vary from the influential "servant leadership" model (Greenleaf, 1991) to those advocating leadership as a "relational and ethical process of people together attempting to accomplish positive change" (Komives, Lucas, and MacMahon, 2007, p. ix). In perhaps the most promising approach to leadership development, Ronald Heifetz and his colleagues at Harvard offer an alternative to the individual model of leadership by defining leadership as "mobilizing people to tackle tough problems" (Heifetz, 1994, p. 15; see also Parks, 2005).

In addition, building on what has been termed the "social change model of leadership development" (Higher Education Research Institute, 1996), a report for the Kellogg Foundation argues that "colleges and universities provide rich opportunities for recruiting and developing leaders through the curriculum and co-curriculum" (Astin and Astin, 2000, p. 3). In calling for greater attention to leadership development in higher education, *Leadership Reconsidered* (Astin and Astin, 2000) declares: "If the next generation of citizen leaders is to be engaged and committed to leading for the common good, then the institutions which nurture them must be engaged in the work of the society and the community, modeling effective leadership and problem solving skills, demonstrating how to accomplish change for the common good" (p. 2).

Toward an Alternative Conception of Public Leadership: The Highlander Folk School

In this chapter, we call for a different but related model of public leadership that is rooted in the community-based struggles for the fullest promise of democracy. This alternative conception of leadership for the common good has taken shape throughout American history. Perhaps not surprisingly, during the 1950s and 1960s, a public idea of leadership education emerged in the heart of the civil rights movement through the efforts of the Highlander Folk School.

The Highlander Folk School was founded in 1932 by legendary democratic educator Myles Horton in the poor, rural area near the small Cumberland Plateau town of Monteagle, Tennessee. After providing educational training for southern unions in the 1930s and 1940s during the labor movement, Highlander became a key partner and gathering place for black and white civil rights activists during the 1950s and 1960s. In a beautiful, natural setting, Highlander brought black and white community leaders together for workshop retreats, or "learning circles," to deliberate and plan for collaborative action in their home communities.

Highlander helped empower an array of leaders during the civil rights movement, including Fannie Lou Hamer, Ella Baker, John Lewis, Bob Moses, and many others. Its most notable student, Rosa Parks, attended a workshop at Highlander the summer before initiating the bus boycott in Montgomery, Alabama, on December 1, 1955.

While the dominant narrative of Rosa Parks most often deeply resembles the individual model of leadership that she was simply a poor, tired seamstress who ignited a movement through her spontaneous refusal to give up her seat on a segregated bus, this is inaccurate. In fact, Parks had been a community leader for many years and was the executive secretary of the National Association for the Advancement of Colored People in Montgomery. She was sent by several local organizations to attend the Highlander workshop on school desegregation because of her local leadership in Montgomery. Learning with others at Highlander proved powerful for Parks. "At Highlander, I found out for the first time in my adult life that this could be a unified society, that there was such a thing as people of different races and backgrounds meeting together in workshops, and living together in peace and harmony," she later reflected (Horton, 1998, pp. 149–150).

And yet the power of the public leadership approach is not individual stories of success. Highlander minimized the importance of positional leadership and technical expertise, instead focusing on the capacity of ordinary people—often with little formal education—to define and then solve problems collectively. Thus, Highlander's approach to leadership education, which can be a model for colleges and universities today, is best expressed in what was a mantra for the civil rights movement: "we are the ones we've been waiting for."

One powerful example of this idea of leadership was seen in the early 1950s through the creation of a leadership and educational program called the Citizenship Schools, arguably the most successful leadership and educational program of the Highlander Folk School and the civil rights movement. Started on Johns Island, one of the largest of the South Carolina Sea Islands, the Citizenship Schools enabled more than a thousand volunteer educators to teach literacy to tens of thousands of African Americans across the South (Clark, 1965). While the direct purpose was using informal education to teach literacy, the larger vision was leadership development, which enabled African Americans to register to vote and, more important, to become first-class citizens.

The selection of the first teacher for the Citizenship Schools is instructive of the conception of leadership. Aware of the limitations of professional expertise, Myles Horton and Septima Clark didn't want a certified teacher because "people with teaching experience would likely impose their schooling methodology on the students and be judgmental" (Horton, 1998, p. 101). Horton and Clark wanted a community-oriented, nonhierarchical leader. Thus, Highlander recruited Bernice Robinson, a black beautician with no training, as a teacher. At first Robinson was hesitant, explaining, "I'm a beautician. I don't know anything about teaching." But Horton and Clark were adamant. Clark later explained, "We knew that she had the most important quality, the ability to listen to people" (Brown, 1990, p. 49).

In 1956, after three months of planning, Robinson began the first class in the back room of a cooperative store by insisting on the theme that would epitomize the Citizenship Schools: we are all teachers and leaders. "I am not a teacher, we are here to learn together. You are going to teach me as much as I'm going to teach you" (Horton, 1998, p. 103). Thus, like all the workshops held at Highlander, the Citizenship Schools were based on the concept that all participants could be contributors and leaders and acknowledged the potential of leadership as a group endeavor. "Our desire is to empower people collectively, not individually," Horton explained (1998, p. 157).

HARRY T. WILKS LEADERSHIP INSTITUTE AT MIAMI UNIVERSITY

As a public university with regional campuses that has made an institutional commitment to leadership over the past decade, Miami University offers an array of curricular and cocurricular leadership programs. It also offers multiple venues for exploring an alternative model of leadership in higher education and public culture (Roberts, 2001, 2007). And while Miami has an array of leadership programs and curricula, including the high-level Integrating Leadership Committee convened by the Office of the Provost and the vice president of student affairs, the newly created Harry T. Wilks Leadership Institute and its focus on collaborative efforts that connect leadership education with civic engagement provides an innovative model for the role of higher education in supporting public leadership. In the tradition of the Highlander Folk School, where students became leaders by practicing leadership together on the issues that most affected them, the Wilks Institute is grounded in the idea that "the best way of educating people is to give them an experience that embodies what you are trying to teach" (Horton, 1998, p. 68).

The Wilks Institute is committed to promoting community-based learning experiences that prepare students to become engaged public leaders and informed global citizens while also enriching and giving back to the communities that surround and support Miami University. By connecting students and communities, in southwest Ohio and around the world, the Wilks Institute advances the understanding and practice of the types of engaged leadership necessary for building a vibrant democratic society today and in the future. With its emphasis on public leadership, the Wilks Institute sponsors a series of innovative civic engagement programs, including courses focused on public engagement and community learning, a high school leadership program, international leadership capacity development, engaged scholarship, and a series of speakers and symposiums promoting leadership for the public good.

Founded through a $5 million gift from philanthropist and alumnus Harry T. Wilks, the institute was launched in 2003 with a sense of urgency about the lack of leadership in our democracy. In the words of the bipartisan National Commission on Civic Renewal (1998): "In a time that cries out for civic action, we are in danger of becoming a nation of spectators" (p. 6). And yet our students are also volunteering in record numbers and engaged in "alternative politics" characterized by community service and relational civic action (Long, 2002). A series of studies has documented that while college students see politics as corrupt, irrelevant, and unresponsive, they tend to try to make change through community service (Longo and Meyer, 2006). Further, young people's views on civic engagement and leadership suggest that giving them the space to explore a model of leadership that is more relational, community based, and collaborative is congruent with how they view leadership in the community. According to research commissioned by Public Allies, for example, young people tend to view leadership as less hierarchical and more collaborative, more bottom-up than top-down, and welcoming, rather than fearful, of diversity. As a result, more and more young people who were involved in community service during high school are seeking opportunities in college to develop new models for addressing problems in local communities that challenge the dominant model of leadership and also value their voices and perspectives (Peter D. Hart Research Associates, 1998).

With this understanding, the Wilks Institute provides programs that promote public leadership and operates with a model of leadership that reflects this approach. For example, the institute is jointly housed in academic and student affairs. Cutting across the traditional compartmentalization that categorizes colleges and universities, the collaboration between student and academic affairs facilitates the connection of public engagement to student life and to the core academic mission of the university.

Another example of the collaboration is CHANGE, a newly created living-learning community for first-year students interested in leadership and civic engagement. In the development of this program, the Wilks Institute worked closely with the Office of Residence Life and several other leadership programs on campus to reimagine how a living-learning community focused on leadership could move beyond positional leadership. This new community replaces a formerly successful living-learning community called Leadership, Excellence, Community, because it was determined that this name implied too much of a positional and individual conception of leadership. CHANGE, on the other hand, focuses on civic leadership and more aptly describes its focus as "emerging community leaders who are dedicated to making the world a better place" among peers who are working toward "finding their voices, building community, and taking positive action on Miami's campus and beyond" (Miami University Office of Residential Life, 2007, p. 5). The new living-learning community features courses on leadership, including a new course entitled Leadership for the Public Good, which uses interdisciplinary scholarship of citizenship, citizenship education, and leadership studies to explore what it means to work in public life and lead for the public good in local, national, and international contexts.

In addition, the Wilks Institute organized a university/school/community project that used public art to promote community leadership. Faculty members and students from the art department partnered with their counterparts from Hamilton High School to create a series of murals at the Booker T. Washington Center, a local community center in the heart of the African American community in Hamilton, Ohio. The ideas for the murals were developed from the stories of local residents who participated in the center over the past decades. After hearing the stories, high school and college students worked in small teams to create several murals to celebrate and embody the history and vibrancy of the community. Given the success of the partnership, the art department again offered the community art course in the spring of 2008 and partnered with Hamilton High School students and teachers to develop new public art in the local community.

To develop additional partnerships with academic departments, the Wilks Institute also supports faculty development through workshops and fellowships to raise faculty awareness of the connections between knowledge production and civic, social, and ethical issues. A faculty learning community focused on community-based education facilitates the development of engaged courses.

Finally, the Wilks Institute has initiated the first in a series of interdisciplinary think tanks to embed public engagement and community leadership into the curriculum through university departments and programs. The first think tank, Acting Locally, an interdisciplinary program located within American studies, is the flagship initiative of the Wilks Institute and is described in detail next. And new think tanks are being developed to embed public engagement and community leadership courses in other departments on campus.

ACTING LOCALLY THINK TANK

> *[Wilks Acting Locally] is very different because we are learning from going out and doing. Most other classes you learn from a book, and in this class you learn from engaging with the community, other students, and the professors.*
> —*Miami University Wilks Scholar*

The first think tank sponsored by the Wilks Institute, Acting Locally: Civic Learning and Civic Leadership in Southwestern Ohio, promotes public leadership through a community-based exploration of the impact of globalization on local communities. Conceived in the fall of 2003 by faculty associated with the American studies program with support from the Office of the Provost and the Miami University Center for Community Engagement in the Over-the-Rhine neighborhood of Cincinnati, the project explores the ways in which local communities of different sorts are created, challenged, transformed, and sustained in a world where global and local forces intersect in complex ways. The first cohort of students enrolled in the two-year think tank curriculum in the fall of 2006.

Acting Locally targets three locales in southwest Ohio—the Over-the-Rhine neighborhood, the city of Hamilton, and rural Butler County—to explore how globalization has affected a decaying urban center, an expanding postindustrial metropolitan city, and a rural agricultural community. Specifically, these three sites provide an opportunity to study and act on a range of topics, including issues of race and class in the context of urban development and decay; increased Latino immigration and migration in the context of service-sector expansion; and agricultural, environmental, and community sustainability in the context of metropolitan sprawl and rural transformation. Designed as an effort to enhance students' understanding of the connections between theory and practice and between analysis and agency, the project centers on the integral relationship between learning and leadership. As one Wilks Scholar explains, "This process has made me see that as students we have so much more power and credibility than I ever thought possible."

Acting Locally grew out of a larger curricular reassessment of the American studies program at Miami. Established in 1944, the program is one of the oldest interdisciplinary programs at the university and among the first wave of undergraduate American studies programs established in the United States. In 2002, the program was one of twenty-five humanities departments and programs nationally to be awarded a National Endowment for the Humanities grant to assess and reenvision its curriculum. The effort began with broad questions: What does it mean to study American culture? Why is it important to do so? As faculty members examined the tensions between national identity and common culture on the one hand and diversity and multiculturalism on the other, they arrived at the concept of "public culture." Faculty then framed additional questions to address the core issues of American studies: What does it mean to be American? How, if at all, do diverse cultures come together in the United States in terms of public culture to examine the process by which diverse individuals negotiate shared meaning? It was important to offer a curriculum that did more than just provide students with the skills to analyze American culture. Faculty members wanted them to understand that they were also *shapers* of American culture. The curricular model that resulted centers on notions of the public: public action, public discourse, public image, public space, public identity, and public belonging. The goal is to support a curriculum that allows students to see the connections between their individual beliefs, values, and actions, and the common cultures they share and create.

These ideas laid the preliminary groundwork for the concept of public leadership that provided the impetus and framework for the Acting Locally think tank project. Faculty began to conceptualize courses that explored issues of identity, diversity, community, and public culture and to develop assignments that encouraged students to link their individual experiences with the larger culture and to move from critical analysis to cultural agency. Students were then propelled to explore bigger questions about the relationship between the global and the local and about developing a shared identity in an increasingly global and postnational culture. As the concept of Acting Locally emerged from these discussions, the faculty imagined an interdisciplinary, community-based curriculum in which a group of selected students and faculty members could partner with local communities to explore the intersections between globalization and local transformation. It was also crucial that students and faculty connect with local communities in an effort to comprehend and experience key civic issues—such as rapid suburbanization, environmental degradation, increased immigration and migration, urban decay, poverty, and racism—as more than abstractions. Thus, faculty sought to integrate learning and leadership through community interaction and problem solving in the three distinct communities and to create a prototype model for a collaborative and interactive curriculum in which students, faculty, and community members work together to share resources, make connections, and develop projects that link critical thinking and learning with public leadership and community development.

As a way to counter the dominant model of the first two years of college, students who are accepted in the Acting Locally program, called Wilks Scholars, enroll as a group in two years of team-taught courses. The cohort model allows students and faculty to build and sustain deeper relationships both with each other and with their community partners. In the first year, Wilks Scholars take an introductory course that critically examines theories of globalization. They then move on to a course on community engagement, in which they engage in guided experiential learning, contextualizing these theories of globalization in local situations. These two courses are based on a standard classroom pedagogical model, encompassing basic concepts, analytical skills, research tools, fieldwork techniques, and service-learning experiences. Faculty members—who are affiliated with American studies and trained in disciplines ranging from geography and history, to political science and Spanish—are challenged to move beyond the role of scholarly expert and to embrace a more democratic form of teaching and learning. This means pushing the boundaries of the traditional classroom, sharing authority with students and community partners, and becoming a facilitator and cocreator of knowledge. In this way, students not only are engaged in public leadership but also are given the opportunity to take on leadership roles in defining the learning process.

Students then participate in a community immersion experience that takes the form of a weeklong summer workshop. Here there is a shift to student-directed learning, drawing from the learning partnership model that stipulates, "Knowledge is mutually constructed via the sharing of experience and authority" (Baxter Magolda, 2004, p. xix). During the summer workshop, students begin to use what they have learned to initiate and expand dialogue with community members to lay the groundwork for community partnerships. In the process, students work together with faculty to define and agree on learning objectives, course material, and assessment criteria. They assume responsibility for working collaboratively to define a community partnership project. In the second year, students complete a yearlong capstone experience focused on developing and implementing their community partnership project.

The first group of Wilks Scholars completed the two-year sequence in the spring of 2008. The projects they developed, which emerged from the students and faculty collaborations in the community, were ambitious and innovative. Students partnered with Latino immigrants in Hamilton to create a series of ongoing Spanish-English language and cultural exchanges in local restaurants, churches, and community organizations using a nonprofessional, democratic approach that centers on one-on-one learning partnerships. Students also collaborated with Latino business owners to host a series of community events, including a neighborhood cleanup and festival, to celebrate and highlight the contribution that immigrants make to this changing industrial city. Students partnered with local farmers to create and sustain a local food network in rural Butler County, including hosting a local-foods dinner to build support for local farmers and developing a food guide to publicize local food options. Finally, students worked on creating a neighborhood coffee shop, along with a job skills training internship program in Over-the-Rhine for former felons.

The goal of this sequence is to draw connections between knowledge production, community engagement, and public leadership. It is critical that students see that knowledge generated in the classroom can be used in partnership with communities to serve the larger needs of society and that knowledge generated in the community is just as valid as curricular knowledge. In addition, the courses are designed to enable students to move from abstract critical thinking to engaged thinking and acting. As students share authority with each other, with faculty members, and with community members, they establish relationships that extend beyond the classroom and begin to appreciate the process of collaborative learning. Most important, students come to understand that their knowledge can only be put into action through these relationships.

This kind of engaged learning can be transformational for students. As one Wilks Scholar explains, "Before, I thought my time as a Miami student was merely an opportunity to gather information in classes and then disengage when I stepped out of the classroom. I now view my time as a student as an opportunity to learn from both my classes and from the community, as a time to build new relationships, and as a chance to understand my place as a member of a community." Another Wilks Scholar wrote, "I realize I am an asset. Though I am younger and have little/no money, my presence still matters and I can still influence what is happening in my communities. My voice is not softer than others, and I am at an institute where I can have the backing of my peers, and as a member of such a large group I have the ability to be noticed and make changes." Students have begun to integrate their academic learning with community learning and action. They see that they can effect purposeful and positive change in their communities. They are beginning to see themselves as public leaders.

Building on the projects developed by this first group of Wilks Scholars, a new cohort of students was recruited to the Acting Locally think tank for fall 2008. Several former Wilks Scholars are community assistants, serving as bridges between the classroom and the community. Although the first cohort of Wilks Scholars did not live together, the second cohort is part of a student-directed living-learning community. This vibrant residential community also provides scholarships to student members.

In addition, the Wilks Institute seeks new think tank proposals focused on public engagement and community leadership from all Miami academic departments and programs. The goal of the institute is to continually provide seed money to departments, programs, and faculty members to support and sustain the integration of permanent public leadership experiences throughout the university curriculum.

CONCLUSION

All the programs supported by the Wilks Institute are grounded in the idea that knowledge is actionable and that individuals coming together to cocreate knowledge empowers them to make positive change in the world around them. Although Miami University benefits from having a funded institute to coordinate and support these kinds of public leadership initiatives, many of these programs can be developed and supported through existing academic and administrative programs. The idea is to shift the driving question from "How does this knowledge or this experience serve me?" to "How can this knowledge or experience be used to serve the broader public?"

Thus, promoting and supporting public leadership means fundamentally changing the way knowledge production and dissemination has been conceptualized at institutions of higher education in recent years. It means shifting the focus of colleges and universities away from the customer service, credential-generating model toward revitalizing the core mission of higher education to create responsible, ethical, and engaged citizens. It means moving from a predominantly individual, private, economic frame to an ecological frame that is based on the principle of interdependence.

The Wilks Institute provides a model for reframing leadership education as comprehensive, relational, and public (Cremin, 1976). When conceptualized in broad terms, this task can seem daunting. However, what our experience has shown us is that seemingly small interventions can have a huge impact.

Thinking *comprehensively* about leadership involves several related aspects. First, it breaks down the leader-follower dichotomy and acknowledges that, as the radically democratic civil rights organizer Ella Baker would argue, "Strong people don't need strong leaders" (Ransby, 2003). Leadership education, thus, means creating space for all stakeholders in higher education (students, faculty, staff, community partners) to use their assets toward public problem solving while, at the same time, further developing their leadership capacity. We have learned that this can begin with the small act of faculty sharing authority with students in their courses, and it can flourish when students and faculty are given the opportunity to move beyond the confines of the traditional semester-long course to address broader, inherently interdisciplinary, questions connected to the larger public good.

Next, thinking comprehensively means considering and valuing all the places where leadership education might take place, including the classroom, the cocurriculum, the residence halls, and the community. Bureaucratic organizational silos discourage collaborative learning. Often universities and colleges isolate or separate themselves from their surrounding communities; academic affairs is walled off from student affairs; sciences are completely divorced from the humanities. However, we have found that community members, students, and most faculty do not think in terms of organizational bureaucratic structures. They want to make connections and forge partnerships. Placing the university's responsibility to the public good over the university's attachment to organizational structure expands opportunities for collaborative learning, which is central to leadership education.

Thinking comprehensively also means thinking about leadership education as part of an ongoing developmental process. The Wilks Institute begins with high school students, offering leadership conferences that bring together students and faculty from approximately twenty high schools in southwest Ohio to build relationships and civic skills. Its programs at Miami span the entire undergraduate experience, commencing with a first-year living-learning community focused on leadership. Courses on public and community leadership range from first-year seminars to capstones courses. In summer 2008, the Wilks Institute cosponsored a national symposium at Miami University on the role of colleges and universities in developing student leadership through civic engagement with leading national organizations, including the McCormick Tribune Foundation, the Center for Information & Research on Civic Learning

& Engagement, Illinois Campus Compact, and Public Allies. The symposium focused on what it takes to educate for publicly engaged leadership among the next generation through presentations and conversations on cutting-edge practices from a diverse range of institutions of higher education and nonprofit partners.

Leadership education should also be *relational*. A key dimension of this type of relationship building is rethinking the more traditional academic model, asking for a longer commitment from students and faculty, and creating sustained university-community partnerships. As described earlier, Acting Locally requires much more than the usual one-term commitment; students and faculty commit to two years of intensive community engagement. This allows deeper relationships not only among the students and faculty but, more important, with the community. And it allows this model of public leadership to go beyond simple volunteerism. As a Wilks Scholar explained, "I plan on establishing as many relationships as I can with people in the community and working with them to help develop their talents and gifts, rather than myself coming in and telling people what I think would work for them."

Finally, leadership education, as this chapter has argued throughout, must be *public*. This means students must be given the opportunity to link theory and practice—to understand that knowledge alone is powerless; it only becomes meaningful when people act on it. Our experience with the Wilks Institute has shown us that when leadership education is connected with community engagement, it becomes clear that leadership can transform publics as well as individuals. An underlying assumption of the work of the Wilks Institute is that by educating a new generation for citizen leadership, we can also partner with our students in the revitalization of public life.

References

Astin, A., and Astin, H. *Leadership Reconsidered: Engaging Higher Education in Social Change*. Ann Arbor, MI: Kellogg Foundation, 2000.

Barber, B. "Neither Leaders nor Followers: Citizenship under Strong Democracy." In B. Barber, *A Passion for Democracy: American Essays*. Princeton, NJ: Princeton University Press, 1998.

Baxter Magolda, M., and King, P. M. *Learning Partnerships: Theory and Models of Practice to Educate for Self-Authorship*. Sterling, VA: Stylus, 2004.

Bellah, R. N., Madsen, R., Sullivan, W. M., Swidler, A., and Tipton, S. M. *Habits of the Heart: Individualism and Commitment in American Life.* New York: Harper & Row, 1985.

Boyte, H. C. *Everyday Politics: Reconnecting Citizens and Public Life.* Philadelphia: University of Pennsylvania Press, 2004.

Brown, C. S. *Ready from Within: Septima Clark and the Civil Rights Movement.* Trenton, NJ: Africa World Press, 1990.

Clark, S. "Southern Christian Leadership Conference Education Program." Horton Papers: Box 10, Folder 9, May 14, 1965.

Cohen, L. *A Consumers' Republic: The Politics of Mass Consumption in Postwar America.* New York: Knopf, 2003.

Cremin, L. *Public Education.* New York: Basic Books, 1976.

Galston, W. A. "Civic Education and Political Participation." *PS: Political Science & Politics,* 2004, *37,* 263–266.

Gibson, C. *Citizens at the Center: A New Approach to Civic Engagement.* Washington, DC: Case Foundation, 2006.

Goethals, G., and Sorenson, G. *The Quest for a General Theory of Leadership.* Northampton, MA: Edward Elgar Publishing, 2006.

Greenleaf, R. K. *The Servant as Leader.* Indianapolis, IN: Robert Greenleaf Center for Servant Leadership, 1991.

Heifetz, R. *Leadership without Easy Answers.* Cambridge, MA: Harvard University Press, 1994.

Higher Education Research Institute. *A Social Change Model of Leadership Development.* Los Angeles: University of California at Los Angeles, 1996.

Horton, M. *The Long Haul: An Autobiography.* New York: Teacher's College Press, 1998.

Komives, S., Lucas. N., and MacMahon, T. *Exploring Leadership: For College Students Who Want to Make a Difference.* San Francisco: Jossey-Bass, 2007.

Levine, P. "Civic Renewal in America." *Philosophy and Public Policy Quarterly,* 2006, *26*(1/2), 2–12.

Long, S. *The New Student Politics: The Wingspread Statement on Student Civic Engagement.* Providence, RI: Campus Compact, 2002.

Longo, N., and Meyer, R. *College Students and Politics: A Literature Review.* (Working Paper No. 46). College Park, MD: Center for Information & Research on Civic Learning & Engagement, 2006.

Mathews, D. "Why We Need to Change Our Concept of Community Leadership." *Community Education Journal,* Fall/Winter 1996, 9–18.

Miami University Office of Residential Life. "*Living on Campus: Housing and Meal Plans 2007–2008.*" Oxford, OH: Miami University Office of Residential Life, 2007.

National Commission on Civic Renewal. *A Nation of Spectators: How Civic Disengagement Weakens America and What We Can Do about It*. College Park, MD: National Commission on Civic Renewal, 1998.

Parks, S. D. *Leadership Can Be Taught*. San Francisco: Jossey-Bass, 2005.

Pelligrini, F. "The Bush Speech: How to Rally a Nation." *Time*, August 29, 2007.

Peter D. Hart Research Associates. *New Leadership for a New Century: Key Findings from a Study on Youth Leadership and Community Service*. Washington, DC: Hart Research Associates, 1998.

Ransby, B. *Ella Baker and the Black Freedom Movement: A Radical Democratic Vision*. Chapel Hill: University of North Carolina Press, 2003.

Roberts, D. "Miami's Leadership Commitment." In C. L. Outcalt, S. K. Faris, and K. N. McMahon, *Developing Non-Hierarchical Leaders on Campus*. Westport, CT: Greenwood, 2001.

Roberts, D. *Deeper Learning in Leadership: Helping College Students Find the Potential Within*. San Francisco: Jossey-Bass, 2007.

CHAPTER TEN

MOVING FROM SERVICE-LEARNING TO CIVIC ENGAGEMENT

Marshall Welch

Over the past decade, both the number of college students participating in community service and interest on the part of educators in preparing students for lives of civic engagement have risen. Historically, volunteerism and community service have focused on meeting an immediate community need. Service-learning adds the components of reflection and reciprocity and is defined as "a form of experiential education in which students engage in activities that address human and community needs together with structured opportunities intentionally designed to promote student learning and development" (Jacoby, 1996, p. 5). Most frequently, service-learning is the integration of service with disciplinary knowledge within an academic course. Proponents and practitioners of service-learning have recently been wondering whether it has been an effective pedagogy for empowering students to bring about positive social change.

Vogelgesang and Rhoads (2006) note that traditional mainstream approaches of service-learning offer students experiences in which they provide direct services to individuals in need that may promote a greater awareness of social issues but have limited to no direct impact on the underlying factors that contribute to those issues. The authors also observe that activism and service-learning have generally been perceived as distinct from one another. Likewise, service-learning educators have assiduously attempted to avoid embracing particular political stances in order to enable service-learning to appeal to all students. While remaining staunch advocates of service-learning, Morton and Enos (2002) characterized themselves as "friendly critics" of the pedagogy as they argued for redefining service-learning to go above and beyond its traditional apolitical orientation to become a political pedagogy that empowers both the community and students and promotes democratic process to bring about social change. Other friendly critics suggest that service-learning is a holdover of the charity model that emphasizes volunteerism rather than teaching about social and systems change (Kahne, Westheimer, and Rogers, 2000). Margaret Himley (2004) wonders whether service-learning focusing on social justice may inadvertently perpetuate oppression and exploitation through a mentality and practice of charity. This is reminiscent of Ivan Illich's provocative speech and essay "To Hell with Good Intentions" (1990) criticizing service activities in general.

New Approaches to Service-Learning

As a result, new models of community service and service-learning emphasizing civic engagement, social change, and social justice have begun to emerge (Vogelgesang and Rhoads, 2006). In this approach, activism and politics move from the margins to the center of learning as students and educators seek creative ways to move from service to civic engagement. In 2001, Campus Compact convened a group of students from across the country at the Johnson Foundation's Wingspread Conference Center to consider how service and politics might be combined to enhance students' civic engagement and efficacy for social change. The Wingspread summit led to two important initiatives: the publication of *The New Student Politics: The Wingspread Statement on Student Civic Engagement* (Long, 2002) and the birth of Raise Your Voice, a three-year campaign that involved hundreds of thousands of college students across the country. Funded by the Pew Charitable Trusts and organized by Campus Compact, the Raise Your Voice campaign empowered college students to use service-learning and other forms of civic engagement to promote political change.

Figure 10.1: Characteristics of Service-Politics

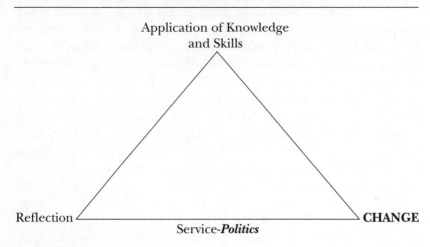

Application of Knowledge
and Skills

Reflection

Service-*Politics*

CHANGE

Its objectives were to increase college student involvement in public life and connect these actions with a larger national student movement around civic engagement, to document student civic engagement activities and issues that are important to college students, and to mobilize higher education in a way that gives more voice to students and makes civic engagement central to student learning. Student leadership teams in fourteen states coordinated a wide variety of activities. The campaign also produced a book: *Raise Your Voice: A Student Guide to Making Positive Social Change* (Cone, Kiesa, and Longo, 2006). The students at the Wingspread conference and those involved in Raise Your Voice saw various forms of service function as a political tool that is characterized as "service-politics" (Long, 2002, p. 18).

Action to bring about social change transcends the traditional apolitical approaches of service-learning. This subtle yet critical difference between application of knowledge and skills to meet a need and action to promote change, combined with critical reflection, is what characterizes service-politics, as depicted in figure 10.1. Service-politics is

the bridge between community service and conventional politics.
. . . Participation in community service is a form of unconventional political activity that can lead to social change, in which participants

primarily work outside of governmental institutions; service politics becomes the means through which students can move from community service to political engagement. Those who develop connections to larger systemic issues building on their roots in community service adopt a framework through which service politics leads to greater social change. (Long, 2002, p. 18)

Thus, service-politics uses service to help bring about policy and political change. This approach may provide a direct service to meet an immediate need while simultaneously effecting social change through an array of tactics, such as policy briefs, consciousness-raising, or community-based research. It would appear that tactics and related skills can be taught and applied in various types of experiential education that promote civic engagement.

There has been a growing interest in explicitly teaching the knowledge and skills required for civic engagement. This pedagogical focus has been referred to as "civic learning" or "civic/citizenship education" (Saltmarsh, 2001, 2004, 2005). In *Civic Engagement across the Curriculum,* Rick Battistoni (2002) provides resources for service-learning faculty across disciplines who seek to use service-learning as a pedagogy to increase civic knowledge and skills. He proposes five conceptual frameworks for civic education, together with their orientations to civic learning, associated civic skills, and disciplinary affinities. The five frameworks of civic learning are constitutional citizenship, communitarianism, participatory democracy, public work, and social capital (Battistoni, 2002). Chapter 3 provides an overview of the Civic Learning Spiral, a recent approach to education for civic engagement.

Educating Citizens: Preparing America's Undergraduates for Lives of Moral and Civic Responsibility (Colby, Ehrlich, Beaumont, and Stephens, 2003) describes the efforts of twelve colleges and universities that take holistic and intentional approaches to educating undergraduates for citizenship. Service-learning emerges as one of the most powerful pedagogies at these institutions for developing moral and civic responsibility. To expand civic learning into the political arena, a sequel, *Educating for Democracy: Preparing Undergraduates for Responsible Political Engagement* (Colby, Beaumont, Ehrlich, and Corngold, 2007), based on the Carnegie Foundation's Political Engagement Project, is a study of twenty-one courses and cocurricular programs that explicitly prepare students for democratic participation.

In a different vein, Dan W. Butin (2007) proposes an approach he calls "justice-learning" that lies at the intersection of service-learning and social justice education. The model builds on feminist poststructuralism, which advocates for social justice while being cognizant of cultural, political, and systemic issues at both the micro- and macrolevels that may perpetuate the oppressive practice of racism, classism, and heterosexual norms (Ellsworth, 1989; Gore, 1993; Jones, 2001; Lather, 1998). In this way, students explore deeper, underlying issues that instigate the need for service and activism while learning and working with the community. It is a messy process that includes reflection and dialogue that often promote debate and action. Justice-learning builds on Himley's observations (2004) that despite its limitations, service-learning "provides a space where students are confronted with the ambiguity, noise, and disruption of their way of thinking about and engaging with the world . . . [forcing] a reconsideration of the taken-for-granted quality of the structures and practices that, beforehand, seemed all too normal. Such service-learning becomes, to be precise, the condition of possibility for justice-oriented education" (Butin, 2007, p. 180). Thus, justice-learning is a process of critically reflecting on unexamined and dualistic thinking to help bring about social change (Butin, 2007).

An emerging body of literature in the area of educating for social justice is evidence of increasing interest in this topic. A brief list of examples of recent publications includes *Learning to Teach for Social Justice* (Darling-Hammond, French, and Paloma Garcia-Lopez, 2002); *Re-Framing Educational Politics for Social Justice* (Marshall and Gerstl-Pepin, 2004); *Race, Poverty, and Social Justice: Multidisciplinary Perspectives through Service Learning* (Calderón, 2007); *Social Work and Service Learning: Partnerships for Social Justice* (Nadel, Majewski, and Sullivan-Cosetti, 2007); and *The Spirit of Service: Exploring Faith, Service, and Social Justice in Higher Education* (Johnson and O'Grady, 2006). Similarly, an entire issue of the professional journal *Equity and Excellence in Education* (April 2007) was devoted to issues related to service-learning and social justice.

Conversely, there has been very little to no research on the impact of integrating service and service-learning with civic engagement or social justice. However, preliminary research has provided promising trends. An investigation of a service-learning course specifically designed to incorporate civic engagement skills and taught for three consecutive years consistently revealed significant student gains in measures of cognitive growth and citizenry skills (Welch, 2007; Welch and Taylor, 2006). Yan Wang and Robert Rodgers (2006) conducted a quasi-experimental investigation on the impact of service-learning and social justice on students' cognitive development. They used the Measure of Epistemological Reflection (MER) to compare students' cognitive growth related to social justice in six service-learning courses with and without an emphasis on social justice (Baxter Magolda and Porterfield, 1985). A multiple regression analysis was conducted using MER pretest scores, age, gender, and course as independent variables and incorporating the MER posttest scores as the dependent variable. Results of the study suggested that students in the social justice group had significantly higher MER posttest scores than students in the non-social-justice group. The researchers concluded that students' cognitive understanding of social justice was enhanced. While these preliminary results suggest service-learning can have a positive impact on students' sense of social justice, more research is necessary (Wang and Rodgers, 2006).

PROGRAM PROFILES

The evolution from volunteer service to civic engagement does not imply or constitute a continuum. In other words, neither students nor institutions necessarily begin their civic engagement with volunteering and "progress" to other, more complex forms. The examples offered in this section illustrate a variety of ways in which institutions have begun to incorporate civic engagement with community service and service-learning to promote social change or social justice. While each example has a focus on civic engagement or social justice, programs range from formal and structured academic opportunities, such as courses or research, to residential life and student organizations.

GEORGETOWN UNIVERSITY: THE CENTER FOR SOCIAL JUSTICE RESEARCH, TEACHING, AND SERVICE

The Center for Social Justice Research, Teaching, and Service at Georgetown University in Washington, DC, promotes and integrates community-based learning with community-based research to advance justice and the common good. Students are encouraged to develop projects to promote social justice, collaboration, and critical analysis of community issues in an attempt to minimize charity-oriented service. Guided by these three values, the student projects include conducting surveys, interviews, or focus groups; recording oral histories; developing asset maps; conducting policy research; writing grants; and participating in education and outreach programs.

There are four options for conducting projects. The Community-Based Learning Credit Program (CBLC) is student initiated, requiring forty hours per semester to earn one additional credit hour in a course related to the project. Goals for the CBLC are determined by the student, the agency representative, and the faculty member. A second option is faculty initiated and requires students to complete a defined community-based learning component of a class. A third option, also faculty initiated, enables students to earn an additional three credit hours by working on a project developed by the instructor or writing a research paper.

The fourth option is conducting community-based research through courses, as part of internship programs, or as independent projects (Strand, Marullo, Cutforth, Stoecker, and Donohue, 2003). For example, Sociology 437: Project DC Urban Research is a course in which students engage in community-based research projects working with a community partner to address a need identified by the partner. Student projects are comprehensive in scope. They include a final formal scholarly thesis consisting of research questions, methodology, and results as well as an extensive Web site with the description and mission of the community partners, the project itself and its products, reflections, institutional review board approval, related links, and final presentations.

There are a number of examples of community-based research projects ranging from health to housing. One study involved agency asset mapping to help combat sexually transmitted diseases.

Another project involved a series of focus groups to create a redevelopment plan for maintaining affordable living units in the District of Columbia and to support resident associations within the housing complexes to address various issues.

LIVING-LEARNING COMMUNITIES FOR SOCIAL JUSTICE AND CIVIC ENGAGEMENT

Discipline-based and other living-learning communities are flourishing on college campuses. However, residential communities focusing on social justice issues and civic engagement are a relatively new development in which students from various majors live and work together to bring about social change.

University of Wisconsin–Madison: Chadbourne Residential College

More than eight hundred undergraduate students participate in a living-learning community at the University of Wisconsin–Madison. The Chadbourne Residential College encourages active involvement and commitment to issues, activities, and programs focused on social change. Two of the groups within the residential college, Global Dialogues and the Social Justice Mission Group, work in partnership with the Morgridge Center for Public Service. In Global Dialogues, international and domestic students discuss, debate, and exchange ideas on an array of issues at the local, national, and international levels. The goal is to exchange perspectives in a respectful climate to gain an understanding of diverse global issues while fostering friendships. A student planning committee organizes the dialogue events on topics such as race, identity, gender, social justice, security, foreign policy, the media, globalization, and politics.

Colorado College: Mathis Hall

Sophomores at Colorado College live together and enroll in a yearlong course designed to teach specific civic skills that address social issues in the local community. The course, In Our Own Backyard: Social Justice in the Southwest, explores the ethical choices made by individuals and society related to social, environmental, and political issues in the American Southwest and the

Colorado Springs area. As residents, the students create a living charter and engage in community-building activities. The students also participate in a two-day retreat at the school cabin to develop leadership skills and plan community-based service-learning projects designed to address identified social issues.

Texas A&M University: L3C Program

The Leadership Living Learning Community (L3C) is composed of sixty-five first-year students from various majors. Students enroll in courses on leadership and peer mentoring that are team-taught by a student affairs professional and a faculty member. The program was named Leadership Program of the Year in 2006 by the Association of Leadership Educators. The L3C program exposes students to theoretically based concepts of leadership, including a relational leadership model that is centered on social justice, challenges freshmen to be globally oriented, stretches students in their development of self and others, and supports Texas A&M's core purpose of developing leaders of character dedicated to serving the greater good.

Columbia College: Social Justice Learning Community

Columbia College, a faith-based liberal arts institution for women in Columbia, South Carolina, offers a Social Justice Learning Community. This community promotes in-depth learning and reflection through communication, collaboration, and discussion of ideas and issues. The program is aligned with the school's mission and the social principles of the United Methodist Church. Approximately fifty courses address a variety of social justice issues and provide opportunities for students to examine social justice through interactive learning activities, case studies, and dialogue. Residents then collaborate to create action plans that address the issues.

UNIVERSITY OF MINNESOTA, MORRIS: CIVIC LEARNING IN STATISTICS COURSES

An innovative example of integrating civic engagement within a disciplinary context can be found at the University of Minnesota, Morris in an introductory course on statistics (Sungur, Winchester, Anderson, and Kim, 2006). Students work with community partners to identify a need leading to the collection and analysis of quantitative data over the course of the fifteen-week semester. They are required to conceptualize, implement, and interpret the findings of their studies and then clearly articulate those findings through narratives and charts to the cooperating agencies. In addition to traditional interpretation and scholarly reporting of results, students in the class create relevant graphic displays and short summaries of their findings for use by the local media. One student worked with the Minnesota Department of Administration to track the number of alcohol-related deaths in five counties as part of a statewide initiative on drunk driving. Another student monitored the increase in rates of children living in poverty in one county through a partnership with the Minnesota Department of Education.

While enhancing their learning of statistical procedures, students also learn from collaboration with community partners and about civic processes. Students learn firsthand about critical social issues and needs coupled with assimilating effective communication and problem-solving skills that enable them to work effectively with others. As a result, the learning experience reflects the pedagogy of engagement as characterized by Ann Colby et al. (2003), which includes a skill set of active learning, learning as a social process, and understanding that knowledge is shaped by contexts, reflective practice, and the capacity to represent an idea in more than one modality.

UNIVERSITY OF MASSACHUSETTS AMHERST: CITIZEN SCHOLARS PROGRAM

A conversation between two University of Massachusetts faculty members in a Washington, DC, train station led to the creation of the Citizen Scholars Program in 1998. The two instructors discussed how they could work together to create opportunities for students to develop their civic engagement skills as part of the undergraduate experience. From that initial conversation arose a three-year grant from the Corporation for National and Community Service that assisted in the development and implementation of the program. The Citizen Scholars Program consists of four service-learning courses designed to help students promote social change (Mitchell, 2007). Students receive a thousand dollars for participating in each of the two years of the program.

The first course, the Good Society, includes sixty hours of service while exploring what constitutes a good society. The Integrative Seminar is the second course, in which students either continue another sixty hours of service from their previous site or identify a new project. Students lead reflection discussions each week to process their experiences. The seminar is followed by Organizing for Change, a course in which students reflect on service experiences and weekly readings on social justice issues before developing and proposing a capstone experience for service and research in the community. The final course, Public Policy and Citizen Action, is the implementation of the capstone project coupled with weekly progress reports, reflection activities, a final essay, and an exit interview. Students also complete an elective course related to their studies and final project. The program includes an induction ceremony, a retreat, monthly gatherings, and a graduation celebration.

The Citizen Scholars Program is designed to help students develop knowledge, skills, and attitudes to be engaged citizens working with other students and community partners to build a socially just society. Student projects are tied to various courses designed as learning circles so participants actively teach, and learn with, each other under the guidance of a faculty member. The program has introduced students to important, yet often unseen, administrative aspects of community organization. As a result, students gain insights into the agency's infrastructure, its funding, and ways to organize grassroots efforts to eliminate the fundamental causes of social problems that the organization strives to eliminate. Some of the social change projects include successfully drafting legislation to increase resources for youth, improving the affordability of textbooks for university students, studying and advocating alternate energy sources, and developing a community-based economic system for local neighborhoods.

UNIVERSITY OF UTAH: SERVICE-POLITICS AND CIVIC ENGAGEMENT

Similar to the genesis of the program at the University of Massachusetts, the Lowell Bennion Community Service Center at the University of Utah created a program known as Service-Politics and Civic Engagement (SPACE) as the result of an informal student discussion on ethical consumerism (Chatwin, Gillespie, Looser, and Welch, 2006). Out of that discussion, students recognized the importance of educating their peers about the underlying issues that necessitate direct service. The goal of SPACE is to promote awareness and action through dialogue and service to help bring about change. The SPACE program integrates community service activities, a service-learning course within the Bennion Center, and outreach to other organizations on campus and in the community to learn and do more about social issues. As a student group, SPACE has hosted a number of forums and film viewings on national and global issues (such as immigration, mass transit, and the conflict in Sudan) and on local issues (such as mass transit and sustainability on campus). Representatives from both sides discuss the issues, and participants are offered an array of options to address those issues, such as contacting their state representative or signing petitions. Students either participate in a weeklong summer training retreat or enroll in a service-learning class designed to teach tactics and skills for service-politics and civic engagement. They learn how to create measurable goal statements and action plans and how to articulate specific goals by including components such as behavior/action, condition, criteria, and duration (Welch, 2004, 2007; Welch and Sheridan, 1995). Action plans include a matrix specifying roles of specific individuals, a list of necessary steps and resources, timelines, locations, and a product or outcome for each step. The course and training also involve collaborative skills, such as running meetings, decision making, problem solving, working with others, conflict management, and communication skills. Students also learn basic principles and practices of public relations. In the course, students apply these skills through working directly with an organization to create, implement, and assess activities that promote systemic change or address policy issues.

St. Mary's College of California: Walk the Talk Initiatives

In addition to promoting social justice in the community, many institutions of higher education are also focusing on what students can do on their own campuses. St. Mary's College of California is one of eighteen campuses selected by the Association of American Colleges and Universities (AAC&U) to participate in the Core Commitments Project, a two-year effort to promote personal and social responsibility among undergraduates. As part of the project, the campus created an ambitious program, entitled Walk the Talk, designed to integrate social justice throughout the curriculum. Courses focusing on social justice have been developed for the January term as well as the fall and spring semesters. Similarly, the college is adding community-based research to its justice and community minor.

Before being selected for the AAC&U project, students and faculty at St. Mary's College had already begun to infuse social justice into a variety of service-learning courses and projects. Examples of efforts include adopting a policy of selling fair-trade coffee at the student union and school sweatshirts in the bookstore that were not manufactured in sweatshops, advocating for a living wage for campus employees, and promoting environmental sustainability. One course on communication and social justice examines theories and principles of justice in the context of communication studies. Students in the course engage in community service, dialogue and deliberation, or projects to democratize the campus. An example of course projects involved expanding an English as a second language program for campus workers.

Another group of students worked off-campus by establishing an organic garden at an underresourced elementary school. In addition to the physical development of the garden space, volunteer students worked with students in the liberal and civic studies program in partnership with teachers at the school to create lesson plans. Campus efforts are coordinated through the Catholic Institute for Lasallian Social Action and the newly formed Social Justice Coordinating Committee, composed of representatives from various offices, such as campus ministries, student life, faculty development, and the Cummins Institute for Catholic Thought, Culture and Action.

TUFTS UNIVERSITY: MEDIA AND PUBLIC SERVICE PROGRAM

The Jonathan M. Tisch College of Citizenship and Public Service at Tufts University in Medford, Massachusetts, offers an array of programs that integrate academic experiences with social justice.

Its media and public service program was created in 2003 through a partnership with communications and media studies to promote the media and arts as an innovative and effective tool for teaching and promoting social change. The program brings community members, artists, students, and faculty together to engage in dialogue and action. Students produce films and other media materials addressing social issues that are presented through campus and local cable-TV channels, film festivals, and the Internet. Courses provide students with various avenues for production projects. One such course on producing films for social change allows students to research and produce documentary films on social issues that have an impact on the campus as well as the local and global communities. Students also critically examine stereotypes presented by and through the media.

UNIVERSITY OF WISCONSIN–STEVENS POINT: THE THAILAND PROJECT

The Thailand Project is a unique combination of using the arts for consciousness-raising and assisting children rescued from child prostitution in gaining an education. Joseph Quinnell, a senior at the University of Wisconsin–Stevens Point (UWSP), traveled to Thailand to document the sex trade industry through a photography exhibit for his class. In the process of capturing the painful scenes and stories from prostitutes, Quinnell also wanted to document hope and efforts to eradicate the sex trade. He visited the Development Education Program for Daughters and Community, a school that provides free education and counseling to children who have been saved from child prostitution and that was started by Nobel Peace Prize nominee Sompop Jantraka. Upon his return to UWSP, Quinnell displayed his photographs at a special showing as a way to incorporate the arts as a catalyst for social justice. As a result, ten UWSP students visited Thailand to engage in a service project at the school during their winter break. Students are now involved in various projects and campaigns for consciousness-raising to combat the child sex trade industry. Quinnell now works with university administration to bring graduates of the Thai school to earn a bachelor's degree at UWSP.

James Madison University: Orange Band

In 2004, a group of students at James Madison University created a grassroots initiative to promote civil dialogue incorporating the simple tool of an orange-colored band of cloth. According to one of the founders, Kai Degner, Orange Band emphasizes dialogue, education, and action over debate in a concerted effort to move away from polarizing talk-radio formats (Jones, 2004). The approach is straightforward and simple. Students write an issue, concern, or topic of interest on an orange strip of cloth and display it in some way, often as an armband, to promote dialogue. The organization characterizes itself as "Rock and Roll Democracy" and, in an essay with that title, lists three key goals:

Civil Discourse, or Respectful Conversation—We're yearning for rich conversations about things that matter, where no organizing body is telling us what should matter to us or how it should matter to us.

Social Capital, or Meaningful Relationships—We're yearning for quality connections with others, and conversation about issues important to us are a basis for meaningful relationships.

Civic Engagement, or Active Citizenship—We're yearning to feel like we have a chance to make a meaningful contribution to change things for the better—or to keep things from changing for the worse. (Degner, n.d.)

The Orange Band program has expanded to other campuses, including San Francisco State University, the University of Connecticut, the University of Oregon, the University of Utah, and Wartburg College.

Social Justice at Community Colleges

Social justice programs are not limited to four-year institutions. Despite a different mission and student population, community colleges have also begun to address social justice. Oakton Community College, located in Skokie, Illinois, has a service-learning program as well as a student club dedicated to social justice. The club, Students for Social Justice (S4SJ), is an extracurricular group committed to achieving genuine democracy and social justice in the United States and globally. The club provides educational events and activities to promote critical thinking and dialogue about various issues surrounding social justice. These issues include economic justice, environmental justice, human rights, and peace. Specific projects have focused on health care issues and oil drilling in the Arctic National Wildlife Refuge.

The Peace and Social Justice Institute at Pasco-Hernando Community College in Florida applies theoretical principles of peace pedagogy through workshops and classes. Students learn practical skills for the promotion of social change taught in ten different classes, including one service-learning course: Introduction to Peace Studies. An interdisciplinary perspective is applied to macro- and microlevels of conflict and conflict resolution. Service-learning projects include working with community agencies to address various types and instances of conflict.

MILLS COLLEGE ALUMNAE INVOLVEMENT

Providing opportunities to learn about and practice civic engagement need not be limited to current students, however, as evident by the efforts at the Institute for Civic Leadership at Mills College to include alumnae. The Institute for Civic Leadership (ICL) offers programs that advance the civic leadership capacities of women during the junior or senior year. Students engage in discipline-based analysis of civic leadership and social policy through projects linked to public policy and social change. The disciplines range from American studies to women's studies. ICL alumnae are eligible to receive grants to develop and complete a project the year following their graduation from the program. They attend an annual weekend conference to discuss their projects with other participants, faculty, and students associated with the ICL program. An impressive array of projects has been conducted in the arts, education, energy policy, faith and social justice, violence, and program analysis. One project, Gender in the Classroom: Classroom Text Analysis, involved a critical review of the textbooks used in two elementary schools to identify how the texts addressed gender stereotypes. The results of the project will be applied to promoting healthy and constructive interaction between the girls and boys in the classroom.

CONCLUSION

The intentional integration of service-learning and civic engagement with other approaches, like service-politics and justice-learning, are both provocative and controversial. When carefully organized and implemented, these approaches can yield substantial benefits in various contexts. Vogelgesang and Rhoads (2006) suggest they reflect Dewey's educational approach (1916) of ensuring that citizens are actively engaged in their communities. They also argue that such approaches have the potential to integrate students' learning with actual and meaningful social change by addressing critical issues.

However, there are challenges. One is how to integrate civic knowledge and skills within discipline-based courses that are not in political science or similar disciplinary areas. Although faculty may be interested in the civic dimensions of their discipline, they may be unfamiliar with how to teach the concepts and practices of civic engagement. Consequently, even faculty members who embrace the notion of service-learning to teach disciplinary content may lack the pedagogical techniques to promote civic learning. Faculty development and support for course design should be offered. Partnerships between faculty and student affairs professionals that strive to offer civic engagement opportunities related to the curriculum are also worth cultivating.

There are also ideological challenges. The concept of social justice implies taking sides and is often associated with partisan liberal activism (Butin, 2007; Westheimer and Kahne, 2007). Joel Westheimer and Joseph Kahne (2007) note resistance to the emerging paradigm of civic engagement and social justice. They cite numerous efforts by various organizations and interest groups to limit or eliminate courses that seemingly promote a liberal political agenda. A specific example is that the National Council for Accreditation of Teacher Education was pressured by groups such as the American Council of Trustees and Alumni (2006) to eliminate all language related to social justice in its accreditation standards (Westheimer and Kahne, 2007). Likewise, Dan W. Butin provides a critical examination of factors that limit the institutionalization of service-learning within higher education. He suggests that "service-learning has a progressive and liberal agenda under the guise of a universal transformative practice" (Butin, 2006, p. 483) that runs the risk of being attacked at best and misappropriated at worst. Butin further suggests that conservatives can argue that "service-learning offices are indoctrinating first-year students into biased, unscientific, and indefensible liberal groupthink practices" (p. 485). He goes on to illustrate the flaw in the argument that service-learning is a universalistic practice appropriate for all political perspectives by presenting a hypothetical counterexample in which Jerry Falwell's Liberty University requires students to block the entrance to an abortion clinic as part of a service-learning course that used reflection, learning circles, and portfolios documenting how their service was linked to the instructional objectives of the course.

Butin suggests the political dimension of service-learning is caught in a no-win situation. On one hand, service-learning faces criticism, censure, and sanctions if it incorporates liberal traditions of political transformation. On the other hand, if it remains apolitical or politically balanced, service-learning is limited in making any real differences in society. Butin claims he is not arguing that service-learning should be void of an ideological agenda, nor should it incorporate conservative missions to provide a balance. Instead, he proposed that we should not continue "to think *about* service-learning as politics to transform higher education and society . . . [but] begin to think through service-learning about the politics of transforming higher education and society" (Butin, 2006, p. 492). He suggests this can be done by viewing service-learning as an academic discipline for community studies, similar to women's studies. In this way, a program of community studies is the focus of inquiry rather than a political project. While there is a degree of credence to the potential dangers raised by Butin, there are a couple of approaches available to address these issues.

First, an instructor can provide an array or menu of projects that represent the political spectrum, ranging from conservative to liberal contexts, for students to choose from. In this way, no student is coerced into an activity or project that presents a moral or political dilemma. For example, the University of Utah has a set of nine criteria that must be met for officially designating courses as service-learning, and one of those criteria is the provision of options for students so they are not forced into a project that is morally or politically aversive. A second way to avoid bias is to allow students to create projects that represent their own interests and concerns. Additionally, a set of guidelines could define criteria for project selection and address bias-related concerns of students, community partners, and faculty. Consequently, it is important to keep in mind the general purpose and intention to provide students with skills for civic engagement and social justice that they can use during and after their college experience. In this way, students, not faculty or staff, choose the issue and approach for the educational experience in any context or for any issue.

This is an exciting and challenging time for the evolving pedagogies of service-learning and civic engagement. We are witnessing burgeoning efforts within the academy to prepare students to become active citizens in a democratic society. To an extent, however, it seems that we are caught in a "damned if you do, damned it you don't" situation. Service-learning has received a degree of legitimate criticism about the extent to which the "service" actually brings about meaningful social change. Attempts to be more political or activist in course design are often deemed as a liberal agenda. As a result, we must continue to be reflective educators, as we have been throughout the evolution of service-learning from its beginnings to its respected position as a pedagogy across institutions and disciplines. As we work to identify and teach a curriculum and set of skills that empower students to become engaged citizens and be critical thinkers that transcend partisan politics, we will be required to revisit culturally entrenched values and norms of the academy and build the infrastructure and resources to support this work. As we have done for service-learning, we will also need to establish and pursue a research agenda that will enable us to empirically assess the impact of service-learning for civic engagement on students, faculty, institutions of higher education, and the community.

References

American Council of Trustees and Alumni. *How Many Ward Churchills?* Washington, DC: American Council of Trustees and Alumni, 2006.

Battistoni, R. M. *Civic Engagement across the Curriculum.* Providence, RI: Campus Compact, 2002.

Baxter Magolda, M. B., and Porterfield, W. D. "A New Approach to Assess Intellectual Development on the Perry Scheme." *Journal of College Student Personnel*, 1985, *26*, 343–351.

Butin, D. W. "The Limits of Service-Learning in Higher Education." *Review of Higher Education*, 2006, *29*(4), 473–498.

Butin, D. W. "Justice-Learning: Service-Learning as Justice-Oriented Education." *Equity and Excellence in Education*, 2007, *40*(2), 177–183.

Calderón, J. Z. *Race, Poverty, and Social Justice: Multidisciplinary Perspectives through Service Learning.* Sterling, VA: Stylus, 2007.

Chatwin, W., Gillespie, S., Looser, A., and Welch, M. "Service-Politics and Civic Engagement." In E. Zlotkowski, N. V. Longo, and J. R. Williams (Eds.), *Students as Colleagues.* Providence, RI: Campus Compact, 2006.

Colby, A., Beaumont, E., Ehrlich, T., and Corngold, J. *Educating for Democracy: Preparing Undergraduates for Responsible Political Engagement.* San Francisco: Jossey-Bass, 2007.

Colby, A., Ehrlich, T., Beaumont, E., and Stephens, J. *Educating Citizens: Preparing America's Undergraduates for Lives of Moral and Civic Responsibility.* San Francisco: Jossey-Bass, 2003.

Cone, R. E., Kiesa, A., and Longo, N. V. *Raise Your Voice: A Student Guide to Making Positive Social Change.* Providence, RI: Campus Compact, 2006.

Darling-Hammond, L., French, J., and Paloma Garcia-Lopez, S. *Learning to Teach for Social Justice.* New York: Teachers College Press, 2002.

Degner, K. "Orange Band: The Rock and Roll of Democracy." http://www.convergingvoices.com/oband, n.d.

Dewey, J. *Democracy and Education.* Carbondale: Southern Illinois University Press, 1916.

Ellsworth, E. "Why Doesn't This Feel Empowering? Working Through the Repressive Myths of Critical Pedagogy." *Harvard Educational Review,* 1989, *59*(3), 297–324.

Gore, J. *The Struggle for Pedagogies: Critical and Feminist Discourses as Regimes of Truth.* New York: Routledge, 1993.

Himley, M. "Facing (Up to) 'the Stranger' in Community Service-Learning." *College Composition and Communication,* 2004, *55*(3), 416–438.

Illich, I. "To Hell with Good Intentions." In J. C. Kendall (Ed.), *Combining Service and Learning: A Resource Book for Community and Public Service,* Vol. 1. Raleigh, NC: National Society for Internships and Experiential Education, 1990.

Jacoby, B. *Service-Learning in Higher Education: Concepts and Practices.* San Francisco: Jossey-Bass, 1996.

Johnson, B. T., and O'Grady, C. R. *The Spirit of Service: Exploring Faith, Service, and Social Justice in Higher Education.* Bolton, MA: Anker, 2006.

Jones, A. "Cross-Cultural Pedagogy and the Passion for Ignorance." *Feminism & Psychology,* 2001, *11*(3), 279–292.

Jones, R. "Not Left—Not Right—Just Orange." http://www.jmu/edu/montpelier/2004Fall/OrangeBand.shtml, 2004.

Kahne, J., Westheimer, J., and Rogers, B. "Service-Learning and Citizenship: Directions for Research." *Michigan Journal of Community Service-Learning,* 2000 (Special Issue), 42–51.

Lather, P. A. "Critical Pedagogy and Its Complicities: A Praxis of Stuck Places." *Educational Theory*, 1998, *48*(4), 487–498.

Long, S. E. *The New Student Politics: The Wingspread Statement on Student Civic Engagement.* Providence, RI: Campus Compact, 2002.

Marshall, C., and Gerstl-Pepin, C. I. *Re-Framing Educational Politics for Social Justice.* Boston: Allyn & Bacon, 2004.

Mitchell, T. D. "Critical Service-Learning as Social Justice Education: A Case Study of the Citizen Scholars Program." *Equity and Excellence in Education*, 2007, *40*(2), 101–112.

Morton, K., and Enos, S. "Building Deeper Civic Relationships and New and Improved Citizens." *Journal of Public Affairs*, 2002, *6*, 83–102.

Nadel, M., Majewski, V., and Sullivan-Cosetti, M. *Social Work and Service Learning: Partnerships for Social Justice.* Lanham, MD: Rowman & Littlefield, 2007.

Saltmarsh, J. "Creating a Personal and Political Culture of Engagement in Higher Education." In H. Boyte (Ed.), *Intellectual Workbench.* Minneapolis, MN: University of Minnesota, Civic Mission Project of the Center for Democracy and Citizenship, 2001.

Saltmarsh, J. *The Civic Purpose of Higher Education: A Focus on Civic Learning.* Unpublished paper, 2004.

Saltmarsh, J. "The Civic Promise of Service-Learning." *Liberal Education*, 2005, *91*(2), 50–55.

Strand, K., Marullo, S., Cutforth, N., Stoecker, R., and Donohue, P. *Community-Based Research and Higher Education: Principles and Practices.* San Francisco: Jossey-Bass, 2003.

Sungur, E. A., Winchester, B. S., Anderson, J. E., and Kim, J. "A Way of Integrating Civic Learning into Statistics Courses: Media Reports." http://www.mrs.umn.edu/services/cst/pubs/2006.ICOTS.full_paper5H3.pdf, 2006.

Vogelgesang, L. J., and Rhoads, R. "Advancing a Broad Notion of Public Engagement: The Limitations of Contemporary Service-Learning." *Journal of College and Character.* http://www.collegevalues.org/articles.cfm?a=1&id=1017, 2006.

Wang, Y., and Rodgers, R. "Impact of Service-Learning and Social Justice Education on College Students' Cognitive Development." *NASPA Journal*, 2006, *43*(2), 316–337.

Welch, M. *Handbook for Service-Politics and Civic Engagement.* Salt Lake City: University of Utah, Lowell Bennion Community Service Center, 2004.

Welch, M. "Identifying and Teaching Civic Engagement Skills through Service-Learning." In L. McIlrath and I. MacLabhrainn (Eds.), *Higher Education and Civic Engagement: International Perspectives.* Burlington, VT: Ashgate Publishing, 2007.

Welch, M., and Sheridan, S. M. *Educational Partnerships: Serving Students at Risk.* Ft. Worth, TX: Harcourt-Brace, 1995.

Welch, M., and Taylor, N. "A Three-Year Study of Service-Learning Courses on Civic Engagement: Quantitative/Qualitative Results and Student Perspective." Paper presented at the Sixth Annual International K-H Conference on Service-Learning Research, Portland, Oregon, October 2006.

Westheimer, J., and Kahne, J. Introduction to *Equity and Excellence in Education,* 2007, *40*(2), 97–100.

CHAPTER ELEVEN

COMMUNITY-BASED UNDERGRADUATE RESEARCH

Collaborative Inquiry for the Public Good

Elizabeth L. Paul

Community-based undergraduate research (CBR) is a promising pedagogical approach that is at the crossroads of three core functions of higher education: undergraduate research, civic engagement, and liberal learning. CBR is scientific inquiry conducted collaboratively by a team of community citizens and leaders, students, and faculty in service of community-identified needs and aims (Paul, 2006a). Like undergraduate research, CBR builds students' skills in inquiry, problem solving, teamwork, and communication. Like civic engagement, CBR cultivates understanding of social realities and social justice, and helps students explore ways to effect change as citizens. Like liberal learning, CBR encourages students to pursue intellectual work together with active engagement in the societal, ethical, and practical implications of their learning. Much can be learned at this crossroads about preparing contemporary undergraduate students for twenty-first-century challenges and opportunities.

This chapter begins with an overview of the pedagogical theory that underlies the powerful learning potential of CBR. It then describes the characteristics and best practices of CBR and presents key challenges in effecting strong CBR partnerships. A variety of models of CBR programs are reviewed, followed by practical guidance for initiating and sustaining CBR partnerships.

Insights about CBR from Learning Theory

Resounding recommendations for inquiry-based *in situ* learning and increased civic engagement have been echoed in several seminal reports, setting a clear agenda for undergraduate learning. These include *Reinventing Undergraduate Education* (Boyer Commission on Educating Undergraduates in the Research University, 1998), *Greater Expectations: A New Vision for Learning as a Nation Goes to College* (Association of American Colleges and Universities, 2002), and *Success in College: Creating Conditions That Matter* (Kuh, Kinzie, Schuh, and Whitt, 2005). All emphasize engagement of undergraduate students in student-faculty collaborative research, facilitation of civic engagement, and encouragement of integration across learning domains. However, there is little recognition of the value of the *intersection* of these avenues for learning.

Constructivist learning theory underlies the recommendations contained in these reports. A constructivist model of learning known as "situated cognition" asserts that learning is potentiated by active engagement in real or authentic activities (Brown, Collins, and Duguid, 1989; Shuell, 1997). Particularly effective is cognitive apprenticeship, wherein novices and experts work together in real situations to accomplish relevant tasks (Lave and Wenger, 1991; Wenger, 1998). In such an apprenticeship, students can observe and model relevant dispositions, skills, and other norms of the milieu, including professionalism and ethics. They receive *in situ* guidance, feedback, and reinforcement. Given the complexity of real contexts, students also have opportunities to integrate new knowledge with prior knowledge, as well as to apply and integrate knowledge from different disciplines or domains (Hunter, Laursen, and Seymour, 2007).

The role of the educator as facilitator of learning is critical in cognitive apprenticeship (Freire, 1990). Educators facilitate novice students' movement from "legitimate peripheral participation" in a novel situation to increasingly full membership (Lave and Wenger,

1991; Wenger, 1998). As such, the educator role moves from direct instruction and modeling of professional practices early on to a less and less central role as students take on responsibility as a full partner in the learning-and-doing context (Brown et al., 1989; Farmer, Buckmaster, and LeGrand, 1992). Frequent opportunities for self-expression, discussion, and reflective thinking guide students and faculty in this evolving relationship. With increasing integration, students learn how to think and act in complex, even ambiguous and uncertain, real contexts (Brown et al., 1989).

Marcia B. Baxter Magolda (2004) asserts that students' intellectual development is facilitated by such authentic learning experiences. In the epistemological reflection model, intellectual development, tied closely to identity development, moves from externally directed (that is, knowledge is situated in and verified by outside authority) to internally directed ways of knowing (that is, thinking for oneself about knowledge as shaped by the context in which it is situated). Students move toward self-authorship as teachers move toward the role of facilitator—rather than supplier or director—of learning (Baxter Magolda, 1999). In this process, students also develop and internalize a personal and professional identity (Baxter Magolda, 2001). Engaging students in community contexts can cultivate development of their cultural and civic identities as well.

Such pedagogical theories suggest several key elements of CBR's potency for undergraduate student learning and development. These include active engagement in real contexts; engagement in real-world complexities and ambiguities; work directed toward the accomplishment of real and meaningful goals; side-by-side collaboration between "novices" and "experts"; and ongoing opportunity for feedback, discussion, and reflection. These elements feature in the ensuing discussion of the characteristics, challenges, and models of CBR.

Defining Characteristics of CBR

CBR partnerships engage community agents together with higher education partners—including faculty, staff, and graduate and undergraduate students—in research projects that address a community-identified question or issue. The term *community agent* is chosen deliberately in this chapter to emphasize the equal, resourceful, and respected role of community partners in CBR partnerships. Community agents include staff of nonprofit organizations or government agencies and community association leaders and members. Community-focused and community-located research projects have occurred for decades and have sometimes been termed problem-centered research, participatory research, participatory action research, collaborative research, participatory inquiry, or practitioner research (Ansley and Gaventa, 1997; Lagemann, 1997). The advent of the label *community-based research* describes a movement that is advancing this type of work as a mainstream undergraduate pedagogy in service of civic engagement and social justice.

CBR recognizes the link between research and democracy in that research contributes importantly to public policy, discourse, and action (Ansley and Gaventa, 1997). Yet the development of knowledge has too often been disconnected from the improvement of communities (Checkoway, 2001). Thus, advocates of CBR urge the engagement of undergraduate students in community-campus research collaborations that address important societal issues as a powerful approach to "educate for citizenship" (Checkoway, 2001, p. 127; see also Boyer, 1987, and Bringle, Games, and Molloy, 1999). In working toward these aims, the following have been identified as key characteristics of productive CBR partnerships: mutual regard among partners, collaborative partnership, clarity of purpose, and commitment to closing the loop.

Achieving mutual regard among partners involves critical deconstruction of social roles and inequalities. There are thick boundaries of social power and politics that have mired many community-campus partnerships and that must be transcended to effect productive CBR partnerships. In too many instances, campus partners are still thought of as the experts and the providers, while community partners are relegated to being the "needy" recipients. Morton (1995) describes such community-campus partnerships as being rooted in charity, a one-way provision of resources to a needy community, rather than in justice, a cooperative focus on sharing mutual resources to effect positive social change for all. In fact, community agents have significant expertise that contributes to all aspects of CBR partnerships, including the planning, implementation, and application of research as well as the pedagogical aims of undergraduate civic education (Nyden, Figert, Shibley, and Burrows, 1997). Moreover, CBR partnerships must recognize the community as a "unit of identity" (Israel, Schultz, Parker, and Becker, 1998), complete with strengths and resources on which CBR projects can be built (Kretzmann and McKnight, 1993).

The CBR collaborative partnership emphasizes "co-learning" (Israel et al., 1998), wherein all partners are at once learners and teachers, contributors, and benefactors (Paul, 2006a). Partners work together in all phases of the research process, integrating knowledge, research, and action (Israel et al., 1998). Such relationships need to be developed incrementally over time to build trust and to slowly dissolve distinctions between the different partner roles (Ansley and Gaventa, 1997). Hideki A. Ishisaka, Nancy Farwell, Sung Sil L. Sohng, and Edwina S. Uehara (2004) observe that CBR partnerships provide opportunities for students, faculty, and agency staff to "struggle together" (p. 331).

It is important for all partners in CBR to achieve clarity of purpose of the partnership. This includes, in part, accepting the "co-learning" relationship just described. Partners must also come to terms with their multiple identities as researchers, practitioners, and social activists, practiced through CBR inquiry, action, and advocacy. CBR challenges the traditional positivist paradigm of research in which researchers are defined as detached and value-free. A prime part of faculty motivation to engage in CBR is civic values. Civic values need not equate with research bias and impropriety. Indeed, maintaining high research ethics and rigorous standards is imperative in all scientific investigations, including CBR. In the case of CBR, the research must withstand both scientific and public scrutiny, making sound research practices imperative (University of Washington, 2008). But there is also need for methodological flexibility. The project must have methodological rigor while also achieving useful results. Important from the beginning of the partnership is open communication about the stakes of CBR: Why is the research important? For what purpose is the research needed, such as making program improvements or securing funding? What information is needed? How will the evidence be used, given the possibilities of both expected and unexpected results? These issues may be especially poignant in the case of program evaluation research, in which evidence of behavior change is so important to assess and so difficult to achieve.

An integral part of the CBR partnership is closing the loop—that is, following through to realize the ultimate aims of the CBR project. While all CBR partners may not have sophisticated analytical skills, they must collaborate in discussing and interpreting the CBR project results. What are the implications of the results? How are the results best communicated to different constituents? How can the results be turned into action? What program modifications or innovations do the results suggest? How can the results be used to seek additional funding for the program? In addition, quality CBR experiences include continual metatalk among the partners about the partnership and the CBR experience, including a concluding debriefing after the project is complete (Schaffer, 1998). Was partner equity achieved in both process and outcome? What did partners learn—about themselves, the community, society, the research process, relevant professional practice, teamwork?

CHALLENGES IN EFFECTING PRODUCTIVE CBR PARTNERSHIPS

Although there has been a movement within higher education to return to its public purpose, today's colleges and universities are "uneven in their commitments, faculty members are unprepared for public roles, and community groups find it difficult to gain access to them" (Checkoway, 2001, p. 127). As such, the most pressing challenges to effecting productive CBR projects include barriers that impede each type of partner from seeking, entering, building, and sustaining a productive partnership. The barriers challenging higher education institutions and community-based organizations, faculty, and students will be discussed in turn.

Many institutions of higher education and community-based organizations have experienced unfortunate misfires in forming community-campus partnerships. Sometimes faculty members have sought community samples on which to conduct their research, alienating communities with their disconnected, one-directional approach. Sometimes service-learning programs—even if conceived with good intentions—have inadvertently reified community-campus disconnections. In some such examples, community agencies have been surprised when groups of students arrive, without warning, to perform service in the absence of faculty or staff engagement during or after the experience. The figurative walls around colleges and universities can easily seem impenetrable to surrounding communities, reflecting disdain and reinforcing ivory-tower stereotypes. Robert G. Bringle et al. (1999) observe summarily that higher education institutions have treated communities as "pockets of needs, laboratories for experimentation, or passive recipients of expertise" (p. 9). Ansley and Gaventa (1997) assert that institutions of higher education need some "lessons of humility, care, and equity" to redress relationships with surrounding communities and realize civic responsibilities (p. 49). They eloquently describe partnership as involving "moving over, making space, and in some instances sharing or giving up certain kinds of power" (Ansley and Gaventa, 1997, p. 50).

Checkoway (2001) identified three obstacles to engaging faculty in CBR partnerships: lack of perception by faculty of a civic component of their professional role, lack of civic socialization in faculty development and academic culture, and lack of recognition of civic engagement in the faculty reward structure. Faculty members have been socialized to affix their allegiance as teachers and researchers to their academic discipline or professional field, not to problems of society or their students' civic development. Slowly reframing the roles of the professorate requires recognizing the different forms of scholarship, including the scholarship of engagement (Boyer, 1987; Bringle et al., 1999; Gibson, 2006), as well as calls for the meaningful integration of research, teaching, and service (Checkoway, 2001; Rice, 1996). Checkoway (2001) observes that engaged scholarship can benefit faculty in many ways, including providing new and different life experiences, stimulating research interests and ideas, and improving teaching.

Undergraduate students are the newest collaborators in participatory research. In many higher education institutions, CBR and other collaborative research opportunities have been restricted to graduate students. Undergraduate students have been viewed as lacking the skills or maturity to participate, have been edged out by graduate education priorities, or have been relegated to positions as distant observers or disconnected assistants. Undergraduates' access to civic engagement has focused largely on service-learning opportunities, in which they provide direct service to community agencies. More recently, involvement of undergraduates in CBR is growing, in part spurred by the strong undergraduate research movement, as well as by national advocacy and educational efforts to expand community-engaged learning, such as CBRnet.org.

While some introduction to research methods is essential, equally critical for student success in CBR partnerships is education about diversity and the social dynamics of power and privilege that enables students to understand principles of democratic society and social justice (Bernstein and Cock, 1997). Students also need ongoing education and reflection on these topics throughout the CBR experience (Paul, 2006a, 2006b). The lack or insufficiency of such education can lead a community-based learning experience to backfire, reinforcing rather than reducing social stereotyping and prejudice.

Lack of preparation can heighten the likelihood of conflicts in fledgling partnerships. In fact, conflicts can arise in CBR partnerships as a result of the absence of trust, inequitable distribution of power and control, differences in perspectives, funding conflicts, and difficulty in maximizing learning benefits from community resources because of stereotypes of community deficit and lack of strategic educational models (Israel et al., 1998). Ansley and Gaventa also identified the challenges of keeping the community involved in driving the research agenda and the importance of constantly tending to issues, including the shifting nature of how funding shapes research priorities, partnership power dynamics, and communicating information in accessible ways. They urge care and caution in ensuring that partnerships avoid becoming "disempowering, nonparticipatory, and misused" (Ansley and Gaventa, 1997, p. 49).

MODELS OF CBR AS UNDERGRADUATE PEDAGOGY

Pedagogical models of CBR vary by the educational context of the project (course-based, independent study, senior thesis, or capstone); faculty involvement (apprenticeship model, senior thesis independent projects); student selection (based on academic achievement, academic risk, interest in social justice); scope of partnership (CBR only, direct service and CBR); length of partnership (a single semester, a year, or longer); and desired learning outcomes (disciplinary or multidisciplinary learning, professional training, liberal learning, student retention). The following are some examples of CBR initiatives that involve undergraduates, selected as examples to represent an array of types of higher education institutions and various program and project models.

Democracy House of Middlesex County College in Edison, New Jersey, engages teams of undergraduate students in integrated direct service and CBR in collaboration with community agencies. For example, at Elijah's Promise, a soup kitchen, students began by assisting in food preparation and helping manage a food donation program. As the partnership grew, a community asset mapping project was conducted, followed by an interview study of potential additional services needed by clients. These CBR projects have resulted in further community partnerships that enrich the resource base of Elijah's Promise, as well as the development of a new bag-lunch program, designed and implemented in collaboration with the Democracy House team. Students are supported with Bonner Leaders Program/AmeriCorps stipends and also participate in CBR projects in specific courses. Notable features of this program include integrated direct service and CBR; a team model, including teams of students and teams of faculty as CBR partners; long-term relationships with community agencies that are supported by Democracy House and an expanding network of associated course-based projects; and the aim of retaining and fostering academic success in students of an open-access community college.

A course-based CBR model is offered through the Center for Excellence in Learning through Service at Berea College in Berea, Kentucky. One example is the Service, Citizenship, and Community course, an introductory course focused on Appalachia. Students participate in a class service project and a team-based CBR project. An exciting innovation is planned for the next three years that involves a collaborative focus of community agencies and service-learning faculty in CBR related to energy use. A broad learning community is being formed that includes Berea College students and faculty in several disciplines, community leaders, and citizens.

Together, they will assess Kentucky's energy needs and assets. They will then use this information to empower the community to engage actively in transforming energy policy and infrastructure, patterns of usage, and implications for the financial security of citizens, particularly low-income families.

Another issue-focused collaborative program is offered through the Center for Community Engagement and Learning at the University of Alaska Anchorage. A network of twenty-three courses and several applied research projects have focused on environmental sustainability in the Chester Creek Watershed. CBR projects involving ecological data collection, management, and analysis feature prominently in this initiative. Projects have emphasized public application of the research findings. In one example, students in human anatomy and physiology courses developed and presented publicly educational materials on endocrine-disrupting chemicals found increasingly in the environment.

The Community-Based Learning Initiative at Princeton University in Princeton, New Jersey, facilitates CBR projects for undergraduate students' senior theses. Princeton University's senior thesis requirement is designed as a culminating independent research project. A recent example was a study of primary care resources for older adults in Trenton, New Jersey. The Public Service Research Program at Appalachian State University in Boone, North Carolina, also offers a yearlong CBR senior thesis course, organized as a learning community composed of students, faculty, and staff working together to conduct research that is useful to a community or organization. Realizing that students would benefit from more preparation for participating in CBR, the university is developing a CBR junior seminar to precede the thesis.

The Trenton Youth Community-Based Research Corps (TYCRC) at the College of New Jersey in Ewing, New Jersey, also includes a preparatory component before CBR engagement. Initially a one-semester course in community-based research methods in which students completed a small demonstration project, TYCRC has now evolved into a three-semester program. Students first enroll in a course entitled Downtown: Inner-City Youth and Families. Downtown is a course within a course—a community course within a college course. Students enrolled in Downtown also partake as citizen participants in the Trenton Community

Orientation Course, an eight-session program fostering youth advocacy skills. Other participants are typically adult social service professionals, retired citizens seeking volunteer opportunities, or philanthropists wanting to learn more about Trenton's needs and assets. Each session focuses on a different issue, such as education or child abuse, and meets at a local social service agency. TYCRC students learn *in situ* about pressing inner-city issues and get to know many Trenton citizens. They learn through observation, interaction, and testimonials about Trenton youth and families. They also learn about numerous social service agencies and those organizations' economic pressures. In addition, they develop familiarity with and comfort in traveling to Trenton. These community sessions are complemented by class sessions at the college that include reflection, relevant social science readings, and discussion with area professionals about the role of research in social service agencies. TYCRC students then enter yearlong CBR partnerships in which they accomplish major research projects with and on behalf of their community partners.

Creative possibilities for CBR projects and models know no bounds. Most important is the fit of the CBR model with student learning outcomes and the community partner (Strand, Marullo, Cutforth, Stoecker, and Donohue, 2003).

PRACTICAL GUIDANCE FOR EFFECTIVE CBR PARTNERSHIPS

The following practical guidance has been gathered from the author's CBR experience, published accounts of CBR projects and programs, and the rich network of practitioners, educators, and scholars involved in CBRnet.org.

Recognize that CBR partnerships can originate in many ways

Partnerships for community-based research can grow out of crisis situations, in which campus and community members may find themselves in a coincidental collaboration, or they can grow out of common concern for an issue or participation in a civic group (Bringle and Hatcher, 2002). CBR partnerships may also arise through a community agency's request for volunteers to the campus service-learning office. Through the process of designing a service-learning project—particularly if this is done as a group involving community agents, faculty, staff, and students—ideas for CBR projects can develop.

There is value to working with a community-based facilitator of CBR partnerships to temper the common power imbalances of community-campus collaborations and ensure community focus. The Trenton Center for Campus-Community Partnerships, for example, is a network of community agency and civic leaders and staff, as well as campus faculty and administrators, dedicated to cultivating CBR partnerships. The director of the center, located in downtown Trenton, has a long history of community work in the city and is also a local community college professor. His groundedness in the Trenton community eases the development of partnerships, ensures that the community is prioritized in the projects, and enables him to provide valuable training to all partners for partnership success. He is also readily available to troubleshoot if a project encounters an obstacle.

Take time to get to know community partners and the mission and work of the agency

Involvement in direct service can be helpful in getting to know agency staff and clientele, building relationships, and understanding the dynamics of the focal issues, as in the Middlesex Community College Democracy House model described in the previous section. This early experience is critical for campus partners to gain footing in a novel situation, to develop cultural competency for working in the agency and community, and to move from peripheral participation to full partnership (Hunter et al., 2007). Early side-by-side engagement of students and faculty in the community setting allows for the feedback, reinforcement, and reflection that is so important for student socialization.

Create the research project goals in a collaborative process

It is important to agree on realistic goals that reflect the needs of all involved. This requires understanding on the part of both campus and community partners of their respective motivations for engaging in the project and the different intended audiences for its results.

Develop a plan for project management

Once the goals are established, a plan that outlines clear responsibilities and lines of accountability is necessary. Setting long- and short-term timelines is a key next step. Regular team meetings, best held in the community, are useful for building relationships, keeping CBR projects on track, and addressing issues or conflicts swiftly. Following each meeting, records of decisions made, work updates, and action plans should be shared with all participants. Team meetings should also include regular opportunities for partnership process reflection, including personal reflections about the partnership experience.

Communicate clearly with students about CBR work expectations

Engaging in CBR partnerships is a novel experience for most undergraduate students. While the work is goal oriented, there is not a preset, detailed syllabus or work plan for students to follow. In fact, students, as full partners, will be involved in defining the work and ensuring its timely, rather than last-minute, completion. The focus of the work is outside the classroom, heightening expectations for the ethics and integrity of student work. Orienting and training students for involvement with the agency and engagement in the CBR project is most effective when it is done with community partners. Topics for training include the content area, the community context, establishing realistic expectations, the specific skills needed, intercultural competence, ethics of the research process, and the appropriate dress and behavior on site.

Use experienced peers to socialize students new to CBR

Students who have previously participated in CBR partnerships are in an ideal position to introduce its concepts and practices to students new to the process. For example, inviting a complete CBR team to share its experience with a new CBR team demonstrates the collaborative nature of CBR. Another strategy is building in a "multigenerational" component to the CBR partnership, wherein a senior student serves as a peer leader and role model for the new team, as in the College of New Jersey's Trenton Youth Community-Based Research Corps and Middlesex Community College's Democracy House. This senior student can help set realistic and productive expectations, moderate the new relationship between students and the community partner (which is especially effective when the senior student's CBR experience was with the same community partner), and contribute to project development and management.

Strive to develop and sustain long-term partnerships

It takes considerable time and investment to develop high-quality, ongoing CBR partnerships, rather than delimiting partnerships by the duration of one CBR project. Longer-term partnerships increase the likelihood that CBR results will be used to affect policies that have substantial benefit to the community (Schaffer, 1998; University of Washington, 2008). Sustained partnerships also lead to deeper institutional commitments to the community.

CONCLUSION

CBR is a promising pedagogy for student achievement of learning outcomes in the six areas of the Civic Learning Spiral described in chapter 3: self, communities and cultures, knowledge, values, skills, and public action (Musil et al., in press). Student CBR partners are empowered by the realness of the work, thereby applying themselves and investing themselves in ways that exceed their own and others' expectations. As the CBR projects advance and students' role as partner blossoms, their personal and professional identity matures to incorporate their emerging sense of self-worth, competence, efficacy, commitment, and possibility (Paul, 2006b).

The undergraduate research movement is certainly encouraging of the strong potential of CBR as powerful undergraduate pedagogy. Recent research on student achievement of learning outcomes through undergraduate research revealed that while students demonstrated skill and professional development, the most significant gain was in personal development (Hunter et al., 2007; Lopatto, 2004; Seymour, Hunter, Laursen, and Deantoni, 2004). Students grew in self-confidence, independence, tolerance for obstacles, and sense of accomplishment. Consistent with the call of many liberal learning advocates, students emphasized that they believed that this growth had many intrinsic merits and benefits that could transfer to their work and personal lives (Schneider, 2003; Seymour et al., 2004).

Recent studies on undergraduate research have also found that strong faculty mentoring is critical to quality experiences (Lopatto, 2006). Strong mentors are friendly and approachable, treat students as respected partners, encourage reflection, and are responsive to questions. Further development of the faculty role in CBR partnerships will be an important catalyst in advancing CBR as a powerful undergraduate pedagogy. Thus, stimulating greater faculty involvement in CBR will require facilitating faculty members' development as citizens and public agents—and recognizing these roles as critical to the higher education enterprise (Checkoway, 2001; Rice, 1996). In a reciprocal role, students may be able to contribute to faculty development. At the College of New Jersey, for example, students with CBR experience are paired with faculty who are new to CBR, to complement the faculty members' introduction to CBR. A critical aspect of this student support role is the stimulation of reflection and dialogue with the professor as they explore this new experience together.

In conclusion, CBR—as the powerful intersection of undergraduate research, civic engagement, and liberal learning—holds tremendous promise for the civic development of both students and their faculty mentors. While achieving tangible project outcomes with real benefits to community partners, CBR also builds each partner's capacity for further civic engagement.

References

Ansley, F., and Gaventa, J. "Researching for Democracy and Democratizing Research." *Change,* January/February 1997, *29,* 46–53.

Association of American Colleges and Universities. *Greater Expectations: A New Vision for Learning as a Nation Goes to College.* Washington, DC: Association of American Colleges and Universities, 2002.

Baxter Magolda, M. B. *Creating Contexts for Learning and Self-Authorship: Constructive Developmental Pedagogy.* Nashville, TN: Vanderbilt University Press, 1999.

Baxter Magolda, M. B. *Making Their Own Way: Narratives for Transforming Higher Education to Promote Self-Development.* Sterling, VA: Stylus, 2001.

Baxter Magolda, M. B. "Evolution of a Constructivist Conceptualization of Epistemological Reflection." *Educational Psychologist,* 2004, *39,* 31–42.

Bernstein, A., and Cock, J. "Educating Citizens for Democracies Young and Old." *Chronicle of Higher Education,* November 14, 1997, p. B6.

Boyer, E. L. *Scholarship Reconsidered: Priorities of the Professorate*. Princeton, NJ: Carnegie Foundation for the Advancement of Teaching, 1987.

Boyer Commission on Educating Undergraduates in the Research University. *Reinventing Undergraduate Education: A Blueprint for America's Research Universities*. Stony Brook: State University of New York, 1998.

Bringle, R. G., Games, R., and Molloy, E. A. *Colleges and Universities as Citizens*. Boston: Allyn & Bacon, 1999.

Bringle, R. G., and Hatcher, J. A. "Campus-Community Partnerships: The Terms of Engagement." *Journal of Social Issues*, 2002, *58*(3), 503–516.

Brown, J. S., Collins, A., and Duguid, P. "Situated Cognition and the Culture of Learning." *Educational Researcher*, 1989, *18*(9), 32–42.

Checkoway, B. "Renewing the Civic Mission of the American Research University." *Journal of Higher Education*, 2001 (Special Issue), *72*, 25–147.

Farmer, J. A., Buckmaster, A., and LeGrand, B. "Cognitive Apprenticeship: Implications for Continuing Professional Development." *New Directions for Adult and Continuing Education*, Fall 1992, *55*, 41–49.

Freire, P. *Pedagogy of the Oppressed*. New York: Continuum, 1990.

Gibson, C. M. *New Times Demand New Scholarship: Research Universities and Civic Engagement*. Medford, MA: Tufts University Press, 2006.

Hunter, A. -B., Laursen, S. L., and Seymour, E. "Becoming a Scientist: The Role of Undergraduate Research in Students' Cognitive, Personal, and Professional Development." *Science Education*, January 2007, *91*, 36–74.

Ishisaka, H. A., Farwell, N., Sohng, S. S. L., and Uehara, E. S. "Partnership for Integrated Community-Based Learning: A Social Work Community-Campus Collaboration." *Journal of Social Work Education*, 2004, *40*(2), 321–336.

Israel, B., Schulz, A. J., Parker, E. A., and Becker, A. B. "Review of Community-Based Research: Assessing Partnership Approaches to Improve Public Health." *Annual Review of Public Health*, 1998, *19*, 173–202.

Kretzmann, J. P., and McKnight, J. L. *Building Communities from the Inside Out: A Path toward Finding and Mobilizing a Community's Assets*. Evanston, IL: Center for Urban Affairs and Policy Research, Northwestern University, 1993.

Kuh, G. D., Kinzie, J., Schuh, J. H., and Whitt, E. J. *Student Success in College: Creating Conditions That Matter*. San Francisco: Jossey-Bass, 2005.

Lagemann, E. C. "*From Discipline-Based to Problem-Centered Learning.*" In R. Orrill (Ed.), *Education and Democracy: Reimaging Liberal Learning in America*. New York: The College Board, 1997.

Lave, J., and Wenger, E. *Situated Learning: Legitimate Peripheral Participation*. New York: Cambridge University Press, 1991.

Lopatto, D. "Survey of Undergraduate Research Experiences (SURE): First Findings." *Cell Biology Education*, 2004, *3*(4), 270–277.

Lopatto, D. "Undergraduate Research as a Catalyst for Liberal Learning." *Peer Review*, 2006, *8*(1), 22–25.

Morton, K. "The Irony of Service: Charity, Project and Social Change in Service-Learning." *Michigan Journal of Community Service Learning*, Fall 1995, *2*, 19–32.

Musil, C. M., Wathington, H., Battistoni, R., Calderón, J., Trementozzi, M., Fluker, W. E., et al. *The Civic Learning Spiral: Education for Participation in a Diverse Democracy*. Washington, DC: Association of American Colleges and Universities, in press.

Nyden, P., Figert, A., Shibley, M., and Burrows, D. *Building Community: Social Science in Action*. Thousand Oaks, CA: Pine Forge Press, 1997.

Paul, E. L. "Community-Based Research as Scientific and Civic Pedagogy." *Peer Review*, 2006a, *8*(1), 12–15.

Paul, E. L. "Facilitating Student Growth as Citizens: A Developmental Model for Community-Engaged Learning." *Diversity Digest*, 2006b, *10*, 7.

Rice, R. E. *Making a Place for the New American Scholar*. Washington, DC: American Association for Higher Education, 1996.

Schaffer, M. A. "Service Learning as a Strategy for Teaching Undergraduate Research." *Journal of Experiential Education*, 1998, *21*(3), 154–161.

Schneider, C. G. *Practicing Liberal Education: Formative Themes in the Reinvention of Liberal Learning*. Washington, DC: Association of American Colleges and Universities, 2003.

Seymour, E., Hunter, A.-B., Laursen, S. L., and Deantoni, T. "Establishing the Benefits of Research Experiences for Undergraduates in the Sciences: First Findings from a Three-Year Study." *Science Education*, 2004, *88*, 493–534.

Shuell, T. J. "Teaching and Learning in a Classroom Context." In D. C. Berliner and R. C. Calfee (Eds.), *The Handbook of Educational Psychology*. London: Prentice Hall, 1997.

Strand, K., Marullo, S., Cutforth, N., Stoecker, R., and Donohue, P. *Community-Based Research and Higher Education: Principles and Practices*. San Francisco: Jossey-Bass, 2003.

University of Washington. "Principles for Community-Based Research." http://www.washington.edu/research/4researchers/cbr.php#com, 2008.

Wenger, E. *Communities of Practice: Learning, Meaning and Identity*. New York: Cambridge University Press, 1998.

CHAPTER TWELVE

PREPARING STUDENTS FOR GLOBAL CIVIC ENGAGEMENT

Barbara Jacoby and Nevin C. Brown

American institutions of higher education universally recognize their fundamental role in preparing students to engage responsibly and productively in a world that is becoming increasingly interconnected and interdependent. Global society is constantly and dramatically being reshaped by "scientific and technical innovations, global interdependence, cross-cultural encounters, and changes in the balance of economic and political power" (National Leadership Council for Liberal Education and America's Promise, 2007, p. 2). The very sustainability of the planet's shared resources is in serious question. Ours is also a world that is threatened by the global spread of communicable disease and terrorism. Local problems—including hunger and homelessness, unequal educational opportunity, crime, and lack of accessible health care—are repeated in cities and communities around the world (Chisholm, 2003). There is virtually nowhere in the United States without an immigrant population. This country is itself an international culture, and nearly all Americans constantly interact with individuals of widely varying backgrounds, cultures, customs, and beliefs. It is therefore essential to educate students to be global citizens who are prepared "to understand, live successfully within, and provide enlightened leadership to a richly diverse and increasingly complex world" (Wilson-Oyelaran, 2006).

In this context, higher education is confronted with the challenge of educating global citizens who can engage with one another to address this dizzying array of factors, including others that emerge regularly. This chapter offers principles to consider in designing initiatives for students to learn about and practice civic engagement internationally. It then provides three general approaches to international civic engagement and programmatic examples. It concludes with a discussion of the barriers and challenges of global civic engagement and steps institutions can take to address them.

Guiding Principles for International Civic Engagement Experiences

In 2003, the International Partnership for Service-Learning and Leadership (IPSL) issued its "Declaration of Principles" that outlined essential elements for structuring effective international service-learning programs (Brown, 2006). The principles are equally effective for developing, implementing, and assessing other opportunities for students to learn about and practice civic engagement in international and intercultural settings. These principles are paraphrased and supplemented with explanatory text here.

Principle 1: There is reciprocity between the community and the college or university

The relationship between the community or organization served and the institution of higher education must be built on mutual respect, trust, and esteem. Reciprocity implies that the partners seek to address goals that are shared or, at least, compatible. Participants in partnerships founded on agreed-on values and vision are viewed as members of a common community that they seek to improve for the sake of their own and each others' benefit (Torres, 2000). Frequent and open communication also characterizes relationships based in reciprocity. When students work in settings based on reciprocal partnerships, they gain "a sense of mutual responsibility and respect between individuals" (Kendall, 1990, p. 22). In a reciprocal relationship, students do things *with* others rather than *for* them and learn to respect and work productively with others across differences.

Principle 2: The learning is rigorous, sound, and clearly connected to the civic engagement activities

It is essential that civic engagement initiatives, whether in the United States or abroad, uphold the highest standards of academic rigor. As is true of all experiential learning, the academic and the field experiences must be thoroughly integrated. Student learning outcomes should be clearly stated, integral to the design and implementation of the program, and communicated to all parties involved. Academic content and pedagogies should be selected to achieve the desired outcomes, and the degree of students' achievement of the outcomes should be regularly assessed. The civic engagement experiences in which the students participate should be designed to enhance learning, and in turn, the academic content should inform students' practical experiences.

Principle 3: The studies should not offer foregone conclusions

In the spirit of academic inquiry, students should be exposed to various points of view, theories, and ideas. They should be asked to critically examine those ideas and their civic engagement experiences to reach their own well-considered conclusions. Given the vast complexities of global civic and social issues, students must be able to recognize when information is needed and to locate, evaluate, and use effectively the needed information.

Principle 4: The service is truly useful to the community or organization

The general principle of service-learning that states that the community or organization is best qualified to define what is useful applies equally to all civic engagement experiences, local and global (Brown, 2006; Jacoby, 1996). The time and quality of student participants' contributions must be sufficient to offset the time spent by members of the community or organization. Anything less amounts to exploitation of the very people that the service intends to assist (Brown, 2006). It is critical to avoid placing students into local or international settings based solely on desired student learning outcomes or on providing services that perpetuate a state of need, rather than seeking and addressing the root causes of the need (Jacoby, 1996). As is the case for student learning, outcomes for community participants and organizations should be clearly stated and addressed.

Principle 5: The experience should be appropriate for the developmental and academic levels of the students, and support services should be provided

To foster student development and to ensure that community needs and expectations are met, it is important that activities are appropriate for the student participants. It is critical that students be well prepared for their experience abroad in terms of culture, academic background, and practical issues. Support services should be readily accessible throughout the experience. Of equal importance is supporting students' reentry to U.S. culture. Students return filled with new ideas and views that can enrich the rest of their college experience and that of their peers. On the other hand, they can also return with a sense of futility in light of the extent and intensity of human suffering that they may have confronted.

Principle 6: Structured opportunities for personal and objective reflection should be built into the program

Structured reflection that is intentionally designed to enable students to achieve the desired learning outcomes is essential. Reflection also allows students to examine their values and beliefs, to consider their own values in the context of different ideas and belief systems, and to put it all into the context of understanding what it means to be a socially responsible global citizen.

OPTIONS FOR GLOBAL CIVIC ENGAGEMENT

This section provides an overview of three general approaches for international civic engagement. There are advantages and disadvantages to each of these approaches.

As more and more colleges and universities offer opportunities across the globe for their students to learn about and practice civic engagement, many are turning to the programs offered by organizations, sometimes called third-party providers, or other higher education institutions. The International Partnership for Service-Learning and Leadership offers fifteen undergraduate programs that combine formal academic study at a university abroad with substantive volunteer service in the local community, plus a master of arts degree in international service (see http://www.ipsl.org). Cross-Cultural Solutions offers a wide range of noncredit volunteer programs in partnership with sustainable local community initiatives around the world (see http://www.crossculturalsolutions.org). The School for International Training offers field-based study abroad programs for undergraduates as well as master's degree programs and certificates. Each of its semester-long programs is built on a theme, including ecology and conservation, culture and development, peace and conflict studies, gender issues, and the arts (see http://www.sit.edu/about.html).

A second option for international civic engagement experiences is to encourage students to enroll in the programs of other colleges and universities. For example, the Center for Global Education at Augsburg College in Minneapolis and Arcadia University in Glenside, Pennsylvania, accept students from other institutions into their wide-ranging and well-established international programs. The Higher Education Consortium for Urban Affairs (HECUA) is a consortium of seventeen colleges and universities that provides its programs to all qualified students. Its offerings include courses combined with internships and other types of experiential learning around the world as well as in the United States, with a focus on urban affairs and social justice issues (see http://www.hecua.org). Similarly, Amizade, through an academic partnership with West Virginia University, offers international service-learning programs for educational credit that focus on academic coursework and meaningful cross-cultural service opportunities (see http://www.amizade.org).

The third option is for an institution to design and operate a program for its own students. The examples in the next section describe a variety of these programs. The advantages to the first two approaches include relying on structures that are already in place and that have been created by experienced personnel who have established international partnerships; they do not require a minimum number of students or a lengthy start-up period. Because the range of possibilities is wide, well-informed advisers can assist students in selecting a program that meets their academic and personal goals and is also appropriate for their developmental level (Chisholm, 2003). On the other hand, when an institution puts the requisite level of effort into the design and implementation of a program to meet institutional and student goals, it has more control over the degree to which desired learning and community outcomes are likely to be achieved. However, the start-up time can be considerable, and the amount of effort significant, both initially and over time. Another disadvantage is that students in an institutionally sponsored program may tend to spend most of their time as a group, limiting their interaction with the people and the culture of the foreign country (Chisholm, 2003).

INSTITUTIONAL EXAMPLES OF INTERNATIONAL CIVIC ENGAGEMENT

This section offers brief descriptions of several examples of international civic engagement initiatives at a range of higher education institutions. While they represent only a small number of programs, they provide a glimpse of the many different possibilities that allow students to learn about and practice civic engagement in international settings.

ST. MICHAEL'S COLLEGE: ILULA ORPHAN PROGRAM

The Ilula Orphan Program at St. Michael's College in Burlington, Vermont, is a combination of a classroom-based interdisciplinary course in journalism and political science on HIV/AIDS in East Africa and a three-week experiential segment in rural Tanzania. Although the course is designated as a service-learning course, it does not involve traditional service. The faculty and students worked with the Ilula Orphan Program to create a Web site, a film, and grant proposals for the program to document its work with orphans and in community development. In the process of researching and designing these products, the students learn about the critical factors that affect the cycle of HIV infection and poverty, including devastating water shortages, gender inequality, lack of educational opportunities, and environmental degradation. The Web site elaborates on these factors, how they are related, and how the Ilula Orphan Program works to break the cycle. The Web site, film, and grant proposals describe the program's outstanding work, its governance by community volunteers, and its needs for additional support. Following the time the students spent in Tanzania, they continued to work on the project back at the college (see http://www.ilulaorphanprogram.org/PROGRAMS_HOME.html).

HAVERFORD COLLEGE: SUMMER INTERNSHIP PROGRAM

The Center for Peace and Global Citizenship at Haverford College in Haverford, Pennsylvania, sponsors and supports several initiatives that involve liberal learning, critical reflection, and social action. The center encourages interdisciplinary collaboration and focuses on social justice. Its summer internship program supports students from freshmen through seniors while they spend four to ten weeks volunteering with and learning from social service organizations around the world. Since the internship program was established, the center has sent students to work in more than thirty countries. Interns have worked with a variety of organizations, from large international development agencies to small community-based groups. They have addressed a wide array of pressing social issues, including postconflict peace initiatives, education, fair trade, environmental degradation, sustainable development, cultural preservation, and the arts. Interns' contributions include conducting research, helping develop networks and fundraising, providing English-language instruction, and collaborating with local colleagues to carry out grassroots programs in communities. Many internships have led to continuing relationships between Haverford students and their host countries, with interns going on to work on international public policy issues, research, education, journalism, and in the nonprofit sector (see http://www.haverford.edu/CPGC/programs/internships_about.htm).

PORTLAND STATE UNIVERSITY: CONNECTING EDUCATIONAL COMMUNITIES

Developed as a community-based learning course, Connecting Educational Communities was organized by a Spanish instructor in response to a request from Guatemala's Liaison for Indigenous Communities. The idea and connections for this course originated in 1997 when the instructor worked in Guatemala City with an advocacy organization for forgotten street children. In the summer of 2003, she returned to Guatemala with another faculty member and fourteen students to pilot a program that would form an ongoing partnership between three Maya communities and Portland State. The students brought funds they had raised and fourteen suitcases of donated educational supplies. They did substantial work on three schools and returned with their suit-cases full of crafts purchased from their Guatemalan partners to be sold to provide a source of sustainable funding for the materi-als needed for the program. The partnership is effective because it allows an American university to contribute resources, energy, and ideas to help marginalized communities survive in the global economy, while providing opportunities for students to learn from indigenous people important lessons and skills in such areas as authentic collaboration and consensus building (Sanders and Wubbold, 2004). Connecting Educational Communities has devel-oped into an eight-credit program that combines campus-based Spanish courses and three weeks in Guatemala. While they are in the rural Maya areas, students work on projects and study Spanish and Guatemalan literature and culture with local teachers and experts (see http://www.guatemala.pdx.edu).

KALAMAZOO COLLEGE: K-PLAN

In 1962, Kalamazoo College in Michigan developed the K-Plan, a liberal learning curriculum enriched by experiential, interna-tional, and multicultural dimensions. Currently, 85 percent of Kalamazoo's students study abroad, and 88 percent of those are in programs that last at least two academic quarters. Recognizing the developmental nature of the undergraduate learning experience, the college's Mary Jane Underwood Stryker Institute for Service-Learning structures service-learning opportunities in a sequence that offers students progressively more responsible service-learning and leadership experiences in culturally diverse settings over four years. Many students are introduced to service-learning in first-year seminars; others participate in cocurricular volunteer programs. These introductory experiences often motivate students to enroll in an academic service-learning course that links their experiences to larger socioeconomic and political contexts. During the sophomore year, students have the opportunity to assume greater responsibility in selecting the nature of the programs in which they participate and the level of leadership they assume. Sophomore-year projects anticipate study abroad, as students immerse themselves in local immigrant communities. After selecting their study abroad sites in the winter quarter, sophomores can opt to participate in the Kalamazoo Project for Intercultural Communication or to begin to develop their integrative cultural research project, which will comprise a significant portion of their study abroad experience. Students participate in a predeparture course that exposes them to the basic principles of intercultural communication, engage in a series of writing assignments while abroad, and as returning students, take a course that encourages reflection on the international experience and how they will be leaders who function effectively in an increasingly interconnected world. Through the senior individualized project and other components of the K-Plan, students are encouraged to extend the depth and breadth of their study abroad experiences to engage further in the work of social justice and community transformation (Wilson-Oyelaran, 2006).

STANFORD UNIVERSITY: OVERSEAS STUDIES ACADEMIC QUARTER PROGRAM IN CAPE TOWN

In the 2005–2006 academic year, students from Stanford University in Palo Alto, California, spent winter quarter in Cape Town, South Africa. Their coursework consisted of three related seminars: community reconstruction and development in postapartheid South Africa, public health and primary health care in a changing community context, and history and politics of South Africa in transition. In addition, students worked on service-learning projects with a nongovernmental organization and also engaged in community-based research. Students participated in one of two group community health assessments with the option of also carrying out their own individually designed research project. The research projects became the academic core of the Cape Town experience. Students found the issues to be complicated and compelling. Their research enabled them to view township life, to meet and engage with residents and service providers in ways that otherwise would have been impossible, and to contribute in modest ways to improve health in the township. The students organized two community forums at which they gave oral presentations of their work. At the end of one forum, the community residents burst into song to express their thanks. In reflection on the experience, the faculty member who organized it recommends that future experiences include a strengthened predeparture orientation, short-term homestays as part of the program, and support from student affairs staff (Stanton, 2006).

UNIVERSITY OF WASHINGTON: BRINGING IT HOME

The University of Washington in Seattle offers a comprehensive three-credit course, Bringing It Home, to students who return from immersion experiences in international settings. The course provides a forum for reflecting on students' experiences, processing reverse culture shock upon returning to the United States, and clarifying values related to the meanings of diversity within the global and local communities. In addition, the class addresses issues of power and privilege, social justice, the differences between tourism and travel, community service versus engagement, and what it means to be civically engaged on the local and global levels. Students in the class volunteer in a community-based organization in Seattle that is connected to their individual interests and career goals.

Course objectives are designed to enable students to sharpen their critical-thinking skills so they can reflect more deeply on their own international experience within the context of global, national, and local social justice. Students acquire language to help them make explicit connections between their experiences and the principles of community, social capital development, democracy, and diversity. They are encouraged to articulate in a complex and thoughtful manner the ways in which the international and the local community service experiences have affected their values, skills, abilities, and career opportunities.

The course is targeted to graduating seniors, advanced undergraduates, and graduate students seeking a more structured, formal, and supportive environment to process their overseas experience and to think deeply about how it will affect their future choices. Class meetings include lectures, seminar discussions, student presentations, and guest speakers (see http://courses. washington.edu/bithome).

Challenges and Barriers to Global Civic Engagement

The scope and variety of the opportunities to learn about and practice civic engagement internationally described in the previous section attest to the value and viability of such labor-and resource-intensive programs. However, there are a number of challenges that remain for U.S. colleges and universities that seek to create these opportunities for their students.

The first challenge involves the lack of administrative integration at the campus level to support global civic engagement. Often offices that support study abroad and civic engagement or service-learning exist in separate silos, even as most students that both offices serve are seeking more opportunities to learn about and practice civic engagement internationally. Successful international initiatives involve cross-campus collaboration. They also involve working closely with other offices that have essential knowledge and services, including financial aid, risk management, and fund-raising.

As more and more institutions are adding to their mission statements a strong commitment to education for global citizenship, there are often academic requirements and expectations that restrict or render impossible student participation in international civic engagement. These include majors, notably in engineering and the sciences, that allow little or no flexibility for electives or experiential learning far away from the campus. In addition, some faculty members may believe that international civic engagement experiences are not academically rigorous or that they do not contribute sufficiently to the student's major to warrant the time and distraction from the academic core. In other cases, faculty and advisers steer students into U.S.-based internships over international civic engagement because they believe that the former more readily lead to postcollege employment. Global civic engagement programs should be designed in partnership with faculty and with these concerns in mind. In addition, opportunities should be provided to educate faculty and advisers about the academic and career development benefits of international study and experiences.

The mismatch between academic calendars and the needs of international partner organizations creates a further challenge. Although traditional study abroad has generally focused on semester- or yearlong programs, there is increasing student demand for short-term international experiences, including spring and winter break experiences that range from one to three weeks in length. The potential upside of this trend is that more students may be able to participate in the shorter experiences. However, a significant downside is that many of the international partners' needs do not lend themselves well to short visits. As stated in the principles in the beginning of this chapter, it is critical that colleges and universities ensure that their partners in international community organizations and government offices do not end up spending more time and resources trying to organize for short-term volunteers than they receive back in benefits.

A final challenge is the narrow demographic range of undergraduate students who engage in international programs. The typical U.S. student in many international programs is a white, upper-middle-class female, in her very early twenties, who attends a small, independent liberal arts college or university. In contrast, many college students are older, work, and have family responsibilities. Minority and first-generation students, as well as those who attend community colleges or who transfer between institutions, are far less likely to participate. It is important for institutions to allow a broader range of their students to have international experiences by helping them overcome financial as well as family or cultural barriers.

CONCLUSION

Research conducted by the International Partnership for Service-Learning and Leadership indicates that global service-learning is a more radical educational experience than conventional study abroad and is more likely to have a long-term effect on participating students. Students in such programs develop significant leadership qualities, including adaptability and resourcefulness, the ability to apply fresh approaches to old problems, and the ability to recast familiar issues in light of broader experiences (Tonkin, 2004). For institutions, the same study found that international service-learning programs are most successful in colleges and universities with a campuswide commitment to experiential learning and civic engagement. On the other hand, large institutions with a weaker tradition of civic engagement and a stronger adherence to traditional pedagogy are less likely to be successful in developing international initiatives. Successful initiatives depend heavily on creative leadership, careful planning, creation of accommodating administrative structures, and buy-in from faculty and administrators at all levels across the institution (Tonkin, 2004). These findings are directly applicable to global civic engagement initiatives other than service-learning.

In conclusion, international opportunities for students to learn about and practice civic engagement belong at the core of undergraduate education because they enable students to develop the very qualities to which liberal education aspires: understanding of our complex and interconnected world, reflection and critical thinking, problem solving, communication, tolerance for ambiguity, appreciation of diversity, and respect for the views of others. Despite the challenges of undertaking it, global learning should be a primary means for higher education to achieve its goals for students, not an add-on. As Kevin Hovland (2005) articulated, "Global learning . . . must challenge students to gain deep knowledge about the world's people and problems, explore the legacies that have created the dynamics and tensions that shape the world, and struggle with their own place in that world. . . . At its best [it] emphasizes the relational nature of students' identities—identities that are variously shaped by the currents of power and privilege, both within a multicultural U.S. democracy and within an interconnected and unequal world. . . . Global questions require students to connect, integrate, and act" (p. 1). Likewise, global questions require institutions to connect, integrate, and act to provide opportunities for their students to be responsible global citizens.

References

Brown, N. "Embedding Engagement in Higher Education: Preparing Global Citizens through International Service-Learning." http://www.compact.org/20th/read/preparing_global_citizens, 2006.

Chisholm, L. "Partnerships for International Service-Learning." In B. Jacoby (Ed.), *Building Partnerships for Service-Learning*. San Francisco: Jossey-Bass, 2003.

Hovland, K. "Shared Futures: Global Learning and Social Responsibility." *Diversity Digest*, 2005, *8*(3), 1, 16–17.

Jacoby, B. *Service-Learning in Higher Education: Concepts and Practices*. San Francisco: Jossey-Bass, 1996.

Kendall, J. C. *Combining Service and Learning: A Resource Book for Community and Public Service*, Vol. 1. Raleigh, NC: National Society for Internships and Experiential Education, 1990.

National Leadership Council for Liberal Education and America's Promise. *College Learning for the New Global Century*. Washington, DC: Association of American Colleges and Universities, 2007.

Sanders, R., and Wubbold, M. "Connecting Educational Communities: Guatemala–Portland State University." *PSU's Faculty Focus*, Spring 2004, 2–3.

Stanton, T. K. *OSP Winter 2005-06 in Cape Town, South Africa: Faculty Leader's Report*. Palo Alto, CA: Stanford Overseas Studies, Stanford University, 2006.

Tonkin, H. *Service Learning across Cultures: Promise and Achievement.* New York: International Partnership for Service-Learning and Leadership, 2004.

Torres, J. *Benchmarks for Campus/Community Partnerships*. Providence, RI: Campus Compact, 2000.

Wilson-Oyelaran, E. "Blending Local and Global Experiences in Service of Civic Engagement." http://www.compact.org/20th/read/blending_local_and_global_experiences, 2006.

CHAPTER THIRTEEN

SECURING THE FUTURE OF CIVIC ENGAGEMENT IN HIGHER EDUCATION

Barbara Jacoby and Elizabeth Hollander

The purpose of this book is to provide a greater understanding of the concept and practice of civic engagement in higher education and how it can and should prepare students for lives of civically engaged citizenship, scholarship, and leadership. Previous chapters have discussed the definition and context of civic engagement in higher education, desired learning outcomes, and many examples of promising practices at all types of institutions. Educating students for civic engagement is a fundamental value of higher education and essential for the future of American democracy and for the health of our global society. However, in practice, civic engagement is one of many competing priorities on campuses and exists at a wide range of levels of support. To survive and thrive as a priority in the long run, civic engagement must be central rather than marginal, institutionalized rather than fragmented, and strong rather than weak. It must also be well grounded in and supported by national organizations and initiatives.

This chapter examines two sets of strategies for securing the future of civic engagement in higher education: campus-based approaches to developing and sustaining civic engagement and leadership beyond the campus to create a national climate that supports and encourages campus efforts.

Campus-Based Strategies

Civic engagement must be woven into the fabric of the institution if it is to be successful over time. However, in reality, this is often not the case. Musil's 2003 observations hold true today: "Unfortunately, too many institutions are marked by a helter-skelter approach to civic engagement. Rather than a cohesive approach to civic engagement, happenstance and impulse more typically govern. . . . All too often, civic engagement is not rooted in the very heart of the academy" (p. 4). As this volume illustrates, many institutions are developing civic engagement initiatives of all shapes and sizes. While some are central and strong, others hover on the margins of their institutions. In fact, there is often disagreement on a campus about whether and how civic engagement initiatives should be implemented and, if so, by whom (Lawry, Laurison, and VanAntwerpen, 2006). This section offers three basic strategies for integrating civic engagement into the core of institutions of higher education.

Institutionalize Civic Engagement

Service-learning educators and advocates have developed a strong, comprehensive, and credible set of models for institutionalizing service-learning through the development of a campuswide infrastructure (Bringle and Hatcher, 1996; Furco, 2001; Holland, 1997; Hollander and Saltmarsh, 2000; Pigza and Troppe, 2003). These models offer assessment tools to enable institutions to determine the degree—ranging from low relevance to full integration—to which service-learning is institutionalized. They are readily adaptable to civic engagement. Although factors vary from model to model, they generally include the following: presence in key documents, such as the mission and strategic plan; whether funding is shaky or secure; the extent to which the president and other leaders mention it in speeches and fund-raising efforts; the breadth and intensity of cross-campus and community partnerships; and the percentage of students, faculty, staff who are aware of the initiatives and are involved in them. The Carnegie Foundation for the Advancement of Teaching created an elective classification for community engagement in 2005 as a means to recognize and classify higher education institutions with a strong commitment to civic engagement. The criteria for this classification serve very well as a template for the institutionalization of civic engagement (Carnegie Foundation for the Advancement of Teaching, 2007).

A less quantifiable but critically important aspect of institutionalization requires changing the campus culture and environment to reflect a deeply embedded commitment to civic engagement. David B. Hoffman (2006) asserts that "students' perspectives and attitudes are shaped by their entire environment, not just the courses and programs designed to teach them" (p. 15). Promising practices in this arena include the democratic classroom (see chapter 5), the use of public spaces, the role of students in campus governance, policies that encourage student initiative, and the overall approach to the role of student affairs professionals. Adam Weinberg describes an ongoing process of rebuilding campus life at Colgate University in Hamilton, New York, that began by thoroughly revising the operating model throughout student affairs away from a "professional service model" to a public work model in which students would think of themselves as innovators, creators, and problem solvers (Brown, 2006).

The extent to which faculty are involved in civic engagement is often identified by scholars as a critical factor in the strength and sustainability of campus-based civic engagement initiatives. To tie civic engagement to the academic core of higher education, it must be recognized and rewarded in faculty promotion and tenure processes. In most universities, particularly research institutions, engaged scholarship, through which faculty apply their academic expertise to public purposes often in an interdisciplinary framework, is not valued as highly as traditional discipline-based research. Substantial work to develop criteria by which the quality and rigor of engaged scholarship can be evaluated is under way and should be supported (Stanton, 2007). Similarly, assessment of faculty productivity needs to be reviewed to recognize pedagogies that enhance students' civic learning and service to communities, as well as to the institution and the disciplines. To ensure the future of civic engagement as an essential aspect of the faculty role, it is important to educate graduate students, many of whom are future faculty members, in engaged scholarship and pedagogies of civic learning and engagement.

It is not possible to talk about the institutionalization of civic engagement without emphasizing the importance of institutional civic engagement, or campus-community partnerships. Students are quick to question the importance of education for civic engagement if they do not view their college or university as engaged in its community and in national and global social issues. Authentic, sustained campus-community partnerships provide fertile ground for teaching that involves service-learning and other active learning pedagogies, as well as service by student organizations and by individual students, faculty, and staff. They offer opportunities for faculty members' engaged scholarship and community-based research that includes undergraduates in all aspects of the research process (see chapter 13). Such partnerships require institutional infrastructure and resources that allow the community to engage with the institution as a whole rather than only with individuals or marginalized programs. They also eschew the traditional one-way expert or outreach models, instead valuing community expertise and shared responsibility in the pursuit of mutually beneficial goals.

Another effective way to bring civic engagement from the margins to the center is to intentionally link it to institutional priorities. Education for civic engagement ties nicely with diversity initiatives because it involves preparing students to understand their own identities, to communicate with people who are different from themselves, to build bridges across cultural differences to accomplish tasks, and to grapple with issues of power and oppression. Global citizenship is becoming increasingly important on campuses, and as chapter 12 demonstrates, study abroad can involve opportunities to learn about and practice civic engagement. The Bringing Theory to Practice Project of the Association of American Colleges and Universities (AAC&U) focuses on engaged learning and civic development as ways to address student mental health and the abuse of alcohol and other drugs—which are serious issues on most campuses. Environmental sustainability has become a critical issue on many campuses, with presidents signing the American College & University Presidents Climate Commitment (see http://www.presidentsclimatecommitment. org). This pledge requires signatories to take immediate steps to reduce carbon emissions, to develop a plan for their institutions to become climate neutral, and to make sustainability a part of the curriculum and other educational experiences. Other priorities that can be advanced by ties with civic engagement include student retention, revitalization of the general education curriculum, and public relations.

Provide Opportunities to Engage *All* Students

Civic engagement initiatives must be intentionally designed and implemented for students of all races, ethnicities, social classes, religions, ages, life situations, political views, learning styles, and interests. On many campuses, the majority of students who participate in service and other civic engagement activities are white, middle class, and female. Scholars have also noted that students' motivations to participate in civic engagement appear to vary according to their race, ethnicity, and class (Stanton, 2007). Civic engagement educators worry that campus-based initiatives "may not attract, be culturally appropriate for, or effectively serve" students of color and those from working-class backgrounds (Stanton, 2007, p. 21). In addition to careful program design, it is important to offer financial assistance to students who otherwise would not be able to participate in civic engagement. This could include civic engagement scholarships that function like athletic and academic scholarships to attract and retain students recognized for past achievement and current involvement in civic engagement. The Bonner Foundation endows such scholarships, and they are also being offered by institutions. Duke University, Brown University, and Miami University of Ohio are examples of institutions that offer campus-based financial aid to encourage and support local and global civic engagement. Federal Work-Study funds can also be used to support student community service.

We need to continue to be thoughtful about how civic engagement can be most effectively integrated into the lives of today's—and tomorrow's—students. Much has been written about the characteristics of the Millennial generation of college students, those born between 1982 and 2002 (DeBard, 2004). The landmark events of their young lives include the Columbine shootings; September 11, 2001; and the Rodney King and O. J. Simpson cases. More recently, they have been shaken by the war in Iraq, the devastation of the tsunami in Southeast Asia and Hurricane Katrina, and the shootings at Virginia Tech. They have been characterized as the most civic-minded generation since World War II (Cone, 2006; Corporation for National and Community Service, 2006). The *2006 Cone Millennial Cause Study* (2006) shows that 61 percent of respondents are currently worried about the state of world affairs and feel a personal responsibility to make a difference. They are angry with adults' apparent inaction on mounting social problems and with what they perceive as adults' labeling them as self-absorbed and apathetic. They are usually not drawn to 1960s-style protests, yet they are uncertain about how to respond to the problems they see around them and worry about future work prospects. This generation is volunteering at increasing rates and seeks to work for and do business with companies that care about how they affect society. Also called Generation Y or the Net generation, Millennials are very technologically oriented. They have never known life without the Internet, and they rely on it for information, communication, social networking, and recreation. Civic engagement educators have an unprecedented opportunity to encourage students to integrate their interests in social change with the potential of technology to transform communication about social and civic issues, to increase political engagement, and to enhance democratic participation and citizen action in new ways.

It is incumbent on us to work with students in ways that are most meaningful for them. In addition to more mainstream volunteer service and service-learning, other approaches are emerging, several of which are described in this book. These include community-based research, service-politics, and public leadership. Other promising practices include community mapping, civic dialogues, community organizing, and advocacy (Cone, Kiesa, and Longo, 2006). Campus Compact's 2006 publication, *Students as Colleagues* (Zlotkowski, Longo, and Williams), provides guidance to educators in expanding the circle of leadership for civic engagement by training students as leaders, engaging students as staff, fostering student-faculty partnerships, and encouraging students as academic entrepreneurs.

DEMONSTRATE THE LONG-TERM EFFECTIVENESS OF CIVIC LEARNING AND ENGAGEMENT

Research and assessment on the effectiveness of civic engagement in higher education is essential to enable its proponents to justify its prominence in the curriculum and the cocurriculum as well as its costs in terms of dollars, time, and effort. This involves assessing the extent to which our initiatives enable students to achieve desired civic learning and engagement outcomes. It is also critical to demonstrate the long-term effects of civic engagement in college. Many questions remain unanswered about what particular initiatives are most effective with what students and to what ends. In addition, new questions constantly arise. Research on the effects of civic engagement is challenging because variables are difficult to identify and define, civic engagement takes place in many ways and settings, causality is hard to determine, and extensive longitudinal research would be required to measure effects over time. As is the case with service-learning, research on the effects of civic engagement on students is necessary but not sufficient. By definition, civic engagement takes place in a social context and must be evaluated based on its societal benefits as well as its individual ones.

Adopting the format of the *Research Agenda for Combining Service and Learning in the 1990s* (Giles, Porter Honnet, and Migliore, 1991), five categories of research questions about civic engagement and its effects are proposed:

The Participant

What are the general effects of civic engagement on the individual student?

> What knowledge do students gain as a result of civic engagement?

> Does participation in civic engagement affect the participant's perception of self and others, social attitudes and behaviors, and view of the world?

> What is the effect over time of civic engagement in college on participants' political involvement, civic professionalism, community building, consumer behavior, engagement in causes, and other civic indicators?

What are the effects of learner characteristics—such as race, ethnicity, socioeconomic status, age, and faith—on outcomes related to civic engagement?

Do different approaches to civic engagement (such as democratic participation, social justice, global citizenship) yield different outcomes?

The Educational Institution

What are the effects of civic engagement on the institution?

How does civic engagement contribute to institutional mission?

Does civic engagement lead to the enhancement of teaching, research, and service?

What are the effects of civic engagement on faculty?

To what extent does civic engagement serve as a vehicle to address institutional priorities?

To what extent does civic engagement contribute to a more positive image of the institution among internal and external constituencies?

Local and Global Communities

What is the effect of civic engagement on communities local and global?

How can partnerships be fostered between campuses and communities to enhance economic growth, improve educational opportunity, and empower individuals and groups?

How can higher education institutions around the world partner with government, business, media, and not-for-profit organizations to sustain social and economic gains for communities?

How can higher education establish partnerships with primary and secondary schools so that education for civic engagement becomes an integral part of learning at all stages of life?

Does civic engagement lead to authentic, sustained campus-community partnerships? Is the reverse true?

What are the benefits and costs to communities as a result of institutional civic engagement?

Theoretical Bases

How can research on civic engagement contribute to the development of theories and models that can further undergird and enrich civic engagement?

How do students develop civic identities?

How can civic engagement help students move from volunteering to social change?

How can research on civic engagement contribute to the development of more comprehensive theories of human development?

How can research on civic engagement contribute to the development of more comprehensive theories of community development?

How can human development, community development, and the scholarship of teaching and learning be used to increase understanding of effective civic engagement strategies?

Program Models

What are the components and outcomes of various approaches to civic engagement?

What strategies, approaches, and models lead to specific civic learning outcomes and long-term civic engagement?

What approaches and program characteristics have enhanced or deterred the institutionalization of civic engagement?

What program characteristics—such as duration, intensity, content, modes of action, and reflection—promote various outcomes?

How can civic engagement be incorporated effectively into the curriculum at various levels (first year through senior year) and in a variety of disciplines?

To address these questions, it is essential to build research and assessment into the design of civic engagement initiatives from the outset. The pool of potential researchers should be expanded to include faculty not necessarily directly involved in civic engagement, graduate and undergraduate students, community partners, foundations, and national associations.

LEADERSHIP BEYOND THE CAMPUS

Securing the future of civic engagement in higher education requires leadership from several key constituencies, including presidents, trustees, academic officers, faculty, staff, students, and alumni. To be realistic about current and future efforts on campus to prepare students for civic and social responsibility, it is important to consider the national context in which these efforts are taking place. This is a time of transition for higher education in the United States. A college education is becoming an economic necessity for increasing numbers of Americans, as jobs increasingly require higher-order skills (Carnevale and Desrochers, 2007). Even so, only 50 percent of young people enroll in college. College costs are rising faster than grant and loan opportunities, and information about the availability of loans is very unevenly distributed to prospective students (McPherson and Schapiro, 2006). All these factors raise serious questions about equitable access to college for low-income and minority students. College retention rates for educationally and economically disadvantaged students raise further questions about the quality of K–12 preparation and the ability of campus programs to help these students succeed (Wyner, Bridgeland, and DiUlio, 2007).

State legislators are increasingly calling for greater accountability from higher education and, at the same time, are reducing public funding for higher education as other state costs, like health care, prisons, and K–12 education, crowd state budgets. On the federal level, the U.S. Secretary of Education's Commission on the Future of Higher Education issued its report in 2006, strongly emphasizing increased accountability from colleges and universities and encouraging a culture of evidence and transparency. The report also argues that educational excellence is required to maintain economic competitiveness (Secretary of Education's Commission on the Future of Higher Education, 2006). However, as Lee Shulman (2006) articulates in his response to the report on behalf of the Carnegie Foundation for the Advancement of Teaching, the report fails to address the urgency "to imbue students with a deep sense of engagement, commitment, and efficacy as citizens in a democracy" (p. 1).

These pressing issues make it more difficult to attract attention to the importance of educating students for civic engagement. To be heard, advocates of civic engagement in higher education must provide visible and vocal leadership at the local, state, and national levels by participating in associations that support the cause. Fortunately, opportunities are much more available and better organized than they were two decades ago. Chapter 1 contains an overview of many of these efforts.

Strategies are emerging to connect civic education to other front-burner issues in higher education. The American Council on Education instituted an advertising campaign to increase public support for higher education and, after a series of focus groups, tied that campaign to the role of the academy in providing solutions to America's problems. A consortium of higher education organizations—consisting of the American Association of State Colleges and Universities, AAC&U, and the National Association of State Universities and Land-Grant Colleges—has received a grant from the U.S. Department of Education to support an initiative on student learning assessment that will include changes in student growth related to civic engagement (AAC&U, 2007).

Campus Compact has taken a similar approach by devising a twentieth-anniversary strategy for the future that ties civic engagement to increasing nontraditional students' access to college and fostering their success (Holland and Hollander, 2006). For example, Massachusetts Campus Compact, in collaboration with Tufts University, received a grant from the Jack Kent Cooke Foundation to launch a college advising corps to recruit and train Tufts seniors to work full-time for one to two years following graduation as advisers to help boost college enrollment of high-achieving, low-income high school students (Massachusetts Campus Compact, 2008).

In the context of these challenges and strategies, leadership opportunities abound for advocates of civic engagement at every level, including presidents, trustees, provosts and other academic officers, faculty, staff, students, and alumni. Each of the organizational efforts described thus far both depends on and provides vehicles for civic engagement advocates to be strong voices for higher education's civic role.

Presidents

Presidents are increasingly engaging their colleges and universities deeply in the civic fabric and future of their communities. There are more and more examples of presidential leadership that directly enhances institutions' civic and economic impact on their communities while providing opportunities for students to learn about and practice civic engagement. In Worcester, Massachusetts, for instance, all the colleges and universities joined together to initiate a consortium with the local government and the chamber of commerce in the innovative UniverCity Partnership. This partnership promotes university investments to support the city's development, markets local businesses to student consumers, and helps coordinate student volunteer activities for maximum effectiveness.

At the state level, it is critical for presidents to raise state legislators' awareness about the social value of higher education in general and its civic role in particular. Such outreach has actually resulted in the allocation of state funds to support the civic mission of both public and private universities. James Votruba, the president of Northern Kentucky University, convinced the state legislature over time that universities could play a key role in assisting local economies and that they required financial support for such outreach. There is now a state appropriation to support public universities in their regional development efforts. Under the leadership of Michael T. Benson, then president of Snow College (now president of Southern Utah University), presidents in Utah nurtured state legislative champions for service-learning and leveraged a hundred thousand dollars in ongoing annual state support for Utah Campus Compact. Because all the colleges and universities in the state are members of Utah Campus Compact, all institutions share the benefits of this effort.

Presidents have an important bully pulpit to promote civic engagement beyond their own campuses—on the local, state, national, and even international levels. At the local level, presidents are regularly asked to speak in such settings as the chamber of commerce or the Rotary Club. Tulisse A. (Toni) Murdock, formerly president of Antioch University's Seattle campus (now chancellor of the Antioch system), tells the story of giving a speech to the Rotary Club of Seattle, one of the country's largest, on the importance of civic education, the movement to reassert it, and her own role as a leader of both the Washington and the national Campus Compacts. This meeting was also attended by academically talented high school seniors and their parents. Dr. Murdock received a standing ovation, and audience members were both surprised and pleased to learn of the important role of civic engagement on college campuses. Presidents can also get the message across by writing opinion pieces for local and national newspapers and by briefing editorial writers about the importance of education for civic engagement and their institutions' civic engagement efforts. For example, an often-quoted *New York Times* editorial written by Judith Rodin (2000) when she was president of the University of Pennsylvania that describes the university's community engagement efforts in West Philadelphia and the reciprocal benefits to the university has inspired other institutional leaders to consider similar engagement in a new light. Campus Compact's Web site contains other examples of presidents' speeches and opinion pieces on a range of topics related to civic engagement that can be accessed at http://www.compact.org/presidents/speeches.

At the national level, it is important for presidents to lend their public support for such federal policy initiatives as the Corporation for National and Community Service, the Peace Corps, student loan forgiveness for students who go into public service, the proposed U.S. Public Service Academy, and other national initiatives for youth civic engagement and education. Some presidents have also added their voices in support of civic education efforts in elementary and secondary schools.

Presidents also can and do promote civic education internationally. The president of Tufts University, Lawrence S. Bacow, organized a meeting of college presidents from around the world in Talloires, France, in 2005, at which they jointly declared the importance of educating students for active citizenship and formed a network to reinforce each other's efforts to do so (Talloires Network, 2005). In addition, the Council of Europe has an initiative that actively involves American presidents, along with those from Europe and beyond, in an effort related to higher education and democratic culture (Council of Europe, 2005).

TRUSTEES

Trustees can be powerful champions for civic engagement. They often bring important connections from within higher education and from other sectors. Trustee support for civic education has been emerging recently in the form of major endowments at such institutions as Amherst College, DePaul University, Duke University, and Tufts University. Eugene Lang, a trustee of Swarthmore College, has made large donations to his alma mater and also has stressed the importance of the trustee role on a broader scale through Project Pericles. Chapter 1 provides further information on this project. Some trustees, such as Steven J. Uhlfelder, who served on the Florida Board of Governors and on the board of Florida State University in Tallahassee, have been champions of student service involvement, including college student service. Uhlfelder expresses his public support by writing editorials and serving as cochair of Florida Campus Compact. However, much more could be done by trustees to rally their peers to actively promote civic education in local, state, and national forums, including business–higher education roundtables, state legislatures, the U.S. Congress, and public and private charitable foundations.

Faculty

Faculty members are in the best position to make the case for building civic learning and engagement into the curriculum. Because faculty stature depends so much on recognition within the disciplines (perhaps even more than on the campus), disciplinary support for civic engagement is essential. It is undoubtedly the faculty who can best influence their disciplinary associations in this regard. In the case of political science, a powerful group of faculty—including such well-recognized names as Robert Putnam, William Galston, Archon Fung, and Wendy Rahn—challenged the American Political Science Association to give more recognition to higher education's civic role in the association's publications and meeting agendas (American Political Science Association's Standing Committee on Civic Education and Engagement, 2004). These faculty members were concerned that the association was heavily engaged in arcane quantitative research at the expense of educating students for engagement in American democracy. One result of this effort is a new journal, *Perspectives on Politics,* that publishes highly accessible articles on current political issues across disciplines (American Political Science Association, n.d.). The committee's work also yielded a book edited by Stephen Macedo and entitled *Democracy at Risk: How Political Choices Undermine Citizen Participation, and What We Can Do about It,* published by the Brookings Institution Press in 2005.

Faculty can be helpful beyond their campuses by submitting articles on their approaches to civic education to such publications as the series on service-learning in the disciplines edited by Edward Zlotkowski (see http://styluspub.com/Books/Series-Detail.aspx?id=35) and journals on teaching in their disciplines. Almost every discipline has such a journal. The full list is available at http://www.ilstu.edu/~sknaylor/sotl.htm. Disciplinary associations can also establish national and regional institutes for faculty interested in civic engagement to provide training in engaged scholarship, teaching and curriculum development, and information on grants and community partnerships.

In addition, faculty members can be catalysts by spreading their exemplary practices in discipline-based civic education across higher education. For instance, William Oakes, the leader of the Engineering Projects in Community Service (EPICS) program at Purdue University, and Ira Harkavy, of the Center for Community Partnerships at the University of Pennsylvania, have successfully sought grants to replicate their work at other campuses, both near and far.

Provosts and Other Academic Leaders

Provosts and other academic officers have a key role on their campuses and beyond in supporting civic education. They have been especially critical in implementing the American Democracy Project by creating and supporting many meaningful initiatives to increase opportunities for students to learn about and practice civic engagement. To facilitate faculty members' use of such civically engaged pedagogy and focus on engaged scholarship, provosts, deans, and department chairs should support ongoing national initiatives to revamp tenure and promotion practices to recognize and reward faculty civic engagement work. They should also review and revise the faculty reward system at their own institutions, as mentioned previously in this chapter.

The Community-Campus Partnerships for Health, Imagining America, and The Research University Civic Engagement Network are some of the national organizations that have put forth ways to evaluate the quality of the scholarship of faculty members whose work is done with, about, or for the public and contributes to the public good. Gibson (2006), writing on behalf of colleagues representing research universities, recommends that academic leaders "develop and agree on a set of standards for what constitutes high-quality 'engaged scholarship'—and then work collaboratively to ensure that these are used by institutions as the basis for tenure and promotion decisions and grant awards" (p. 23).

As a result, there is much work for academic officers to do on both the national and the institutional level to create a climate that encourages faculty civic engagement. However, in general, provosts have not played a major role beyond their institutions in this regard, often leaving this work to their presidents. There are exceptions, like William Plater, former provost at Indiana University–Purdue University Indianapolis, who has written extensively about the importance of civic education and has served on the National Review Board for the Scholarship of Engagement. To increase the participation of provosts in advancing civic engagement, AAC&U has organized special institutes for chief academic officers about best practices in liberal education, including civic engagement.

PROFESSIONAL STAFF

Senior student affairs officers and other professionals in both student affairs and academic affairs who work in community service, service-learning, and civic engagement centers must engage together in professional development, share best practices, and advocate for civic engagement on and beyond their campuses. Higher education associations—including AAC&U, Campus Compact, NASPA–Student Affairs Administrators in Higher Education, and ACPA–College Student Educators International—provide important forums for staff to document, disseminate, and discuss the civic education work on their campuses. Professional staff members also participate in conferences and read journals about current research on civic engagement.

But what of the role of staff in influencing state and national policy? While some staff may be reluctant to take a stand without clearance from their institutional president's or public affairs office, seeking approval from those offices to advocate for civic engagement on the national and state levels can help inform campus leaders and colleagues about the issues and enlist their support. Staff who work with community service, service-learning, and civic engagement have long advocated for causes that affect their work, including funding for national service and loan forgiveness for students who go into public service employment. Staff can work with students to help them express their views about enhancing civic engagement opportunities on and off campus or other issues of interest to them to the U.S. Congress and local and state representatives.

Professional staff in all functional areas have much to contribute to advancing civic engagement. Financial aid officers can encourage their peers to learn how to use Federal Work-Study funds to support student work in communities and can support efforts in Congress to increase the percentage of Federal Work-Study funds that must be earned by students involved in community service. Institutional researchers can exchange information on how to assess civic learning and engagement and encourage such assessments to be conducted at colleges and universities across the country. Career center staff can develop and share best practices for helping graduating seniors find employment in public service and nonprofit organizations, as well as postcollege national and international service opportunities. Alumni affairs staff can organize civic engagement activities for alumni and encourage them to support civic engagement at their institutions and nationally.

Students

Students, of course, are natural advocates on behalf of their own interests in civic engagement and are increasingly being viewed as a resource to support civic engagement on campus and beyond. Campus Compact's Raise Your Voice campaign resulted in several powerful student statements about civic engagement and two publications that focus on mobilizing students to be effective leaders for change while enhancing their academic and civic learning. The Campus Compact Web site contains links to other resources for student advocacy and engagement (see http://www.compact .org/students). In several states—including Oklahoma,

Massachusetts, Illinois, Indiana, and Pennsylvania—students gather regularly to discuss and participate in a range of civic engagement activities. Campus Compact state offices organize most of these initiatives.

At the moment, there is no national student-led organization dedicated to promoting civic engagement or service-learning. The Campus Outreach Opportunity League (COOL), organized in the mid-1980s, merged with Idealist.org in 2004, and in 2007 they announced that they would not hold a 2008 national conference. However, building on COOL's spirit and legacy, an ad hoc group of students and staff held a national conference in 2008 called IMPACT: the National Student Conference on Service, Advocacy, and Social Action.

In addition to this example of entrepreneurial student energy for national organizing, there are many other student-driven national efforts that address civic and social issues, such as the National Student Campaign against Hunger and Homelessness, a twenty-year-old organization born out of the state Public Interest Research Groups (PIRGs) that are based on college campuses. This organization's annual conference provides student training in relief efforts, fund-raising, and advocacy. The National Student Partnerships is another student-initiated national effort to deploy college students to assist low-income individuals on a one-on-one basis. Started in 1998, it now operates centers in thirteen cities. College students organize both within and across political parties to mobilize young people to be informed voters and active participants in national, state, and local elections.

Graduate students are another important constituency who are finding their voice about their own civic engagement and are becoming advocates for civic engagement in graduate education. Perhaps the most common examples of graduate student public service and civic engagement are individual students who have become involved in community efforts on their own initiative. Individual graduate students undertake these activities for many reasons, as an extension or component of their graduate programs or as a respite from their studies. However, there is generally no expectation that such activities be reported as part of a graduate student's program of study or that he or she be recognized for this work. Similar activities are sometimes embedded within graduate programs and enjoy institutional support, primarily in fields such as medicine, dentistry, social work, education, law, architecture, engineering, clinical psychology, and public policy. However, they rarely appear as an integral part of degree programs in core academic disciplines, such as biology, English, history, and the arts (Stanton and Wagner, 2006).

As an example of advocacy, the Publicly Active Graduate Education Collective is a national alliance of graduate students focused on publicly engaged scholarship. They are involved in guest-editing a special issue of *Reflections*—a peer-reviewed journal on writing, community literacy, and service-learning—on engaged scholarship (Stanton, 2007).

Conclusion

This book began with a clarion call for higher education to prepare students to assume their roles as civically engaged citizens, scholars, and leaders to meet the demands of our democracy and of our complex and interconnected world. The introduction states that, in the past two or three decades, higher education's foremost experts, as well as its critics, have been urging colleges and universities to more intentionally and more thoroughly educate students to be informed, committed, and active participants in local, national, and global affairs. Research indicates that when students have high-quality, accessible opportunities to learn about and practice civic engagement, they readily take advantage of them (Colby, Beaumont, Ehrlich, and Corngold, 2007; Kiesa et al., 2007).

As this volume clearly demonstrates, it is no longer simply a matter of acknowledging that there is important work to be done. The chapters of this book are filled with specific examples of successful initiatives at a wide range of higher education institutions. These examples assure us that the work can be done and that— when done well—it makes a difference. They also demonstrate that education for civic engagement supports the missions of institutions across the entire spectrum of higher education, including liberal arts colleges, historically black colleges and universities, research universities, community colleges, and faith-based institutions. This book describes multiple approaches, together with lessons learned, ongoing challenges, and specific action steps.

This final chapter puts forth strategies, both at individual campuses and in a much broader playing field, to secure the future of civic engagement in higher education. As strong advocates of civic engagement, we believe that we have reason to be optimistic about its future. We believe that graduates of effective programs like the ones described in this book will themselves seek ways to create and sustain institutions and environments that will prepare and motivate future generations of engaged citizens. Our democracy and the well-being of the world depend on it.

References

American Political Science Association. "Perspectives on Politics." http://www.apsanet.org/content_4522.cfm, n. d.

American Political Science Association's Standing Committee on Civic Education and Engagement. "Democracy at Risk: Renewing the Political Science of Citizenship." http://www.princeton.edu/~apsaciv/apsaciv_final_review_ch1.pdf, 2004.

Association of American Colleges and Universities. "Association of American Colleges and Universities Awarded $2.4 Million Grant from Department of Education to Lead Collaborative Project on Student Learning Assessment." http://www.aacu.org/press_room/press_releases/2007/fipsegrant.cfm, 2007.

Bringle, R., and Hatcher, J. "Implementing Service Learning in Higher Education." *Journal of Higher Education*, 1996, *67*(2), 221–239.

Brown, D. "Public Work at Colgate: An Interview with Adam Weinberg." *Higher Education Exchange*, 2006, 12–26.

Carnegie Foundation for the Advancement of Teaching. "The Carnegie Classification of Institutions of Higher Education." http://www.carnegiefoundation.org/classifications/index.asp?key=1213, 2007.

Carnevale, A. P., and Desrochers, D. M. "Benefits and Barriers to College for Low-Income Adults." In B. Cook and J. E. King (Eds.), *Low Income Adults in Profile, Transforming Lives through Higher Education*. Washington, DC: American Council on Education, 2007.

Colby, A., Beaumont, E., Ehrlich, T., and Corngold, J. *Educating for Democracy: Preparing Undergraduates for Responsible Political Engagement*. San Francisco: Jossey-Bass, 2007.

Cone. *The 2006 Cone Millennial Cause Study*. http://www.2164.net/PDF-newsletters/2006MillennialCause.pdf, 2006.

Cone, R. E., Kiesa, A., and Longo, N. V. *Raise Your Voice: A Student Guide to Making Positive Social Change*. Providence, RI: Campus Compact, 2006.

Corporation for National and Community Service. *College Students Helping America*. Washington, DC: Corporation for National and Community Service, 2006.

Council of Europe. "Declaration on Higher Education and Democratic Culture: Citizenship, Human Rights and Civic Responsibility." http://dc.ecml.at/index.asp?Page=Declaration, 2005.

DeBard, R. *Serving the Millennial Generation*. (New Directions for Student Services, No. 106). San Francisco, CA: Jossey-Bass, 2004.

Furco, A. "Institutionalizing Service-Learning in Higher Education: Findings from a Three-Year Study (1997–2000)." Paper presented at the Forum on Volunteerism, Service, and Learning in Higher Education, College Park, MD, June 2001.

Gibson, C. M. *New Times Demand New Scholarship: Research Universities and Civic Engagement*. Medford, MA: Tufts University and Campus Compact, 2006.

Giles, D., Porter Honnet, E., and Migliore, S. *Research Agenda for Combining Service and Learning in the 1990s*. Raleigh, NC: National Society for Internships and Experiential Education, 1991.

Hoffman, D. B. "The Campus as Civic Community: Shaping Institutional Culture to Motivate and Empower Students as Citizens." *Journal of Cognitive Affective Learning*, Fall 2006, *3*(1), 13–21.

Holland, B. "Analyzing Institutional Commitment to Service: A Model of Key Organizational Factors." *Michigan Journal of Community Service Learning*, 1997, *4*, 30–41.

Holland, B., and Hollander, E. "Framing Essay." http://www.compact.org/20th/framing, 2006.

Hollander, E., and Saltmarsh, J. "The Engaged University." *Academe: Bulletin of the American Association of University Professors*, 2000, *86*(4), 29–31.

Kiesa, A., Orlowski, A. P., Levine, P., Both, D., Kirby, E. H., and Lopez, M. H., et al. *Millennials Talk Politics: A Study of College Student Political Engagement*. College Park, MD: Center for Information & Research on Civic Learning & Engagement, 2007.

Lawry, S., Laurison, D. L., and VanAntwerpen, J. *Liberal Education and Civic Engagement: A Project of the Ford Foundation's Knowledge, Creativity and Freedom Program*. http://www.fordfound.org/elibrary/documents/5029/toc.cfm, 2006.

Massachusetts Campus Compact. "College Advising Corps." http://ase.tufts.edu/macc/programsCAC.htm, 2008.

McPherson, M. S., and Schapiro, M. O. *College Access: Opportunity or Privilege?* New York: The College Board, 2006.

Musil, C. M. "Educating for Citizenship." *Peer Review*, Spring 2003, 4–8.

Pigza, J. M., and Troppe, M. L. "Developing an Infrastructure for Service-Learning and Engagement." In B. Jacoby, *Building Partnerships for Service-Learning.* San Francisco: Jossey-Bass, 2003.

Rodin, J. "Working with the Neighbors." *New York Times,* Dec. 30, 2000, p. A15.

Secretary of Education's Commission on the Future of Higher Education. *Final Report of the Secretary of Education's Commission on the Future of Higher Education.* http://www.ed.gov/about/bdscomm/list/hied-future/reports/finalreport.pdf, 2006.

Shulman, L. "A Response to the Final Report of the Commission on the Future of Higher Education." http://www.carnegiefoundation.org/news/sub.asp?key=51&subkey=1927, 2006.

Stanton, T. (Ed.). *New Times Demand New Scholarship II.* Los Angeles: University of California at Los Angeles, 2007.

Stanton, T., and Wagner, J. *Educating for Democratic Citizenship: Renewing the Civic Mission of Graduate and Professional Education at Research Universities.* Unpublished paper, June 2006.

Talloires Network. "The Talloires Declaration on the Civic Roles and Social Responsibilities of Higher Education." http://www.tufts.edu/talloiresnetwork, 2005.

Wyner, J. S., Bridgeland, J. M., and DiUlio, J. J., Jr. *Achievement Trap: How America Is Failing Millions of High Achieving Students from Low Income Families.* Lansdowne, VA: Jack Kent Cooke Foundation, 2007.

Zlotkowski, E., Longo, N. V., and Williams, J. R. *Students as Colleagues: Expanding the Circle of Service-Learning Leadership* Providence, RI: Campus Compact, 2006.

Name Index

SUBJECT INDEX

A

Activism, as civic engagement, 9

Accreditation, and disciplinary capstones, 119

Acting Locally: Civic Learning and Civic Leadership in Southwestern Ohio (think tank): centered on integral relationship between learning and leadership, 165; challenge to faculty in, 166–167; community immersion experience in, 167; integration of academic learning with community learning in, 168; interdisciplinary and community–based curriculum in, 166; and local impacts of globalization, 164; "public culture" concept in, 165

American Association of Community Colleges, service–learning projects of, 17–18

American College & University Presidents Climate Commitment pledge, 230

American culture: contemporary turn toward the larger public good in, 156; Reagan's consumerization of, 156–157

American Democracy Project initiatives, 17

AmeriCorps, 12–13

Antioch College, first–year seminars on civic engagement and experiential education in, 75

Applied learning, as essential learning outcome, 51

Associated New American Colleges, mission of, 20

Association of American Colleges and Universities (AAC&U): call for liberal education focused on civic learning, 100; educational philosophy of, 16; on essential learning outcomes, 16, 50–51; student's narcissistic perspectives on their education, 49–50

B

Beginning College Survey of Student Engagement (BCSSE), 72

Beloit College Mindset List, 79

Berea College's Center for Excellence in Learning through Service, course–based community–based research model in, 204–205

Bonner Scholars Program, 20

"Bowling Alone: America's Declining Social Capital," 14

Bringing Theory to Practice Project (BTtoP), AAC&U partnership with, 16–17, 230

Brown University's independent study capstones: interview and fellowship experience in, 125; Society of Royce Fellows as example of, 125–126

C

Campus Compact: formation of, 12; mission and civil engagement work of, 15; network of state compacts, 15–16; strategy tying civic